Masterclass: Fashion & Textiles

Guide to the World's Leading Graduate Schools

Frame Publishers

Contents

Introduction

There are many things to consider when choosing a graduate school and *Masterclass: Fashion & Textiles* aims to make this process easier. The focus of a master's degree course can differ greatly from school to school, as can the expectations of the different institutions and the lifestyles that can be enjoyed in the various cities. This book explores what future students can expect from each school and what opportunities await them.

This guide features 28 of the world's leading graduate design schools extensively. The articles are fact-filled and follow a similar format for ease of comparison. All the useful school specifications, such as programme description, application details and requirements, lecturers and alumni, student demographics, tuition and scholarship details, and full contact details, can be found herein.

An introduction by the dean or programme leader gives a good insight into the focus of the fashion/textiles programme at each school, as well as its specific educational approach. Photos and descriptions of student work and an interview with a successful alumnus provide additional, more personal information along with further insight into the depth of each programme.

Since location plays an important role in the school selection process, Frame gained insight from numerous interviews with current and previous students. How do students experience the city they live in? The various quotes included give an almost personal guide to each city and answers many of the questions future students might have. Each school profile contains information about the school's location regarding housing, transportation and the cultural scene from a student's perspective. A world map indicating the demographic spread of the presented schools is also included.

The featured graduate schools are selected based on a list of criteria including the quality of the student work that Frame has seen over the years. Furthermore, successful players in the fashion/textile design fields were asked to state which schools they felt best prepare students for their careers. We looked at the list of notable alumni, guest lecturers and current teachers as an indicator of the school's quality. The school's general reputation and other media attention it receives were additional factors. Last but not least, the aim was to create a global overview and thus select schools that offer master's degree courses in fashion and textiles from across the world.

A summary table can be found at the end of this guide, which gives a good overview of some important specifications. As part of the selection process, when a shortlist of schools of interest has been made, we encourage all future, potential students to go along and visit as many schools as possible during their open days. Take this guide along and use the notebook section at the end of the book for any findings. Explore the website of each institution, listed on the opening page of every school profile, to learn more about visa requirements for foreign students, how to apply for possible scholarships and the exact application details. Also tuition fees and application dates may have changed since the publication of this book.

All the information offered in this guide results in a very clear impression of what the listed schools have to offer, on every thinkable front that is relevant to potential students. We are confident this guide can help students find a master's course in the field of fashion/textiles that is right for them.

Aalto University School of Arts, Design and Architecture

Aalto University School of Arts, Design and Architecture
Hämeentie 135 C
00560 Helsinki
Finland

T +358 50 522 3296
viestinta-arts@aalto.fi
aalto.fi

Entrance to Media Centre Lume which also has a gallery that is open to the public.
Photo Julia Weckman

Course
Fashion and Clothing Design

School
Aalto University

Introduction

'Students are encouraged to work independently in order to develop their original thinking'

Pirjo Hirvonen, head of the Department of Design

Photo Anni Hanén

When was the school founded and has it changed much over the years?
A craft school was founded in Helsinki in 1871. After various incarnations, the modern day school was established as the University of Art and Design Helsinki in 1993 and a decision was taken in 2007 to merge the School of Art and Design, the School of Science and Technology and the School of Economics to form Aalto University. Five years later, Aalto University School of Arts, Design and Architecture was created and the new school continued in the footsteps of its predecessors that were internationally recognised and celebrated for their expertise.

What is studying at this school all about?
Study is based on studio work, lectures and working as part of a team on different projects and productions. Studying is communal and emphasises personal artistic development and problem-solving skills. However, students are also encouraged to work independently in order to develop their original thinking. Studies combine theoretical and practical professional understanding and involve finding ways of expressing students' own artistic ambitions. Furthermore, developing communication and collaboration skills is as important as acquiring specialised knowledge.

What is the strength of this department?
The school's core strength lies in experience-based thinking that combines visionary and user experience-based design. The main focus points in research are design, digital media, audiovisual communication, art, visual culture, and architectural solutions to issues of wellbeing and community and city planning.

What kind of teaching methods do you use?
Learning through practical assignments and projects. Aalto University is all about learning in practice: there are numerous ongoing projects created and led by students.

Why should students choose this school?
Aalto University combines technical sciences, business sciences and art in a single entity. The university takes great pride in its cross-disciplinary nature. In fact, it is the only university in the country that offers students the possibility to think outside the box and combine the best of the three fields within their degree. Located in the Helsinki metropolitan area, it is an international university built on Finnish values of equality, integrity and transparency.

Programme

The MA Fashion and Clothing Design programme allows students to focus on deepening the professional skills and knowledge achieved in previous studies or at work, and diversifying and developing their artistic expression. The objective is to produce creative specialists to meet the changing needs of society and business. We encourage the unique qualities of each student by providing each one with an individual study plan. This is achieved through a modular study system as well as minor studies, which both stimulate personal specialisation paths.

Opportunities for combining an academic approach with the strengthening of creative skills are vast and encouraged: thinking and doing, and concepts and practice are equally valued in experimentation. Also, collaborations with fellow students, from other fields of design and other disciplines are seen as a valuable means of gaining new knowledge and experiences. This kind of openness lies at the core of the philosophy of the programme. It results in a great diversity of graduate projects, ranging from the creation of commercial collections, academically conducted research and artistic expression, to everything found in between.

After completing the programme, students possess a deep understanding of their strengths and are able to apply their own personal design skills, thinking and values to the context of the international fashion industry and society at large. With this personal approach, they are equipped to give their own creative contribution to the development of the shared world.

Lume Gallery has a bright and airy atmosphere thanks to the all-glass ceiling.
Photo Julia Weckman

The Library and Information Centre Aralis at Aalto University is a combination of art, science and public libraries.
Photo Riittaliisa Leskinen

Programme
Fashion and Clothing Design

Leads to
Master of Arts

Structure
The 2-year full-time programme consist of modules that focus on the degree programme's core competences, as well as changing project modules in which students participate in teamwork and contests. The course is designed to be completed in a minimum of six terms. The school asks that the first three terms be completed contiguously with a strong recommendation to do four terms uninterrupted in order to ensure an immersive learning experience with the same cohort. The fifth and sixth terms are dedicated to a final project and are often spread out over the course of a year to accommodate internships.

Head of programme
Pirjo Hirvonen

Mentors and lecturers
Jasmin Julin-Aro and Tuomas Laitinen.

Course
Fashion and Clothing Design

School
Aalto University

School Facts

Duration of study
2 years

Full time
Yes (40 hours a week)

Part time
Not recommended

Female students
88.5%

Male students
11.5%

Local students
80%

Students from abroad
20%

Yearly enrolment
10

Tuition fee
Free

Funding/scholarships
No

Minimum requirements for entry
Bachelor's degree in fashion or equivalent in design

Language
English

Application procedure
All applicants must fill out the online application form. The following additional documents must also be delivered to the school (in person or by post) in order to complete the application:
- two copies of printed application form
- two copies of your degree certificate, one of which needs to be officially certified
- two copies of an official transcript of study records, one of which needs to be officially certified
- language certificate (if appropriate)
- your portfolio, maximum size A3; no samples in electronic or digital format will be accepted
- two copies of your curriculum vitae
- two copies of your study plan (letter of motivation)
- photocopy of your passport or ID card (with photo).
Selection for master's degree programme is done through a two-stage selection process. Candidates reaching the second phase will be interviewed in April and the selected

applicants will be informed of the result by email.

Application details
aalto.fi/en/studies

Application date
By 31 January

Graduation rate
High

Job placement rate
High

Memberships/affiliations
EDII, BEDA and ICSID.

Collaborations with
Various, including: educational institutions, such as the Royal Collage of Art, Central Saint Martins, Parsons NY, Design Academy Eindhoven, Donghua University Shanghai; cultural bodies, such as Design Museum Helsinki, EMMA Museum for Modern Art, Tilburg Textile Museum, COMON Como; and companies, such as H&M, Diesel, Marimekko, Stockmann and Lapponia.

Facilities for students
Lecture rooms, workspaces, well-equipped studios (knitting, weaving, sewing, printing/dyeing and pattern studios), IT classrooms and library.

City
Helsinki

Country
Finland

Student Work

The New Old (2012)
by Aiwei-Foo

An exploration of fashion and clothing consumption, the project investigated the significance of used clothing and created a strategy for making do with existing objects and up-cycling them through personal involvement. The material was collected via clothing donors from all walks of life and through the process of making is juxtaposed with the identity of the creator. Through this encounter, the project aims at inciting both emotionally and aesthetically ambitious experiences and cutting consumption.

Shirts (1–5) (2012)
By Alisa Närvänen

By designing, producing and sharing five copies of the same shirt, Närvänen set out to undertake a social experiment. Once leaving the designer's hands, the shirt becomes subject to different people in different situations and each seemingly identical garment begins a life of its own. The shirts' lives are interpreted and presented in the form of an installation representing multiple cultural processes, categories and principles, revealing fascinating and ambiguous stories, traces and memories of people, time and places.

Garment in Landscape (2012)
By Satu Maaranen

A study of the relationship between haute couture garments and land art, this project gave perspective to the subject through the camouflage phenomenon, landscape painting and Finnish pattern design. The collection shows how clothing can be found harmonic or discordant in relation to the constructed and natural landscapes one moves in. As we experience rather than just see the landscape, the garment is an object creating the landscape while simultaneously the landscape creates the garment and dresses us.

Course
Fashion and Clothing Design

School
Aalto University

Immediate Invisible (2012)
By Liisa Pesonen

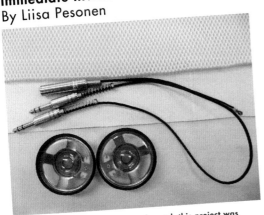

Combining fashion, electronics and sound, this project was executed in collaboration with Media Lab student Waltteri Wikström and composer Samuli Tanner. The collection consists of outfits that are able to read physiological data such as pulse and muscle contractions from the wearer's body. This data is used to modify musical soundscapes which are played by speakers built into the outfits.

Regulating Line (2012)
By Laura Juslin

Approaching the garment following the principles characterised by modernist architecture, primary shapes and Le Corbusier's regular line have guided the design process in this project. Clothing was based on leanness and simplicity, removal of decoration and the harmony of optimal shape, surface and cut. Theory is transformed into a concrete set of finished garments.

Fashion Openness (2012)
By Natalia Mustonen

Investigating an open source approach to fashion practice reveals its benefits for creating a more environmentally, socially and economically sustainable fashion system. At the breaking point of the industrial and post-industrial era, we are experiencing the trend of openness in many fields, increasingly escaping from hierarchical thinking and one-way communication, as well as striving for sharing structures and user empowerment. So what is open (source) fashion?

Alumna

Name Noora Niinikoski
Residence Espoo, Finland
Year of birth 1972
Year of graduation 2001
Current job Head of fashion design at Marimekko
Website marimekko.com

Why did you choose this school?
After studying in Helsinki, Paris and London in1995 (I graduated from Central Saint Martins in 1998), I worked for a while in Italy at the Benetton Group. In 2000, I decided to return Finland and did my master's at Aalto because I wanted to go deep into my own personal creative process. The course was the perfect way to do it, and I knew the facilities at Aalto University were superb.

What was the most important thing you learned here?
I worked with the textile designer Piia Rinne for the whole 2 years of the course, so I learned a lot about teamwork and sharing the creative process.

Are you still in contact with the school?
Yes. I taught there for a while and I still go back to give a lecture for the students.

What are you doing now?
Now I work for Marimekko. As the head of fashion design, I'm responsible for the womenswear, bags and accessories collections.

How did the school prepare you for what you are doing now?
While studying I had time to study my creative process. In my opinion, that process is the essential tool for a designer. All is very systematic, although the ideas can often be abstract. In my job now, I need to develop ideas very fast and then this effective process is the key to survival!

What was your graduation project?
I did a collection of mostly printed clothes together with Piia Rinne.

Was the transition from graduation to working life a smooth one?
I started to work with Piia Rinne at the school and then we continued to work together for 10 years.

Any words of advice for future students?
Work hard and do what you love the most. Don't give up!

For her graduation project, Niinikoski developed a collection of printed clothes together with Piia Rinne.

Course
Fashion and Clothing Design

School
Aalto University

Current Students

'My favourite workshop was the textile project called PatternLab. I had no experience in making textile patterns before that course, so we really learnt from scratch how to make patterns using different techniques. In a team you develop marketing themes that you follow for developing your pattern collections.'
Varvara Zhemchuzhnikova

'Work hard, use the amazing studios and workshops that are provided, and have a lot of fun while doing it! It's all about the attitude.'
Anna-Mari Leppisaari

'I chose this school because of its reputation, international cooperations and cross-disciplinary possibilities.'
Timo Helin

'There is an encouraging yet highly driven and motivated spirit and atmosphere among us students. This means that people constantly help and support each other, but also push and challenge each other to do greater things.'
Anna Alanko

'When I started this course my aim was to become conceptually and technically more professional, whilst developing a unique style.'
Ting Yun Huang

City Life

Helsinki is the capital of Finland. It is located in the south of the country, on the shore of the Gulf of Finland. The population of the city is around 600,000 making it by far the most populous municipality in the land. Helsinki is Finland's major political, educational, financial, cultural and research centre. Approximately 70 per cent of foreign companies operating in Finland have settled in the Helsinki region.

In 2009, Helsinki was chosen to be the World Design Capital for 2012 by the International Council of Societies of Industrial Design primarily due to the city's approach to 'embedded design', which has tied design in the city to innovation. This has seen the creation of global brands, such as Nokia,

Kone and Marimekko, popular design-related events, outstanding education and research institutions, and exemplary architects and designers. The city features several buildings by the world-renowned Finnish architect Alvar Aalto (1898–1976), recognised as one of the pioneers of architectural functionalism.

Located in the heart of the city is Helsinki Cathedral and Senate Square, designed by Carl Ludvig Engel and completed in 1852.
Photo Mikko Raskinen/Aalto University

Finland

Helsinki

1 Aalto University
2 Designmuseo
3 Kansallismuseo
4 Suomenlinna Island
5 Design Forum Finland
6 Kauppatori
7 Arabia Factory Outlet
8 Cafe Regatta
9 Train Station

Gulf of Finland

 Park

 Water

Railway

Main road

Course
Fashion and Clothing Design

School
Aalto University

City Facts

Helsinki Design Week
Helsinki Design Week brings together the international design community and local artists. The event spreads from the Cable Factory to the Old Customs Warehouse.
helsinkidesignweek.com

Designmuseo 2
Helsinki's Design Museum offers fantastic surroundings for different types of events, like an auditorium, a cafe and several exhibition spaces.
designmuseum.fi

Kansallismuseo 3
The new permanent exhibition of the National Museum of Finland tells the story of 20th-century Finland. The focus is especially on the daily life in Finland, cuisine, traffic and communication, as well as developments in politics and state.
kansallismuseo.fi

Artek
Originally established by Alvar and Aino Aalto, this home ware, glassware and furniture store maintains the simple design principle of its founders.
artek.fi

Suomenlinna Island 4
An ideal day trip from Helsinki is to pack a picnic and take the regular ferry to the island fortress of Suomenlinna. A great deal of Helsinki's history was shaped here.

Marimekko
Marimekko is a leading Finnish textile company that designs, manufactures and markets high-quality clothing, interior decoration textiles, tableware, bags and other accessories, both in Finland and abroad.
marimekko.fi

Vappu
Walpurgis (Vappu) witnesses the biggest carnival-style festival held in the streets of Finland. Student traditions are one of the main characteristics of Vappu.

Design Forum Finland 5
The promotion organisation of Finnish design. A small exhibition space and shop also operate in these premises.
designforum.fi

Kauppatori 6
Famous market on the waterfront. Fishmongers still sell from boats moored at the quay, with local handicrafts and souvenirs at (sometimes) inflated prices.

Arabia Factory Outlet 7
Stylish products for the home can be found at the Arabia Factory Outlet, the largest single sales centre for Arabia, Iittala and Hackman products. The store includes special discounts and mark-down prices.

Cafe Regatta 8
This is a well-loved countryside-style cafe, located in a traditional 115-year-old cottage. It is positioned in beautiful surroundings next to the sea and is open every day around the year.

How to get around
Around 200 international flights a day arrive at Helsinki-Vantaa Airport, which is situated 19 km from the centre of Helsinki and can be reached by car in approx. 25 minutes. It is also possible to take a taxi, the Finnair airport bus or bus 615 to the central railway station 9. A taxi to city centre costs approx. EUR 30. There are excellent train connections from Helsinki to all major towns in Finland as well as to Lapland. There is also a daily train service to St. Petersburg and Moscow. The Central Railway Station is a landmark itself in Helsinki. Buses from all around Finland arrive to the central bus station, from the largest cites almost every hour. There are daily ferry services to Helsinki from Estonia, Sweden and Germany. All the ferry companies offer also possibility to take a car with you. The main building of the School of Arts, Design and Architecture is located in Arabianranta, the oldest part of Helsinki.

Arranging housing
Never a problem

Housing support by school
No

Cost of room in the city
Between EUR 200 and EUR 700 per month

Cost of campus housing
n/a

Academy of Arts, Architecture and Design in Prague

The fashion and textile labs are bright spaces where students' creativity abounds.

The impressive school building in central Prague was built between 1882 and 1885, the project designed by František Schmoranz junior and Jan Machytka.

Academy of Arts, Architecture and Design in Prague
nam. Jana Palacha 80
11693 Prague
Czech Republic

T +420 (0)251 098 111
info@vsup.cz
vsup.cz

Introduction

'Our teaching methods nurture creative thinking, development and excellent craftsmanship'

Rony Plesl, head of the Department of Applied Art

When was the school founded and how has it changed over the years?
The Academy of Arts, Architecture and Design (AAAD) in Prague was established in 1885. It has changed over the years in its interconnection of individual disciplines, especially between the fine art disciplines and those of applied arts and design. Students receive a comprehensive education in this field, with the possibility of combining traditional craft techniques with new media or to process design assignments conceptually.

What is studying at this school all about?
This school of ours has a great advantage in the genius loci of the place where it's located, in the tradition that it builds on. Czech art is generally fond of complexity and nostalgia and it is dominated by peripheral themes. Our school is not seeking a simple profile. It doesn't seek students with uniform faces. We are pleased to describe that the school has an atmosphere of 'pragmatic craziness'.

What kind of teaching method is applied?
The educational methods are liberal and varied in the individual departments and disciplines.

What is expected from the students?
A student of ours shouldn't blend in with the crowd, even with an artistic crowd. Ours seek new paths and shouldn't be afraid to fight for them, even in the face of lack of understanding.

What is the most important thing for students to learn during this course?
The mixture of creative thinking, development and excellent craftsmanship.

What is the most important skill to master for a fashion/textile designer?
Obsession with work, perceptiveness, openness, humility and diligence.

In what kind of jobs do your fashion/textile graduates mostly end up?
Former students mostly join one of the bigger industrial companies or small design companies, create their own company or connect with other young Czech designers.

Programme

The MA Applied Arts programme is taught across all the studios in the department, including fashion art, fashion and footwear design and textile art. While the department is most closely related to design, the concept of learning – grounded in a close relationship with materials and workshop production – is quite specific, notwithstanding rapid development and common objectives.

The main idea behind the concept of the programme is a focus on a creative conception of the clothing form. The concentration on the development of creative thinking, should have the final form that goes beyond previous types of clothing, footwear and accessories towards a free artistic form. Fundamental is the path to excellent craftsmanship. Students have to know who they are and understand their possibilities so they can fullfill their potential.

The main aim of the programme is to develop and eestablish a personal identity, strongly obsessed with work that is susceptible, open, humble and diligent.

Fashion project work on display at the end-of-year show.

Setting up the degree show can be fun – the chaos before the calm!

The school's historic building is an ideal setting for exhibition the work of master's students.

Programme
Applied Arts

Leads to
Master of Arts

Structure
The 2-year full time course is structured into semesters. Throughout the course, students get to work in the various studios of industrial clothing design and fashion design within the entire scope of artistic, technical and marketing approaches. The study programmes cultivate original creative work, as well as artistic training in traditional techniques and new digital media.

Heads of programme
Pavel Ivancic, Libena Rochová, and Jitka Škopová.

Mentors and lecturers
Pavel Ivancic, Lenka Kohoutová, Vojtech Novotný, Libena Rochová, Jitka Škopová and Markéta Vinglerová.

Alumnus
Monika Drápalová, Zdenka Imreczeová, Pavel Ivancic, Jindra Jansová, Zuzana Kubícková, Daria Makeeva, Pavla Podsedníková, Markéta Šohajová, Mirka Talavašková, Josef Taptuch amd Hana Zárubová.

Course
Applied Arts

School
Academy of Arts, Architecture and Design in Prague

School Facts

Duration of study
2 years

Full time
Yes (20 hours a week)

Part time
Possible

Female students
52%

Male students
48%

Local students
70%

Students from abroad
30%

Yearly enrolment
12

Tuition fee
Free for all students with a basic level of the Czech language

Funding/scholarships
Yes

Minimum requirements for entry
Bachelor's degree in relevant field

Language
English and Czech

Application procedure
Your application should include the following:
- your contact details
- your curriculum vitae
- application form
- portfolio
- proof of language (if applicable). Candidates are invited to take an entrance examination, for which an application exam fee, to verify their artistic talent and a capacity for independent creative activity in the chosen studio and a level of professional and general education and cultural knowledge. Successful applicants will be informed by email.

Application details
studijni@vsup.cz

Application date
By 30 November

Graduation rate
56%

Job placement rate
High

Memberships/affiliations
Erasmus, Socrates and Leonardo programmes.

Collaborations with
Camper, Simple Concept Store, Swarovski, Pietro FIlipi, Bata, Intel, Czech Centres, Chevrolet, Hi-Tech and Skoda Auto.

Facilities for students
Fashion and textile labs, specialised workshops for printing, glassmaking, ceramics and email facilities, as well as a computer centre, canteens and a library.

Student Work

Awkward Rococo (2013)
By Lucie Jelínková

A collection inspired by Queen Marie Antoinette, depicting her troubled life since her youth until the moment of her execution.
Photo Martin Faltejsek

Moments of Weakness & Strength (2013)
By Renata Sedláková

A collection focused on women's clothing using a couture technology components. The main linking element is playful contrast. Feminine tenderness of a light organza material against coarseness of wool with latex and foil layer. Femininity and power.
Photo Petr Jandera

Ready To Wear (2013)
By Filip Hieke

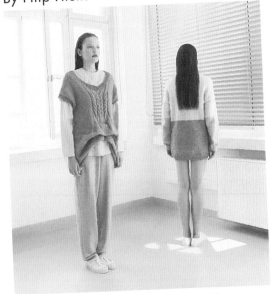

This is a collection which includes traditional craft techniques, modern design, non-limiting form and traditional values.
Photo Jean-Claude Etegnot

Candy Yunn (2013)
By Filip Jakab

Candy Yunn is a symbolic name for 'modern witches'. The project used the technique of mix&match colours, textures and materials for to create an imaginary feminine world.
Photo Bambi Christa

Course
Applied Arts

School
Academy of Arts, Architecture and Design in Prague

Fantasy Mystery Sci-fi (2012)
By Pavla Podsedníková

This collection was based on the theme of the film and music festival Fantasy Mystery Sci-Fi, and focused more on the artistic forms of the fashion objects.
Nikola Šrajerová

Havana Wall (2010)
By Linda Kaplanová

White transparent decorative paper relief designed as a light. Curved paper strips pf textile fabric playfully deal with the shadows.
Photo Linda Kaplanová

Accidental Meeting (2010)
By Daria Makeeva

This was a collaborative project with the jewellery KOV Studio of Eva Eisler on the topic of celebrating dinner in the palace.
Photo Nikola Šrajerová

Bata Bullets (2011)
By Karolína Juríková

This project was a collaboration with the Bata company to redesign of the once iconic Bata Bullets sneakers, based on a graphic composition and collage combining the original sneaker as a representative of a cheap series of shoes with a 'luxury' leather riding boot.
Photo Nikola Šrajerová

Alumna

Name Daria Makeeva
Residence Prague, Czech Republic
Year of birth 1987
Year of graduation 2013
Current job Freelance fashion illustrator
Clients Stylesight, Esprit

Why did you choose this school?

I knew that AAAD was the most respectable school with a fashion department in the whole the Czech Republic. At the same time, I was captivated by the family atmosphere in the school as a whole.

Are you still in contact with your fellow class mates?

Many of us remain good friends now. And as friends we meet periodically and consult our projects which each other. Those meetings are very inspiring for me, those moments are truly exciting!

What was the most important thing you learned here?

Probably the most important was how to be really and deeply sincere in my creative expression. I think it is not easy today to find your own place is this vast universe of fashion production. There are many ways (more or less difficult) of how to be involved in the industry, but only sincereness can make you feel really satisfied with your designs.

What was the most interesting project you did?

The most interesting project for me was at the same time the most difficult. It was a group project to create an exhibition concept for our department exhibition at the end of the semester. It was in some way an experiment: nobody in our department had done a fashion exhibition concept before. But we wanted to try it very much, and we are very grateful to our department leader for all that support she gave to us. We learned a lot in this project.

Was there any class you found particularly difficult?

It is hard to say because each class can be passed in a range of ways. So, it is usually up to you and how serious your interest in this subject – this determines how much energy you are going to invest in it.

What was your graduation project?

In my graduation project I worked with my family history: I tried to imagine my ancestors (Russian peasants) and compared their everyday clothes with my everyday fashion routine. The result was a womenswear collection, supported by a book of visual research, atmospheric short film and exhibition concept.

What was your favourite place to hang out?

Usually it was some park or riverside. But beside this, I remember many lovely evenings spent in our department studio working all together and telling bizarre stories of almost everything.

Any words of advice for future students?

Trust your soul, not ambitions.

One of Makeeva's student projects involved a womenswear collection in a range of pastel colours, inspired by flowers in full bloom.

Course
Applied Arts

School
Academy of Arts, Architecture and Design in Prague

Current Students

'My favourite workshop is the Technology and Producing Accessories class. You prepare the patterns for your design, which is followed up with a visit to a workshop in the South Morava where you get to see the item you designed being produced.'
Kristýna Nováková

'The master's degree course at AAAD prepares students creatively, instilling them with the knowledge to enter the real-world fashion business.'
Filip Jakab

'Public transport in Prague is very good and not very expensive for students. To get around the city, I often take the tram, since Prague is not very convenient for bikes unfortunately.'
Marie Petráková

'My favourite places to hang out are Galerie DOX (contemporary art gallery with it also has interesting lectures and a good bookshop), Museum Kampa (great exhibitions and very close to the park) MeetFactory (international centre for contemporary art) and Naplavka, which is near to the river where you can meet a lots of nice people – it is a perfect place to spend a nice summer evening!'
Monika Krobová

City Life

Prague is the capital city of the Czech Republic. It is one of the oldest in the Europe and is situated right in the historic centre, in front of the Rudolfinum Gallery. You can watch the Moldau river and Prague Castle from the school's studios.

The city has got an easy-going atmosphere, good prices, lots of culture spots and lively art scene. It is also very safe with a perfect infrastructure. Every year, millions of tourists visit Prague, but there are still quiet areas like Vinohrady, Dejvice or Vršovice.

The city is notable for its well-preserved city centre which is very compact. There are also lots of green areas right in the city centre, where you can exercise, study or read. Even though Prague is the capital city, it is quite small and not over-crowded.

Prague offers several design shops, student design shops and the art, design and architecture student suburb is wide as well as the tight connection between the people thanks to the relatively small city.

The view across the historic city of Prague at night time, when it is especially dramatic thanks to the buildings being illuminated.

Czech Republic

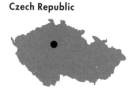

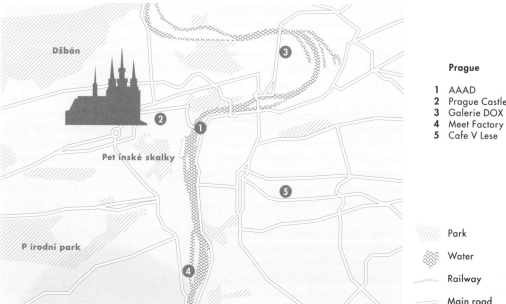

Džbán

Pet ínské skalky

P írodní park

Prague

1 AAAD
2 Prague Castle
3 Galerie DOX
4 Meet Factory
5 Cafe V Lese

Park

Water

Railway

Main road

Course
Applied Arts

School
Academy of Arts, Architecture and Design in Prague

City Facts

Prague Castle ②
Prague Castle is a dominant aspect on the city's skyline and one of the most important cultural institutions in the Czech Republic. It is considered to have been founded around 880 by Prince Borivoj of the Premyslid Dynasty (Premyslovci). A UNESCO World Heritage site, it consists of a large-scale composition of palaces and ecclesiastical buildings of various architectural styles.
hrad.cz

Galerie DOX ③
The DOX Centre for Contemporary Art, Architecture and Design was originated as a private initiative and opened to the public in 2009. It has presented more than 80 exhibition projects and over 300 educational programmes. The DOX Centre is located in Holešovice, a dynamic district of Prague which has recently undergone a fundamental transformation.
dox.cz

MeetFactory ④
MeetFactory was founded in 2001 by David Cerný in order to make contemporary art and culture accessible to the public. It connects art, theatre, film and music with educational programmes. It also provides facilities for resident artists, who come from all around the world.
meetfactory.cz

Cafe V Lese ⑤
This is a popular cafe for students. Its name translates as 'coffee in the forest' and due to its location by the river, it is also an attractive meeting point for many people even from outside the city.
cafevlese.cz

Náplavka
The Náplavka Farmers' Market is an institution in Prague. It takes place every Saturday and draws visitors from far and wide.

Müller House
In the autumn of 1928, Frantisek Müller commissioned Adolf Loos and Karel Lhota to design the new house for the Müller family. It is located in the Strešovice district and has a modernistic architectural style.

Baba Hill
In the north of Prague, there is a hill called Baba. Take the no. 131 bus to U Mateje and then it is a short walk through the woods of Divoká Šárka to reach the ruin at the top of the hill. Noone knows the exact history of this monument – although it is claimed to be a former wine-press built in 1622. From here, you can get a great view across the city.

Designblok
This is an annual event that takes place in October as the Prague Design and Fashion Week. During this week, the city is filled with design and creativity which pervades every street corner and it is truly the centre of life and inspiration.
designblok.cz

How to get around
The nearest airport is a distance of 19 km away is Prague Václav Havel airport, accessible by buses and trains into the city centre. You can get around the city by trams, bus, underground, walking or bicycles. The nearest stops for public transport to the school are trams 17 and 18 at the stop Staroměstská. There is also a nearby subway A stop Starom stská and bus no. 207 stop Starom stská.

Arranging housing
Quite easy

Housing support by school
Yes

Cost of room in the city
CZK 7250 per month (approx. EUR 280)

Cost of campus housing
CZK 5500 per month (approx. EUR 212)

ArtEZ Institute of the Arts

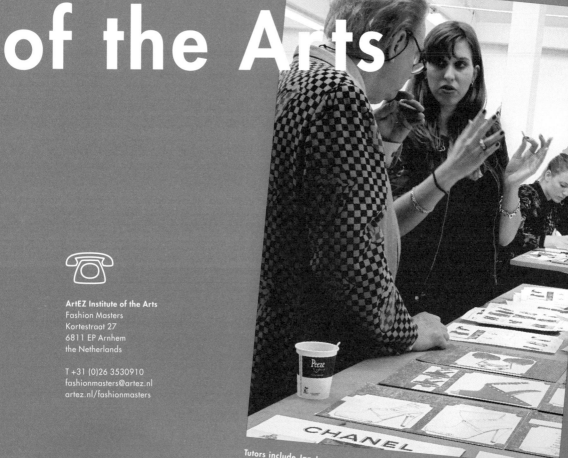

The landmark main building of ArtEZ dates from 1963 and was designed by the famous Dutch architect Gerrit Rietveld.

ArtEZ Institute of the Arts
Fashion Masters
Kortestraat 27
6811 EP Arnhem
the Netherlands

T +31 (0)26 3530910
fashionmasters@artez.nl
artez.nl/fashionmasters

Tutors include Jan Jansen, the renowned Dutch shoe designer, seen teaching here.
Photo Sarah Meers

Course
Master Fashion Design

School
ArtEZ Institute of the Arts

Introduction

'Our aim is to educate fashion professionals who question current mainstream fashion'

Mascha van Zijverden, Master Fashion Design course director

When was the school founded and how has your programme evolved?
We celebrate our 60th anniversary in 2013. The fashion master's degree programme started in 1998 and, in 2008, was fully accredited – it is funded by the Dutch Ministry of Education and now comprises a 2-year full-time curriculum, with English as the language of instruction. As of 2009, the programme received its present name: Master Fashion Design. Together with the Master Fashion Strategy, it is known as the 'ArtEZ Fashion Masters'. In 2010, shoe design was added as a new specialisation.

What is studying at this school all about?
Our aim is to educate fashion professionals who question the current mainstream fashion system and seek out the boundaries of the prevailing discourse through research and design. Our master's programme is geared to talented fashion and shoe designers who want to develop their skills in order to better position themselves in the international high-end fashion industry.

Tell us about your teaching methods.
We teach students how to design and complete collections according to the design (research) cycle. Research is not merely viewed as a theoretical activity, but as a vehicle for design and experimentation. We train our students to become fashion professionals with an investigative, research-oriented mind set. As such, we do not only educate students for particular professions in the world of fashion – they should also be able to reflect critically on the fashion world through their work.

Why should students choose ArtEZ and what is expected of them?
Our personal approach is within the framework of a research community, emphasising the individual strengths of each student. They need to be prepared to question the mainstream fashion industry in critical ways, and examine their own role within it.

What is the most important thing for students to learn during this course?
To reflect critically on themselves as a designer and on their work, as well as to position themselves in the international professional field of fashion.

What is the most important skill for a fashion designer to acquire?
The capacity to innovate.

In what industries or in what kind of jobs do your former students mostly end up?
Mostly as fashion or shoe designers in well-known international fashion houses such as Louis Vuitton, J. Lindeberg and Viktor & Rolf. A significant number set up their own fashion label, or position themselves as a designer within a multidisciplinary field of fashion and the arts.

City
Arnhem

Country
the Netherlands

27

Programme

The ArtEZ Fashion Masters programme looks looks for designers who critically question the current mainstream fashion system and seek out the boundaries of the prevailing fashion discourse through research and design. Students are capable of thinking conceptually, a distinctive feature of fashion education in Arnhem, and of translating these concepts into relevant collections.

The fashion master's degree offers a small-scale research community where supervision is provided in both personal and critical ways. We attract talented designers who are skilled, who do not shy away from experimentation and interdisciplinary collaboration, and who manage to develop a clear perspective on their own role within the professional field of fashion. They are not afraid to change course when they need to.

In the first year, fashion and shoe design students follow a theoretical programme together with students of the Master Fashion Strategy, and they are stimulated to collaborate with each other. This theory programme is developed in partnership with the ArtEZ Fashion Professorship.

Students receive individual supervision from experienced professionals in the national and international field of fashion. This guarantees students' academic, creative and professional development and also allows them to build their own international network. The students conclude their degree work by designing a clothing or shoe collection, writing a thesis and putting together an extensive portfolio. Students are stimulated to reflect on alternative presentation and dissemination formats such as film and exhibitions. Each year the graduation collections are presented to an international audience.

Students have access to a range of workshop facilities.
Photo Sarah Meers

The atelier in the Master Fashion Design building.
Photo Sunanda Koning

Programme
  Fashion Design

Leads to
  Master Fashion Design

Structure
  The 2-year full-time course has a curriculum which consists of four semesters (orientation, reflection, creation, presentation), each of 21 weeks duration, and it focuses on three different domains: the artistic, theoretical and professional domain. In addition, workshops, lectures and an international exchange project constitute major elements of the curriculum.

Head of programme
  Mascha van Zijverden

Lecturers and tutors
  Lilian Driessen, Martin van Dusseldorp, Oscar Raaijmakers, Bibi Straatman, José Teunissen and Mark van Vorstenbos.

Notable alumni
  Monique van Heist, Claes Iversen, Bas Kosters, Spijkers & Spijkers, Jan Taminiau, and many others.

Course
Master Fashion Design

School
ArtEZ Institute of the Arts

School Facts

Duration of study
2 years

Full time
Yes (40 hours a week)

Part time
No

Female students
81%

Male students
19%

Local students
53%

Students from abroad
47%

Yearly enrolment
10

Tuition fee
EUR 1835 for EU citizens and EUR 8780 for non-EU citizens. There are exceptions – visit website for full details.

Funding/scholarships
Yes, ArtEZ scholarships for non-EU applicants are available on a competitive basis. Each year the fashion master's programme nominates outstanding students for the Huygens Scholarship.

Minimum requirements for entry
A bachelor's degree in fashion design. Candidates who want to apply for the specialisation in shoe design must have a bachelor's degree in fashion design, industrial design, product design or 3D design.

Language
English

Application procedure
Apply by registering online at studielink.nl and submitting the following:
- your curriculum vitae
- a letter of motivation
- a digital portfolio.
Based on this, an initial selection will be made. Selected applicants will be sent an admission assignment. If the assignment is evaluated as adequate, the applicant will be invited for an interview before an admission committee.

Application details
fashionmasters@artez.nl

Application deadline
Before 1 May

Graduation rate
99%

Job placement rate
High

Memberships/affiliations
n/a

Collaborations with
Parsons (United States), University of Creative Arts (United Kingdom), Hochschule für Technik und Wirtschaft Berlin (Germany).

Facilities for students
All students have their own studio workspace in a well-equipped atelier in the Master Fashion Design building which is open 7 days a week. There is a computer room with scan and print facilities and a kitchen for communal lunches. In addition, all facilities of ArtEZ Institute of the Arts are available for master's students, such as photography, print and silkscreen workshops, knitting room, library, etc.

Student Work

fake_me (2012)
By Matthias Louwen

'Fake' is part of our daily life, so better face it instead of avoiding it. To visualise the concept of fake_me, prints are used which make you look twice to find out whether something is fake or real. If this strategy is aimed at creating an illusion, the fabrics and cuts are also designed to play with the imagination and the thoughts of the spectator.
Photo Freudenthal/Verhagen

Synch (2012)
By Yohji van der Aa

The Synch collection is a backlash against the homogeneous idea/ concept of a collection. By realising an array of archetypes – that allow for unlimited combination – this work celebrates style, and identity through style. The outcome is a nonchalant yet 'dressed' collection where polished looks are to be avoided.
Photo Isolde Woudstra

Waltzing Lights (2012)
By Sabela Tobar Salazar

Waltzing Lights is inspired by the lifecycle of the jellyfish. Using the jellyfish as a metaphor, an evolving collection was created relying on the idea of metamorphosis and the fascination of the duality of such beautiful creatures being so deadly.
Photo Valentina Vos

Course
Master Fashion Design

School
ArtEZ Institute of the Arts

Jessy says 'Booo!!!' :) (2012)
By Gladys Tumewa

'The only real voyage of discovery consists not in seeking new landscapes but in having new eyes,' Marcel Proust. This collection is based on the idea of transgression in the bodies of children. Jessy's wardrobe closet is a contemplation of boundaries in the child's body: what is proper to wear, what do we culturally consider to be wrong, where are the limits of dress, and where are the taboo zones for children?
Photo Meinke Klein

The Beauty of Constructed Fusion (2012)
By Jenna Lievonen

This is a collection inspired by the construction of shoes. It is divided into the three elements which make a shoe complete – silhouette, texture and structure.
Photo Rein Janssen

Dangerous Liaisons (2012)
By Deniz Terli

This collection by Terli is the result of her own personal search for what it means to be a woman. Femininity and the performance of seduction are the collection's common threads. The shoes challenge and emphasise the set stereotypical rules on femininity, by playing with proportions, silhouette, graphics and materials.
Photo Pim Top and Mathijs Labadie

Conscious Imagination (2012)
By Amber A A Verstegen

The designer of this collection used her educational background in art history and shoe design to create and explore the boundaries between the two disciplines. As a result, her designs are a rare reflection on the similarities as well as differences between these two fields.
Photo Simon Claassen

Alumna

Name Pauline van Dongen
Residence Arnhem, the Netherlands
Year of birth 1986
Year of graduation 2010
Current job Designer own label
Website paulinevandongen.nl

Why did you choose this school?
Because of its forward thinking approach, the variety of courses and the international experts who are invited to share their knowledge. Also, its highly respected group of alumni convinced me of the school's influence and distinction. I enjoyed the fact that it has a relatively small group of graduates each year.

Are you still in contact with the school?
Actually at the moment I have my studio in Arnhem, so I'm still close by.

What was the most important thing you learned here?
Through the guidance of great professionals, I was able to further develop my own signature style, which someone later described as 'sculptural science'. The course in shoe design led me to develop a new approach and working method which formed the basis for my current work. I improved my skills and knowledge in pattern cutting and garment construction, and I also expanded my network in fashion and my vision of my own position within it.

What are you doing now?
Right after graduating, I founded my own fashion label. Since then I've been working on various collections and exciting projects and collaborations. With my work, I aim to infuse fashion with technology; currently I am investigating the use of flexible solar cells in fashion. I am also embarking on a PhD in fashion and technology at the University of Technology in Eindhoven – the first fashion designer in the Netherlands to get this opportunity.

What was your graduation project?
I graduated with my collection Morphogenesis. I'm fascinated by the interaction between people and their surroundings. With this collection I explored the void between the body and the garment. Alienating shapes or capsules floating around the body are turned into clothes, like organic sculptures. Metal knitwear and the contrast between dark shades and bright tops create a sharp, minimalistic feel. As part of this collection, I developed one of the first fully 3D-printed heels in collaboration with Freedom Of Creation.

Was the transformation from graduation to working life a smooth one?
During the course, you're already being taught to work independently. After graduating, I was curious about having my own studio. I wouldn't say it's a smooth transition to start your own brand, but I love the challenges.

Any words of advice for future students?
Be open to new ideas, concepts and collaborations. Try to get the most out of every experience and never stop learning!

For her latest collection Kinetic Landscapes, van Dongen was inspired by eroded natural forms.

Course
Master Fashion Design

School
ArtEZ Institute of the Arts

Current Students

'My favourite hang out in the city is ZafVino and StijnKookt – always a nice atmosphere.'
Mirjam Colombo
Photo Sunanda Koning

'The best thing about this school? The lecturers – plus the ceramics workshop and a product development studio where you can explore a lot of other facilities.'
Stéphanie Baechler
Photo Sunanda Koning

'They teach you how to be an independent designer here. You really have to give it your all if you want to succeed .'
Laura de Weijer
Photo Sunanda Koning

'My advice to future students would be to have a long-term career view. Focus on it and make the best of it by seeking out the boundaries of your creativity, individuality and skills.'
Hilda Wijnhoud
Photo Sunanda Koning

'ArtEZ gives you a strong theoretical background alongside the practical aspects of fashion design, making your decisions more informed and congruent with contemporary fashion thought.'
Simeon Morris
Photo Sunanda Koning

'You learn how to make a professional collection and to think about how you want to position yourself in the fashion field.'
Barbara Langendijk
Photo Sunanda Koning

'The course gives you the insight of the whole process of building a big collection, from first drawing to sample to final garment, what the steps are in between, and how to organise these and meet with the deadlines.
Roos van Woudenberg
Photo Sunanda Koning

City Life

Arnhem, located in the eastern part of the Netherlands, has a sound reputation as city of fashion and design. It is home to a large number of designers and other professionals from a variety of disciplines such as art, music, dance, theatre and architecture. Upcoming young designers as well as established entrepreneurs in the creative industries offer a major impetus to the city's dynamic and entrepreneurial climate. The creative industries form the fastest growing sector of the Dutch economy. Arnhem plays a central role due to the high quality and concentration of its fashion activities. Various institutions and organisations – such as the Museum of Modern Art Arnhem, MoBA (Mode Biënnale Arnhem), Design Platform Arnhem and Arnhem Mode Incubator, aimed at young and promising fashion designers – further enhance the city's creative climate. The landmark main building of ArtEZ, located on the River Rhine, dates from 1963 and was designed by the famous Dutch architect and designer Gerrit Rietveld, associated with the De Stijl movement.

The MoBA fashion biennale takes place in June/July every 2 years, with events open to the public covering all aspects of fashion in different locations across the city.

the Netherlands

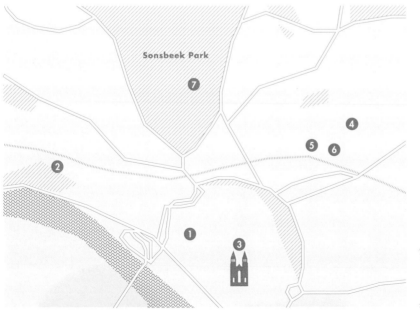

Sonsbeek Park

Arnhem

1 ArtEZ Institute of the Arts
2 Museum of Modern Art
3 Arnhem Coming Soon
4 Arnhem Fashion Quarter
5 Hotel Modez
6 Arnhem Mode Incubator

///// Park

Water

Main road

Course
Master Fashion Design

School
ArtEZ Institute of the Arts

City Facts

Museum of Modern Art Arnhem ②
MMKA, which displays art from the 20th century, pursues a dynamic and high-quality collection and exhibition policy.
mmkarnhem.nl

Kröller-Müller Museum
Located about 20 km from Arnhem in the Hoge Veluwe national park, this museum and has a world-leading collection of mainly 19th and 20th century fine art, including the biggest collection of works by Vincent van Gogh outside Amsterdam and an excellent sculpture garden.
kmm.nl

Mode Biënnale Arnhem
Known as MoBA since 2013, every 2 years this event offers a fresh look at the latest trends in lifestyle and fashion, fashion design and fashion culture at an international level.
moba.nu

Arnhem Coming Soon ③
This concept and design store in Arnhem concentrates on Dutch Design. Its assortment is an original mix of fashion and products by both promising young designers and established Dutch labels.
arnhemcomingsoon.nl

Arnhem Fashion Quarter ④
This area has a dense concentration of ateliers and shops run by young and upcoming designers.
modekwartier.nl

Hotel Modez ⑤
A unique style in this hotel – its entire interior and 20 individual rooms – has been created by 30 different fashion designers. The elevator alone, called 'the smallest fashion museum in the world', is worth a visit. Step in, close the door, push the button to the top floor and watch photographed fashion history develop – bottom to top – on various themes as you slowly make your way up.
hotelmodez.org

Arnhem Mode Incubator ⑥
This space offers facilities and advice to starting fashion designers, while designers offer fashion-related products or services.
arnhemmodeincubator.blogspot.com

Sonsbeek Park
The largest and most beautiful park in Arnhem, measuring some 67 hectares and set on a hillside is well worth a visit.
parksonsbeek.nl

How to get around
The ArtEZ Fashion Masters building building is in the inner city, not far from the ArtEZ Institute of the Arts main building and close to the railway station. Arnhem is only 1 hour by train from Amsterdam and 40 minutes from Utrecht. Arnhem has an attractive city centre which has much to offer in terms of shopping, entertainment and culture, and in addition to its large Sonsbeek Park it is surrounded by lovely green, hilly nature. A medium-size city, Arnhem is easy to get around by bike, while its public transport system is efficient and not over-crowded.

Arranging housing
Average

Housing support by school
No

Cost of room in the city
EUR 400 per month

Cost of room on campus
n/a

Bunka Fashion Graduate University

The knit computer lab, with its machines and state-of-the-art equipment, is fully accessible to students.

The mission of Bunka, with its campus in central Tokyo, is to ensure the next-generation of designers are educated to be fully integrated into the global fashion business.

Bunka Fashion Graduate University (BFGU)
3-22-1 Yoyogi
151-8521 Shibuya, Tokyo
Japan

T +81 (0)332 992 701
otoiawase@bfgu-bunka.ac.jp
bfgu-bunka.ac.jp

Course
Fashion Design

School
Bunka Fashion Graduate University

Introduction

'We foster the ability in students to explore and experiment freely'

Sanae Kosugi, dean

When was the school founded?
The Graduate School was founded in 2006, consisting of three courses: fashion design, fashion technology and fashion business management. Historically, the school has its foundations in Bunka Gakuen, an educational foundation dating back to 1922.

Has it changed much over the years?
Yes. Fashion is a mirror of society: it continuously changes. To educate future fashion designers who can meet the needs of society, our curriculum and teaching method is regularly revised and updated.

Why should students choose this school?
Our philosophy is to educate creative talent that can be competitive in the global market. With this in mind, we focus on fashion design as well technology and business. Not only equipped with skills to design clothes, but to have the technical skills to understand how their design would actually be made, and whether it is marketable or not.

What is studying at this school all about?
Studying at Bunka is about finding the seed of your own, unique creations. We foster the ability in students to explore and experiment freely before they go out in to society as a professional designer. School is like a research lab. They can be bold and crazy, but their designs always need to be feasible.

What kind of teaching method is applied?
We don't use a guidebook or specific format, as teaching is particular to each student. Our education is more like a one-to-one approach. We don't assign themes or concepts to work on, students need to propose these for themselves, then develop them under our guidance.

What is expected from the students?
They must be dedicated and focused in the pursuit of their original concept. Students are also expected to manage the entire process of their fashion design. They will come to understand that the design process is not just about giving attractive form to fabric, but needs to be a compromise with economy, whether it is adoptable for factory manufacturing.

What is the most important skill to master?
To be original. If one's design is similar to something already in the market, who will buy it?

Programme

The MA Fashion Design programme is focused on creating unique designers capable of competing in the international market, while allowing students to master the means necessary to connect design with business success. Our mottos are: realise creative design underlined by masterful skills; not to create something replaceable; aspire to be number one in the world; and pursue your own ideas.

The course includes concept work, seminars and practice sessions, further strengthened by classes in the management field which includes global business and business enterprise.

The ultimate goal of the programme is for students to design and produce their own fashion collection consisting of 10 to 15 pieces and present them in runway-show form.

Bunka's training educates students in the very latest methods used by the industry.

Bunka Gakuen Costume Museum is a vast source of inspiration for students from Japanese ceremonial dress to ethnic costumes of the world.

Programme
Fashion Design

Leads to
Master of Arts

Structure
The 2-year full time course begins in early April with students establishing their own theme and concept to work on. Alongside this they will take seminars, practices and classes, including 18 units of design field classes to deepen and cultivate their skills in creative design, as well as classes on fashion business management. The course also has 7 units of technology field classes for future designers to be well informed about how their design can be realised. These include classes on CAD operation, characteristics of materials, fashion production, human engineering and strategies for globally competitive fashion.

Head of programme
Shinichi Kushigemachi

Mentors and lecturers
Sanae Kosugi, Shinichi Kushigemachi, Yhoji Yamamoto, Atsurou Tayama, Hiroko Koshino, Junko Koshino, Kichisaburou Ogawa, Yoshyuki Miyamae, Tamae Hirokawa, Hiroyuki Horihata, Akira Minagawa and Nicola Formichetti.

Alumnus
Yusuke Takahashi

Course
Fashion Design

School
Bunka Fashion Graduate University

School Facts

Duration of study
2 years

Full time
Yes (25 hours a week)

Part time
No

Female students
76%

Male students
24%

Local students
36%

Students from abroad
64%

Yearly enrolment
53

Tuition fee
JPY 1,450,000 per year includes enrolment fee (approx. EUR 11,000)

Funding/scholarships
Yes

Minimum requirements for entry
Bachelor's degree in relevant field

Language
Japanese

Application procedure
Your application should include the following:
- your personal and contact details
- your curriculum vitae
- application form
- portfolio
- proof of Japanese proficiency. Candidates are invited to take an examination, for which an application exam fee of JPY 35,000 (approx. EUR 270) must be paid. Successful individuals will be informed by email.

Application details
otoiawase@bfgu-bunka.ac.jp

Application date
By mid-February for April intake

Graduation rate
83%

Job placement rate
90%

Memberships/affiliations
Association of Private Universities of Japan

Collaborations with
St. Petersburg State University of Technology and Design (Russia), Central Saint Martins and London Colleges of Art and Design (United Kingdom), Domus Academy and Istituto Marangoni (Italy), Fashion Institute of Technology (France) and Beijing Institute of Fashion Technology (China).

Facilities for students
Library, costume museum, knitting computer application room, costume reference room, textile laboratories (including digital textile machinery), research laboratory for fashion textiles and production management application room.

Student Work

Underside Heaven (2013)
By Harue Nagamoto

This collection is inspired by the story of a fictional queen and her bodyguard.
Photo Josui Yasuda

Parade (2013)
By Akie Ueda

Visualisation in fashion of Japanese writer Yasutaka Tsutsui's 1993 science fiction novel *Paprica*, in which the leading actor infiltrates human dreams.
Photo Josui Yasuda

Inclusion (2012)
By Ayako Kadoya

Inclusion refers to the foreign material within minerals. The design aims at expressing the beauty of having inclusion rather than eliminating the inclusion as a defect. The design brings to light a rather unique aspect of having inclusion in a form of fashion.
Photo Josui Yasuda

Course
Fashion Design

School
Bunka Fashion Graduate University

Whalabout (2013)
By Hiroshi Akiha

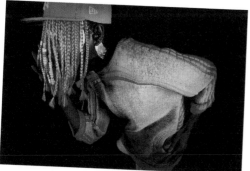

This fashion collection is all about sports knitwear, with inspiration coming from African colours and Afro-American culture.
Photo Siva

Anomie (2012)
By Junnosuke Kato

An urban collection, inspired by the collision of social order, morals and values – abandonment of universality.
Photo Norifumi Fukuda

Creative Evolution (2012)
By Tatsuya Tamada

Taking inspiration from the paintings of Polish decadent artist Zdzisław Beksiski, design is formalisation in fashion about the next evolution of human body.
Photo Eri Nakazawa

Contingency Theory (2013)
By Kaori Tanaka

The theme of this project came about by thinking outside the box of what a garment is all about. Tanaka applied unrestricted, contingent theory to fashion design.
Photo Momiji

It Is Alive (2012)
By Saeyoung Bird Park

Exploring life, colour and a freewill of expression resulted in a collection with a vibrant potency.
Photo Jun Matarai

Alumnus

Name Ikuma Fujikawa
Residence Tokyo, Japan
Year of birth 1984
Year of graduation 2010
Current job Fashion designer
Website amakiru.com

Why did you choose Bunka?

I did my undergraduate studies there and decided to stay as I knew the graduate school has outstanding facilities, as well as a flexible curriculum to further strengthen one's creativity in fashion.

What was the most interesting thing you studied?

I was into developing new materials – designing textiles is at the core of my creativity. Experimenting with printing, dyeing, texture and playing with the combination of these elements were fascinating aspects of design for me.

What was the most important lesson you learnt at Bunka?

To hand in your best possible work within the time limit. This is fundamental thing, but it is hard as a student to produce more than 10 pieces for the final presentation while you are expected to apply for other contests as well. Now that I own a company of my own brand, to be able manage all the production schedule is something I cherish learning at school.

How was the transition from studying to working life?

As I founded my own company, the difficulty was to get work. But being an owner of your brand means you get direct responses.

What are you doing now?

I am the owner of fashion brand Amakiru, meaning 'the clouds block the light from the sun'. I also design costumes for musicians and performers for commercial advertisements, music videos and live concerts.

Are you still in touch with the school?

I send out invitations to the teachers when I have shows or events. Teachers kindly come over when they have time. As we are in the same industry, occasionally we come across each other. As for my classmates, I am connected via social media. There are several others who have their own brand like me, so we exchange information and help each other when we can.

Any advice for future students?

To think thoroughly what it means to produce things in this society full of objects. In the fashion field, one needs to think about the over saturation of clothes, decline in consumption, downslide of prices and the value of design. To become a fashion designer means to design the whole environment surrounding a single piece of clothing.

Fujikawa designs womenswear that has urban chic qualities.

Course
Fashion Design

School
Bunka Fashion Graduate University

Current Students

'The class I enjoyed most was learning the complexity of traditional menswear, especially the pattern making and the detailing.'
Ruri Tayama

'I come from Korea and was attracted to the school because of its famous name. I like the classes where we learn the latest fashion trends, as well as the different technologies and pattern making that shape garments.'
Park Minseo

'Students from abroad need to be highly motivated as they need to have a certain level of Japanese language skills for presentations. However, there are many foreign students who take on this challenge and study at the school. I think it will be an enormous asset for one's future to experience Japanese culture and research amongst unrivalled facilities like those at Bunka.'
Yukari Shimizu

'My teacher in Shanghai recommended the school. You get to work on knitting, design drawing, CAD for fashion, all of these classes give practical knowledge for becoming a designer. I don't feel homesick here because the good thing about Tokyo is that you will surely find good Chinese food!'
Cui Lina

'I think the facilities at BFGU are top level. You can't get a better environment to learn fashion. I like it when we visit textile factories, weavers and sewing factories and actually see the technology in practice.'
Syouhei Kinoshita

City Life

With some 13 million people living and working in Tokyo, it is an exciting city that seemingly never sleeps. Fashion-obsessed youngsters create a world-famous street culture. Hidden in small areas in Tokyo, one can find artisanal workshops and factories alongside the city's skyscrapers which underline high-quality Japanese crafted objects. There is no difficulty finding materials needed for student projects, research inspiration and reading materials. There is a wealth of exhibitions and events giving plenty of opportunities for students to immerse themselves in the world of fashion.

Close to the school is the Shinjuku area, which is one of the largest commercial and business centres in Tokyo, providing everything from high-end shopping to electrical appliances and endless choices of restaurants and bars. The choice of dining and entertainment venues is endless, and coupled with a well-serviced network of public transportation means students can get the most out of Tokyo.

The school is in downtown Tokyo, only a short distance from the world's busiest travel hub, Shinjuku Station.

Japan

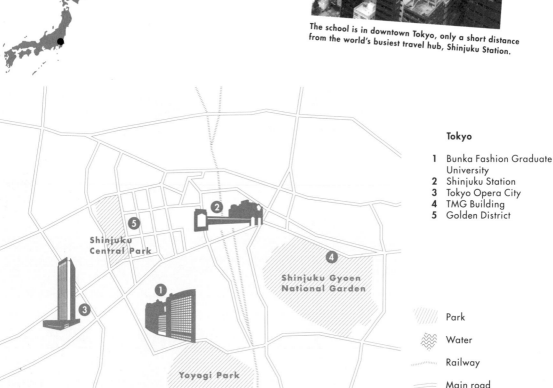

Tokyo

1 Bunka Fashion Graduate University
2 Shinjuku Station
3 Tokyo Opera City
4 TMG Building
5 Golden District

Shinjuku Central Park

Shinjuku Gyoen National Garden

Yoyogi Park

Park

Water

Railway

Main road

Course
Fashion Design

School
Bunka Fashion Graduate University

City Facts

See more Tokyo City Facts on p. 245

Shinkuju Station ②
Shinjuku Station is classed as the world's busiest transport hub (according to the *Guinness World Records* in 2007). It serves as a hub to connect central Tokyo with the western suburbs.

Tokyo Opera City Art Gallery ③
This is a well-known gallery for exhibiting all kinds of contemporary art. It was opened in 1999 and holds special exhibitions four times a year.
operacity.jp/en/ag

Shinjuku Gyoen
Shinjuku Gyoen National Park is the place to go to witness the amazing cherry blossoms in the springtime. Originally constructed on the site of a private mansion, it was opened to the public after the Second World War. It has a circumference of 3.5 km and three distinct styles: French Formal Garden, English Landscape Garden and Japanese Traditional Garden.
env.go.jp/garden/shinjukugyoen

TMG Building ④
The Tokyo Metropolitan Government Building provides probably the best observation deck to see the Tokyo skyline and Mount Fuji.
metro.tokyo.jp

Golden District ⑤
Deep inside the dense area of Kabuki-cho, one can find the rows of tiniest bars as if kept within a time capsule from back in the days.

How to get around
BFGU is located in the Shibuya ward, just south of Shinjuku. Students mostly travel using public transport, such as subways and trains. The school is only a 7-minute walk from Shinjuku Station, and there are good connections to other stations such as Shibuya, Ikebukuro, Ueno and Shinagawa and the full railway network. For those living near the school, bicycles are also a popular mode of transportation. The nearest airport is Haneda Airport, which is about a 30-minute journey by train. Narita International Airport is about 90 km from the school.

Arranging housing
Average

Housing support by school
Yes

Cost of room in the city
JPY 80,000 per month
(approx. EUR 650)

Cost of campus housing
JPY 60,000 per month
(approx. EUR 500)

De Montfort University

Specialist machine rooms are among the facilities on offer.

De Montfort University (DMU)
School of Fashion and Textiles
Leicester LE1 9BH
United Kingdom

T +44 (0)116 250 6249
adh@dmu.ac.uk
dmu.ac.uk/adhpg

Trinity House at DMU is one of the oldest buildings on campus and it is the location of the vice chancellor's office.
Photo Jack O'Sullivan

Course
Fashion and Bodywear

School
De Montfort University

Introduction

'Studying here is all about creative and technical design – the two cannot be separated'

Julie King, head of the School of Fashion and Textiles

When was the school founded and how has it changed?
Our school at De Montfort University dates back to 1875, with a historical connection to the tremendous number of textile mills and associated industries in the region. We developed a programme in contour fashion in response to the local corsetry industry 66 years ago, and a decade later started a footwear design course, again responding to local demand. The master's degree in fashion was established in 2006.

What is studying at this school all about?
It's all about creative and technical design – the two cannot be separated.

What kind of teaching method do you use?
We use a variety of teaching methods, including the traditional practitioner approach which is very hands on, along with lectures and small group seminars. We have introduced a range of TEL resources recently, including screencasts of popular software programs and 'how to do it' film clips on our virtual learning blackboard.

Why should students choose this school?
Our strength lies in our very close relationships with industry, Students work on live industry briefs, and have opportunities for internships overseas with brands, such as Gap and Clover, and we pride ourselves on developing highly industry-ready graduates.

What do you expect from students?
We expect everyone to work hard and be passionate about the subject, naturally, but we also strive to develop a balance in our students between the creative and the technical.

What is the most important thing for students to learn during this course?
Technical skills and how to balance them with creativity, how to work with unusual materials and how to push their design skills to the limit.

What is the most important fashion skill to master for a fashion designer?
Understanding your strengths and developing them to the utmost.

What career paths do your graduates embark on?
The programme prepares its graduates for a variety of roles, ranging from design, product development, buying and garment technology, to working freelance or starting up a small business. Graduates to date have gone on to work for both national and multinational companies, specialising in fashion outerwear and intimate apparel, such as Bravissimo. There is also the possibility of advancing research initiated on this course to PhD level.

City
Leicester

Country
United Kingdom

47

Programme

The MA Fashion and Bodywear course offers a predominantly practical, design-led experience in fashion and intimate apparel aesthetics. The distinctive strengths of the School of Fashion and Textiles with its long standing heritage in contour design offer a unique learning environment for this fusion of design disciplines.

Practical study is offered in the areas of fashion and contour design under the direction of specialist tutors. These areas can include fashion outerwear, jersey wear, lingerie, corsetry, bra making, swimwear and lounge wear. Access to a range of industry-standard resources and machinery for both outerwear and intimate apparel provides the opportunity for design ideas to be realised to a professional standard.

The programme concentrates on extending and deepening existing creative, technical and intellectual knowledge, in order to develop new skills and design capabilities. A philosophy of developing independent learners is promoted. Tuition builds on individual learners' skills and knowledge in order to develop new capabilities of design investigation, experimentation, analysis and production. Supported by specialist staff, students are encouraged to negotiate and direct their own learning. The development of critical and reflective analytical skills alongside design practice is emphasised. Networking opportunities to extend learning through collaborative working practices are encouraged to uncover new potential in design research and innovation. Participation in key national and international competitions is a feature of the learning experience.

Students have the opportunity to broaden their practical skills in all areas of fashion and textiles.

Designs by students on show at New Designers, the annual exhibition for graduate work held in London.

Programme
Fashion and Bodywear

Leads to
Master of Arts

Structure
The 1-year full-time course is divided over three semesters and is modular (taught and research). The first two semesters include research methodologies/design innovation modules to support students in the production of individual and creative 2D/3D designs. Other modules include business planning for the creative practitioner and critical perspectives on ethical and sustainable fashion, and fashion marketing/design research and development. The third semester is dedicated to the major project in design.

Head of programme
Rachel Toner

Mentors and lecturers
Emily Baines, David Morris, Dee Parker, Alison Prince, Gillian Proctor, Julia Reeve, Rachel Toner and Laurie Truscott.

Notable alumni
Unknown

Course
Fashion and Bodywear

School
De Montfort University

School Facts

Duration of study
1 year

Full time
Yes (40 hours a week)

Part time
Yes (over 2 years)

Female students
80%

Male students
20%

Local students
37.5%

Students from abroad
62.5%

Yearly enrolment
15–20

Tuition fee
- GBP 4200 for EU citizens (approx. EUR 4850)
- GBP 12,200 for non-EU citizens (approx. EUR 14,000)

Funding/scholarships
Yes, see ed.ac.uk/schools-departments/student-funding

Minimum requirements for entry
Bachelor's degree in related field and/or 2 years of professional experience

Language
English

Application procedure
Your application should include the following:
- your personal and contact details
- your curriculum vitae
- application form
- digital portfolio showing 10 images of your strongest work
- evidence of pattern cutting and garment manufacture
- 200-word description of your proposed direction of study
- proof of language (if applicable). Successful applicants will be informed by email.

Application details
By 1 July

Application date
Before 30 June

Graduation rate
High

Job placement rate
High

Memberships/affiliations
n/a

Collaborations with
n/a

Facilities for students
Specialist machine rooms, CAD labs, product design and textile multimedia workshops, library with specialist books, journals, trend-forecasting packages, online learning platform, study skills support and language support for international students.

Student Work

The Dys-Appearing Body (2012)
By Ania Sadkowska

A collection of moulded-leather and hand-knitted pieces utilising traditional craft techniques to embrace the natural beauty of the materials. This project aims is to analyse and explore the concept of the 'dys-appearing body' understood as the literal and metaphorical ageing of the female body leading to its social invisibility.
Photo Fraser West

Geometric Nature (2012)
By Judith Bell

A lingerie and lounge wear collection inspired by succulents and the mathematics of nature, commenting on notions of minimalism combined with excess. Geometry is explored from both a construction and surface-pattern perspective.
Photo Nigel Essex

Loungerie (2011)
By Maggie Liu

A collection fusing lingerie with lounge wear to create a sophisticated and elegant range of garments for the strong contemporary woman. Key inspiration comes from Renaissance painting, in particular the chiaroscuro technique with its contrasting effects of light and dark.
Photo courtesy of Nigel Essex

Course
Fashion and Bodywear

School
De Montfort University

Bodywear (2011)
By Penny Newton

A collection of fashion and bodywear incorporating traditional tailoring and corsetry techniques, together with digital print and perspex moulding.
Photo Grace Elkin

Femme-Enfant (2012)
By Karena Meng

A fusion of fashion and musical instruments, inspired by Man Ray's provocative Le Violon d'Ingres (1924), showing the metamorphosis of woman into instrument. Garments explore the female body through the refined and contoured forms of the violin and cello, with other surreal touches added, such as oversized glove patterns.

Morphogenesis (2012)
By Pratytush Kumar

A young, sporty collection. The colour palette consists of brights associated with the sport of skiing and with cellular images of morphogenesis. During mutation of cells, bright colours are noticed, and a grid-like structure is also formed, which inspired the print artwork.
Photo Nigel Essex

Alumna

Name Lisa Mansel
Residence Stafford, United Kingdom
Year of birth 1986
Year of graduation 2011
Current job CAD lingerie designer
Clients Sainsburys, Peacocks,
Factory Shop, Figleaves
Website elsieloves.carbonmade.com

Why did you choose this school?
I chose to study at De Montfort as it is renowned for its contour and lingerie programmes. It seemed the perfect way for me to further my knowledge in this specialist area.

What was the most important thing you learned here?
The most important thing was about discovering myself. I discovered strengths I did not know I had. It boosted my confidence levels, self-motivation and commitment to the course. This has since made me able to future my career in lingerie.

What was your most interesting project?
The most interesting project was exploring lingerie, swimwear and outerwear. This was a capsule collection that portrayed femininity and highlighted the erogenous zones through the use of fabrics, style lines and a vibrant and loud, yet silent colour palette. Using sensuous silks, combined with woven fabrics and power nets helped me to provide a story of sophistication, simplicity and stimulation.

What subject do you wish you paid more attention to?
I think I paid attention to all subjects equally, as I knew I had such a short window to cram all the information from the course into my brain.

What was your graduation project?
My graduation project was entitled 'Self vs Self'. This was a collection of underwear and outerwear garments exploring the simultaneous presence of modesty and exhibitionism fuelled by the philosophical theories of Freud's three constructs of the mind, the link between fashion and identity, body manipulation and the Baroque period.

Any words of advice for future students?
Utilise the staff there to soak up as much information and knowledge on the subject. Make the most of your time and use it to explore the topic areas, but also yourself. Embrace the learning curve.

Where did you live at the time?
At the beginning of the course, I lived in a one bedroom flat very close to the University. For the last 6 months I house-shared with a class mate as we got on so well, so it was a perfect set-up.

What was your favourite place to hang out?
My favourite place to hang out was definitely The Polar Bear, a bar with a great atmosphere! Oh and The Firebug, my brother was also studying his degree at De Montfort at the same time so we always had a good catch up here – great memories.

Was the transformation from graduation to working life a smooth one?
It did take a while for me to enter into working life; having to make sure I really stood out from every other fashion graduates in the ever-competitive industry. I tried to publicise my work in many different ways to get myself noticed.

In Mansel's graduation project saw influences from the Baroque period to create embellished pieces.

Course
Fashion and Bodywear

School
De Montfort University

Current Students

'For me, the key factor was the great international reputation of DMU and its recognition for contour fashion. This unique combination allowed me to integrate and develop my design interest in both underwear and outerwear structures.'

Anna Maria Sadkowska

'The pattern-cutting workshop was very valuable. I progressed significantly with the skills I acquired and learnt to love pattern-cutting as an art.'

Judith Bell

'The choice and freedom on this course was most valuable. It was inspiring to have so many specialised facilities, resources and workshops within my reach. I could experiment in the workshops, and really enjoyed exploring the shoe design department too. The guidance was accurate and professional but never suffocating – I'm grateful to the staff for giving me the chance to develop my design voice by myself.'

Chiyono Jaeger

'The most important part of the course was getting to specialise in one form. We had the full freedom to practice this through different materials and techniques, as well as all the resources during the master's course.'

Pratyush Kumar

City Life

Leicester is in the heart of England. It is a bustling destination with shops and cafes in a lively, safe atmosphere among pleasant open spaces. The city itself is thriving and fast-evolving centre of business, with prestigious companies and creative enterprises jostling for position.

The city is a cosmopolitan hub, with much to see and do, including attractions such as the National Space Centre and Curve Theatre. It also has a new, sate-of-the-art shopping complex housing a multiplex cinema. Bars, pubs, restaurants and cafes are in abundance so there is never a long walk between friendly venues offering food, drink or entertainment.

The city is also very green, with a number of large expanses of parkland available for relaxation. The closest to town is Victoria Park, which is where many students like to hang out in the summer thanks to the vicinity to campus and areas where students live. A short drive away there is also Abbey Park in the north and Braunstone Park in the west.

United Kingdom

The Magazine Gateway Monument, *circa* 1410, is a mediaeval gateway that was once part of Leicester Castle.
Photo Jack O'Sullivan

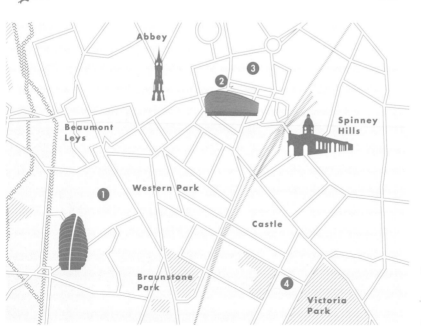

Leicester

1 DMU
2 Curve Theatre
3 Phoenix Square
4 De Montfort Hall

Park

Railway

Main road

Course
Fashion and Bodywear

School
De Montfort University

City Facts

Curve Theatre ②
Leicester's iconic performing arts centre was designed by world-famous architect Rafael Viñoly and has hosted stars such as Marc Warren and Oscar-winner Juliette Binoche.
curveonline.co.uk

Phoenix Square ③
Partly-funded by DMU, with three cinema screens showing art house (as well as popular) cinema on advanced digital screens with a digital exhibition space and digital production facilities it is also a space for new creative businesses. This is also the location of DMU Cube, an interactive digital arts space showcasing cutting-edge work.
phoenixsquare.co.uk

De Montfort Hall ④
This is a beautiful concert venue set within its own grounds with a full programme of events throughout the year, including pop concerts to classical recitals – from Motorhead to Mozart. It is located adjacent to the city's Victoria Park.

National Space Centre
This is the largest dedicated space and astronomy centre in the United Kingdom and one of the leading visitor attractions in the East Midlands. From the futuristic rocket tower to the domed cinema and planetarium, it's an out of this world experience.
spacecentre.co.uk

Museums
Dinosaurs, mummies, Roman remains, classic and modern art, steam and industry, even Wallace and Gromit, Leicester's museums appeal to all ages and interests.
leicester.gov.uk/museums

Local Music Scene
There is a healthy live music scene in Leicester at venues, such as The Musician and The Shed. De Montfort Hall is also an excellent venue for seeing more established bands and artists. The annual Summer Sundae festival, held in the grounds of De Montfort Hall, is a very popular event with a relaxed atmosphere.
summersundae.com

How to get around
Leicester is a young city, having a large contingent of students – with a number of universities located in the city. DMU's campus, comprising 10 modern halls of residence offering around 3000 university rooms, is just a 10-minute walk from the city centre. Getting around the city is easy using the bus and public transport system, taxis and also cycling, with many dedicated cycle paths connecting different parts of the city. The train station has local and high-speed train links to the rest of the country, with London just over 1 hour away by train (69 minutes to be precise). The nearest airport is East Midlands airport which is only 30 minutes away by shuttle bus (Skylink).

Arranging housing
Average

Housing support by school
Yes

Cost of room in the city
GBP 400 (approx. EUR 465)

Cost of campus housing
GBP 350 (approx. EUR 400)

Domus
Academy

Student facilities include strategically placed workstations dotted around the school.

Domus Academy
Via Darwin 20
20143 Milan
Italy

T +39 02 4241 4001
info@domusacademy.it
domusacademy.com

Teaching encourages a practical but personal approach to fashion.

Course
Fashion Design

School
Domus Academy

Introduction

'We value the individual approach and try to balance this with craft and vision, all within the context of real market demands'

Barbara Trebitsch, head of the School of Fashion

When was the academy founded, and how has it evolved over time?
Domus Academy was founded in 1982 by leading figures in the Italian art and design world. Our academic programmes enhance and match the growing needs of contemporary society. Since 2009, the academy has been part of Laureate International Universities, a leading international network of more than 70 innovative higher education institutions, thus offering our students more opportunities.

What is unique about this school's vision?
Since the founding of the fashion master's course in 1983, we have strived to be an open environment conducive to reflection and criticism, bringing together students and companies to pursue real-world projects on the most important aspects of contemporary life. We have a professional network-based development experience that is deeply rooted in the Milan fashion system. We value the individual approach and try to balance this with craft and vision, all within the context of real market demands.

What is your approach to teaching?
It is based on a 'learning by designing' methodology, through which students learn by actively carrying out their projects under the mentorship of experienced, professional designers, a system which puts processes at its core, maintaining the human being as the focal point of any project.

Why do students pick this school?
Because of Italian design culture and the Italian approach to design, plus our concept of diversity as a value and of learning by designing. Our entire faculty is made up of professional designers (Alessandro Dell'Acqua, Elio Fiorucci, Ennio Capasa, Diego Dolcini and Ildo Damiano) and we involve international companies in educational activities (Fendi, Cartier, Moschino, Pomellato, Vionnet, Versace and others). Domus Academy is repeatedly rated among the world's top design schools.

What can students expect here?
Students coming here are experienced design professionals seeking advanced and highly reputed degrees for business applications. They have the chance to carry out important projects together with leading companies and must challenge themselves in a 'close to reality' learning environment.

What's the main thing you teach students?
We enable them to develop their own signature as designers and to join the job market with high professional skills.

City
Milan

Country
Italy

Programme

The objective of Domus Academy master's programme in Fashion Design is to bring students into direct contact with the real fashion world, in Italy and abroad, in order to render them employable or in a position to manage the start-up of their own brand.

The course is geared towards providing the tools not only to help students understand how things are done, but also to help them to understand the reasons why they are done that way. The structure of the programme is based upon the project experience, with a one-to-one emphasis which supports students in the development of a personal yet advanced approach to design processes and to outline their own design identity. At the end of it, students will: understand the trends, cultural and contemporary issues influencing the fashion design domain; produce innovative solutions with awareness of the global fashion system; foster a personal creative style and individual expressive language; generate ideas and specify appropriate means of production; demonstrate a deep degree of awareness concerning production in the fashion system; and establish an individual mode expression.

The course is aimed at high achievers with a good honours degree in a fashion- or textile-related subject, and those with substantial experience in the fashion industry who want to develop and refine their skills through postgraduate study.

Just some of the 9000 books in the academy's library.

The main entrance of the Domus Academy, which opens up the world of Italian design to its students.

Programme
Fashion Design

Leads to
Master in Fashion Design

Structure
The courses provide the tools necessary to acquire an in-depth fashion culture and to explore marketing practices. Offering an overview aimed at the knowledge of the field, the programme includes a series of four workshops that is intended to exploit, reach and challenge opportunities of cooperative projects with companies and professionals. The academic master's degree includes the possibility of an internship as the final step of a pathway, with a deep and balanced evaluation of the student's skills and aspirations, in order to build a career which fits the student's aims. The last phase involves the development of a final master project.

Head of programme
Sara Desimoni

Mentors and lecturers
Antonella Antonelli, Riccardo Grassi, Roberta Valentini, Sara Maino, Raffaello Napoleone, Alessandro Dell'Acqua, Antonio Berardi, Antonio Mancinelli, Carlo Rivetti, Carlos Osman, Cav. Mario Boselli, Emanuela Bacchiani, Diego Dolcini, Ennio Capasa, Felice Limosani, Gianluca Cantaro, Ildo Damiano, Marco Giani, Martino Scabbia Guerrini, Maurizio Galante, Maurizio Modica and Pierfrancesco Gigliotti.

Notable alumni
Diego Dolcini, Oscar Carvallo, Anna Dello Russo, Carlos Osman, Chul Young Choi, Erkan Coruh, Fabio Cammarata, Lorenza Baschieri, Giovanni Morelli and Alessia Xoccato.

Course
Fashion Design

School
Domus Academy

School Facts

Duration of study
1 year

Full time
Yes (40 hours a week)

Part time
No

Female students
88%

Male students
12%

Local students
0%

Students from abroad
100%

Yearly enrolment
25

Tuition fee
- EUR 16,500 per year for EU citizens
- EUR 23,790 per year for non-EU citizens

Funding/scholarships
Yes. The Domus Academy financial aid consists of a partial reduction of the tuition fees that can be granted to deserving students with financial constraints.

Minimum requirements for entry
Bachelor's degree or professional experience

Language
English

Application procedure
The following documents are required for registration:
- a completed application form
- a curriculum vitae
- a statement of purpose
- a portfolio of projects
- a copy of your BA degree certificate
- a copy of your IELTS language certificate or recognised equivalent certificate (if appropriate)
- two letters of recommendation issued by your school, teacher or employer
- a copy of your passport
- a copy of the receipt of the application fee payment.
In order to apply and be considered for admission, an application fee of EUR 100 must be paid. Applications are reviewed by the Admission Committee. Within 10 working days, candidates will be provided with feedback on whether the outcome is positive or negative.

Application details
domusacademy.com/site/home/how-to-apply/admissions--registration-guidance.html

Application date
Before 5 August for courses starting in September and before 30 November for courses starting in January

Graduation rate
100%

Job placement rate
67%

Memberships/affiliations
Piattaforma Sistema Formativo Moda, Fashion Colloquia Series and Patronage Camera Nazionale della Moda Italiana.

Collaborations with
Companies: 7 For All Mankind, Alessandro Dell'Acqua N°21, Antonio Berardi, Costume National, Eastpak, Fay, Fiorucci Love Therapy, Fondazione Gianfranco Ferrè, Frankie Morello, Havaianas, Hogan, Maurizio Galante – Tal Lancman, Interware, Meltin 'Pot, Napapijri, Neil Barret, Nike, SAOBC (South African Ostrich Business Chamber), Stefanel, Ter et Bantine, Versace, Vueve Clicquot, Victor Bellaish, Virtus Palestre and Ermenegildo Zegna.

Facilities for students
A libary, computers and workstations all wireless enabled, laboratories for model-making, metal, wood, plastic and 3D section, plus a fashion lab with a workroom for students to make their prototypes. The lab is equipped with swing machines, mannequins, irons, a sewing table and additional tools. A dedicated Career Services office supports students and graduates in the development of a successful professional path.

City
Milan

Country
Italy

Student Work

The Seven Deadly Sins (2012)
By Alina Bianca Ciobotaru

A project based on wrath, greed, sloth, pride, lust, envy and gluttony and the quality that glues the world together: debauchery.

In Between (2012)
By Tea Chakhnashvili

The concept is to show the huge gap between the individual perception and reality ; the main aim is to create a well-constructed collection, balanced with clean lines fusing with a woman's sensuality.

Course
Fashion Design

School
Domus Academy

In the River of Time (2012)
By Se Lee Lee

A search for the cultural and historical traces of time, implemented in a collection by visualising important life moments.

Solve et Coagula (2012)
By Cora Maria Bellotto

A link between body and spirit, merging together alchemy, Christianity and psychology into a whole where opposites unite. Ecclesiastical costumes inspire shapes, details and finishing.

Supreme Virginity (2012)
By Yueh Lin Tsou

In physical geography, tundra is a zone where tree growth is hindered. By making tundra scenery and wildlife movement the main language of the design, the collection aims at nature's clarity of strength.

Simultaneity in Picasso's Work (2012)
By Areum Roh

An attempt to design applying the method used by Picasso and the cubists. Several sides coexist which cannot be seen from the front, representing the other's point of view as well as our own imagination.

Alumnus

Name Carlos Osman
Residence Milan, Italy
Year of birth 1965
Year of graduation 1989
Current job Accessories designer
Website carlososman.com

Why did you choose to attend this school?

I did a degree in architecture in my own country, Colombia, and while I was finishing university my main interest became focused on fashion design. Domus Academy was the perfect place for someone with my background, because of the mix of fashion and design and so many topics that I hadn't expected: history of fashion, anthropology, arts and other things besides – all of which gave me a higher conception of the fashion world. In addition, the director of the fashion department was Gianfranco Ferré, who was not only one of the most important Italian fashion designers, but also an architect like me.

What was the most important thing you learned at Domus Academy?

That fashion is not only a matter of design. It's a very complex field with so many opportunities and things to explore.

What are you doing now?

I'm an accessories designer. I've also worked as a consultant for many Italian brands designing leather goods.

How did the school prepare you for what you are doing now?

It taught me the concept of research, the process of developing my own ideas and it gave me the rigour to get the results I'm looking for.

What was your graduation project?

It was something about coats and the primordial concept of protection.

Was the transition from graduation to working life a smooth one?

Yes. I was lucky, Milan then was the world centre of fashion.

Any words of advice for future students at the academy?

The school is the best there is for research and it teaches you to understand the freedom of your mind – don't miss out on that chance! Actually, I'd love to back to school again!

Today, Osman is a successful accessories designer with two of his creations shown here.

Current Students

'My favourite workshop keeps changing – it is always the one I am working on now! The research is the most interesting part, it gives you the chance to experiment new ways of expression even if the formula is more or less the same. It gives you the opportunity to work on your personal interpretation of it. The most valuable classes are those when professionals in the field share their experiences and stimulate you to succeed with the same passion for what you do.'
Francesca De Giorgio

'At Domus, you have the chance to learn how to express yourself better and to act in a professional way while working in the industry.'
Zeynep Guntas

'I love to be able to go to Pitti Uomo in Florence and visit the textile exhibitions. We have great collaborations with different companies and fashion designers, like Frankie Morello.'
Elizabeth Soon Li Qian

'I received a place on the course here after taking part in a competition in Japan. I find the connection to Italian fashion houses through our workshops extremely valuable.'
Keita Ebihara

'I have many favourite hangouts all around Milan, each place having its own appeal – anything from an old church, art museum, gallery, the fashion district, gelato cafe ,flea market, etc. I also enjoy day trips out of the city, perhaps going to another town to find fabric or supplies. This type of roadtrip always brings me a fresh idea for my designs.'
Natalia Gunawan

City
Milan

Country
Italy

63

City Life

Milan, with a population of 1.3 million, is not only Italy's capital but also its creative heart of design and fashion. All the important furniture factories are located in Lombardy, the area around Milan. The major design and fashion events worldwide take place in Milan every year, with the pinnacle being the Salone del Mobile with its Fuorisalone events. This is why you can live design and fashion 24/7 in Milan better than in any other city all over the globe. The city combines this with ancient arts and history, as well as looking to the future. The Duomo di Milano, the Sforzesco castle, numerous ancient churches and the Last Supper by Leonardo Da Vinci are important traces of the past, while Milan is welcoming future talent by creating the new fashion district, and planning the 2015 Universal Exposition. The most important design and art galleries are located in the Ventura Lambrate area and all the fancy fashion shops can be found in the golden triangle. Domus Academy is in a specialised art and design education campus in the Navigli area, one of the liveliest places in Milan where you find many interesting shops, restaurants and markets.

Piazza del Duomo with the arch that marks the entrance to Galleria Vittorio Emanuele (on the left) and the Duomo, Milan's famous Gothic cathedral on the right.
Photo Giorgio Galeotti

Italy

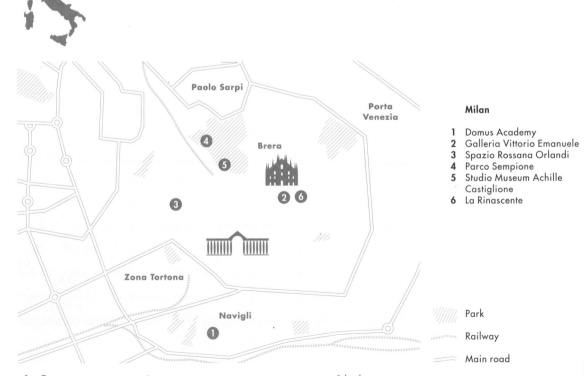

Paolo Sarpi

Porta Venezia

Brera

4

5

3

2 6

Zona Tortona

Navigli

1

Milan

1 Domus Academy
2 Galleria Vittorio Emanuele
3 Spazio Rossana Orlandi
4 Parco Sempione
5 Studio Museum Achille Castiglione
6 La Rinascente

Park

Railway

Main road

Course
Fashion Design

School
Domus Academy

City Facts

See more Milan City Facts on p.165

Galleria Vittorio Emanuele ②
Named after Vittorio Emanuele II (the first king of Italy), the galleria was designed in 1861 and built between 1865 and 1877. The structure of the double arcade is formed by two glass-vaulted arcades intersecting in an octagon.

Spazio Rossana Orlandi ③
Rossana Orlandi's shop and gallery are located in a former tie factory and aim to forecast and promote young and upcoming designers, discovered all around the world.
rossanaorlandi.com

Parco Sempione ④
This park is adjacent to Sforzesco Castle and the Arch of Peace, two of the prominent landmarks of Milan. The design was conceived with the intent of creating panoramic views encompassing both monuments.

Studio Museum Achille Castiglione ⑤
As a tribute to the late industrial designer Achille Castiglioni (1918–2002), his heirs transformed his former studio into a museum. The guided tours are usually managed by his wife Irma and daughter Giovanna.
achillecastiglioni.it

Via Durini
Via Durini is the best shopping street when it comes to design. Showrooms of all the renowned Italian design brands, like B&B Italia and Cassina, can be found here.

Chinatown
Like every major city in the world, Milan too has its very own Chinatown. It has a number of fantastic, interesting, authentic shops and trades that offer traditional Asian products that you get nowhere else in Italy.

Fiera Milano City
Milan's old trade fair, located near the city centre. Fiera Milano City hosts smaller exhibitions with more limited logistical requirements, in addition to events that cannot be held outside the city.
fieramilano.it

Corso Magenta
This historical boulevard features a vibrant combination of palaces, hidden gardens and exclusive shops. For example Pasticceria Marchesi, Milan's most antique pastry shop and bakery. The interior is still original.

Corso Vercelli
A gorgeous modern shopping street outside the city centre that offers a wide range of small boutiques and department stores.

La Rinascente ⑥
This is not your average department store. Besides the usual selection, La Rinascente also offers a design supermarket with famous work by Italian and international designers.
rinascente.it

Navigli area
While markets and antiques and artists' shops can be visited here during the day, the Navigli (canals) area is the best place to visit bars and clubs at night time. Some of them even offer free delicious traditional Italian food around dinnertime, as long as you buy enough drinks.

How to get around
Milan has an extensive internal transport network and is also an important transportation node in Italy, being one of the country's biggest hubs for air, rail and road networks.
The city is served by three major airports: Malpensa Airport (60 km from the city centre), the biggest in northern Italy, Linate Airport (6 km from the city centre), mainly used for domestic traffic and Orio al Serio Airport (50 km from the city centre), used mainly by low-cost airlines. Because of its position, Milan is also the main gateway for international passenger traffic to Europe.

The internal public transport network includes the metro, suburban railway, tram and bus network, as well as taxi, car and bike sharing services. Domus Academy is surrounded by many tram stops. The nearest metro stop is Romolo, accessible with Linea 2.

Arranging housing
Quite easy

Housing support by school
Yes

Cost of room in the city
Between EUR 300 and EUR 600 per month

Cost of campus housing
n/a

City
Milan

Country
Italy

École nationale supérieure des Arts Décoratifs

École nationale
supérieure des Arts
Décoratifs (ENSAD)
31 rue d'Ulm
75240 Paris
France

T +33 (0)1 4234 9700
ensad.fr

The graduation show of 2013 exhibited works from all the students on the master's programme during which time they had chance to discuss their projects with potential future clients.
Photo Laurence Sudre

Course
Fashion Design

School
École nationale supérieure des Arts Décoratifs

Introduction

'The course aims to foster a personal interpretation of clothing'

Gilles Rosier, head of the Fashion Design Department

When was the school founded, and has it changed much over the years?
The origins of the École nationale supérieure des Arts Décoratifs (ENSAD) date back to the École Royale Gratuite de Dessin, founded in 1766. In 2007, the curriculum was reformed and a competitive entrance examination was instituted to bring the course into line with the European harmonisation of degree courses (LMD). In 2010, a master's degree was granted to the École. In 2012, the École introduced a doctorate program (SACRe) in partnership with the best Parisian schools of higher education, PRES (Pole of Research and Higher Education), and PSL (Paris Sciences et Lettres).

What is studying at this school all about?
The École's mission is to provide artistic, scientific and technical training for creative designers who are involved in design and research in all aspects of the decorative arts. The École has 10 departments: animation, art, fashion design, graphic design/multimedia, interior design, photography/video, printed image, product design, stage design and textile/texture design.

What is the school's educational approach?
The training aims to master the process of conception and production in fashion design, costume and accessories, in every context, from mass production to bespoke pieces, and via research.

What is the most important thing for students to learn here?
The course aims to foster a personal interpretation of clothing, an innovative approach, and an ability to anticipate the function of tomorrow's clothing (design, realisation, structure and composition).

What is the most important skill to master for a fashion designer?
The school's training focuses on the technical specificities of fashion, within the general framework of applied arts courses. The school adopts a design-oriented approach, in which clothing has a complementary role (highlighting the body, forms, accessories, and innovative clothing functions) and a supportive role (theatrical costumes and a scenographic approach to clothing).

In what kind of jobs do your former fashion students mostly end up?

Graduates generally enter the luxury goods industry (couture and accessories), a sector in which craftsmanship and technology are combined.

Programme

The MA Fashion Design course incorporates the various contemporary design practices and focuses on the technical specificities of fashion. The programme combines theoretical and practical classes as a methodical and reasoned approach to mastering the processes of design and production in the fields of clothing design, fashion, suiting and accessories. The course is based on a set of activities directed towards the outside world in the form of international exchanges, study trips, partnerships, competitions, exhibitions and professional internships. The courses offered correspond to every form of production, from mass production to the bespoke piece, and include strategic foresight.

Final year projects include designing and creating a collection of at least seven garments and accessories, along with presentations using images, videos, sketchbooks, and so on. The work is then presented to a jury of professionals from the world of fashion. The students can then conclude their final year with a display of their work in scenographic installations that are presented to the media and professionals from the fashion industry.

Master's student Grouazel Marin in front of the jury during the final project viva.
Photo Laurence Sudre

Students produce a final collection (this is by Inès Dufay from 2012) which is then judged by professionals.
Photo Laurence Sudre

Programme
Fashion Design

Leads to
Master of Arts

Structure
The MA Fashion Design programme at the École is a 2-year full-time course, divided into four semesters. Each year consists of 30 credits per semester. The course includes a mandatory professional internship of at least three months. At the end of the final year, students defend their senior project before a jury.

Head of programme
Gilles Rosier

Mentors and lecturers
Joël Dagès, Jocelyne Imbert, Lea Peckre and Farid Chenoune.

Course
Fashion Design

School
École nationale supérieure des Arts Décoratifs

School Facts

Duration of study
2 years

Full time
Yes (25 hours a week)

Part time
No

Female students
87.5%

Male students
12.5%

Local students
87.5%

Students from abroad
12.5%

Yearly enrolment
8

Tuition fee
EUR 637 per year

Funding/scholarships
Yes, through the school
and foundations

Minimum requirements for entry
Bachelor's degree or 5 years of
experience in this field; all candidates
onto the master's programme
must pass a competitive entrance
examination

Language
French

Application procedure
Apply by submitting the following by
normal post:
- A completed application form
- a copy of your passport
- a copy of your qualifying degree
(plus a certified translation for
languages other than French)
- for foreign residents, a copy of the
authorisation of stay
- a EUR 51 cheque for the registration
fee (EUR 26 for grant holders)
- a copy of your DALF or TCF language
certificate (if appropriate).
Appropriate candidates will receive
an invitation for a test by mail. Those
candidates must send in their portfolio
accompanied by a motivation letter
and their curriculum vitae. They will
also have a 20-minute interview
with the jury. All candidates will
be informed about their admission
before the end of June.

Application details
ensad.fr/admissions

Application date
Before end of January

Graduation rate
100%

Job placement rate
High

Memberships/affiliations
Cumulus and ELIA.

Collaborations with
Hermès, IFF, Lanvin and
Maison Martin Margiela.

Facilities for students
Studios, fashion ateliers, personal
worstations with individual IMacs,
3D printers, library, cafeteria and
workshop facilities.

City
Paris

Country
France

Student Work

L'Eve Future (2012)
By Lysmina Attou

This collection was inspired by a fascination with fashion designers' skill in creating an ideal female form. A strange medical world is evoked, where the female form is reshaped with protective shells and transparent membranes.
Photo Dan Perez

Metamorphosis (2012)
By Anna Belyavina-Normand

The male wardrobe provides the basis for hybrid forms realised by the technique of tufting, which enables materials to be combined and fused. The female wardrobe introduces a more lively touch, with drapery and pleats that alter outlines.
Photo Dominique Feintrenie

Bushido (2012)
By Inès Dufay

This collection was inspired by Japanese armour, which is somewhere between being clothing and an 'object' and has protective, technical and performance qualities.
Photo Dominique Maitre

Palimpseste (2012)
By Juliette Gouraud

This collection was inspired by the codes of the male wardrobe. Material is removed to enable combinations of superimposed jersey, knitted and woven fabrics.
Photo Dominique Maitre

Course
Fashion Design

School
École nationale supérieure des Arts Décoratifs

Flowing (2012)
By Kristina Guseva

The details and finishing of the flowing garments are fixed in place by inlaying silicone in luxurious materials. The material follows the suppleness of the female form, either by clinging to it or liberating it.
Photo DR

Vestiges (2012)
By Marion de Raucourt

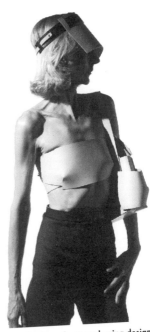

This collection adapts packaging designs to clothes. Unstitched leather pieces are held in place using a system of trimmed forms that fit together. Laces enable the pieces to be secured and tightened around the body. Flowing material adds a counterpoint of softness and lightness to the coarse and angular leather pieces.
Photo DR

Muein (2012)
By Jennifer Pineau-Ledreny

Inspired by interlacing and intertwining designs and organic complexity, braids and pleats play a key role in this collection's designs.
Photo DR

Alumnus

Name Tristan Lahoz
Residence Paris, France
Year of birth 1988
Year of graduation 2011
Current job Freelance designer for YSL and Chanel Jewellery
Website tristanlahoz.jimdo.com

Why did you choose this school?
ENSAD looked like a creative 'paradise': I wasn't from Paris and I was dreaming of this new *parisien artistique* life... It was super-challenging because of the tough competition to get in, but also it seemed very different from other schools.

Are you still in contact with the École?
Yes, every year I go to the graduation show.

What was the most important thing you learned here?
I learned team spirit. ENSAD gave me the opportunity to meet people I will love and work with for the rest of my life. And the nice surprise is that these people are all from different design categories (graphic designers, artists, movie makers) and our collaborations are strong because we recognise each other's talents and believe in each other. For me, this is the biggest reward of studying at the school.

What are you doing now?
Nowadays, I'm a freelance designer, working for Saint Laurent and Chanel, and I am also working on my own brand with Anne-Line Desrousseaux from ENSAD too, that's a summer accessory brand called Chichi.

What was your graduation project?
I presented a men's collection entitled Epidaure. It consisted of summer items, sleeveless shirts and short trousers, with a lot of fabric exploration: leather engraving, laser cuts on cotton, accessories with wood. Epidaure is a classical city in Greece, when I went there I felt something very special and I really wanted to associate this collection with that feeling of space. I also proposed a fragrance to add another dimension, and creating this fragrance was an amazing collaboration.

Was the transition from graduation to working life a smooth one?
It was very special. You work so much for your graduation – and you expect so much from it – but real life comes after that, and it means a new start. At the beginning it is not easy, but it quickly becomes exciting I think.

Any words of advice for future students?
Look around you, enjoy the people you meet at the school, believe in your dreams, and have a martini or two!

Tristan Lahoz's graduation work featured highly experimental materials as well as a collection fragrance.

Course
Fashion Design

School
École nationale supérieure des Arts Décoratifs

Current Students

'For me, the great strength of the school are the students. Students from other years, other classes and other countries. Every day we make new collaborations and have new experiences that are rich and valuable to prepare us for the professional world.'
Charles Pottier

'I chose this school for its variety of departments, which means a great deal of input from different minds, all in the same place. The most important aspect for me is self-reliance. It is not offered to you on a plate, you need to know what you want out of it. Future students can expect plenty of workshops here, so it is a great opportunity to take.'
Elodie Louzaouen

'My time here was the most intense and it was where I learnt the most! We developed a personal collection, realising our pieces with the help of two technicians in an atelier in the school, and then presented it in a flurry of press and media.'
Marion de Raucourt

City
Paris

Country
France

City Life

With an estimated population of over 2.2 million inhabitants, Paris is the capital and largest city of France. The river Seine divides the city in two parts.

Paris is today one of the world's leading business and cultural centres, and its influences on politics, education, entertainment, media, fashion, science and the arts all contribute to its status as one of the world's major global cities. It hosts the headquarters of many international organisations, such as UNESCO, OECD, the International Chamber of Commerce and the European Space Agency. Paris is considered to be one of the greenest and most liveable cities in Europe. It is also one of the most expensive. Three of the most famous Parisian landmarks are the 12th-century cathedral Notre Dame de Paris on the Île de la Cité, the Napoleonic Arc de Triomphe and the 19th-century Eiffel Tower.

Ever since the beginning of the 20th century, Paris has been famous for its cultural and artistic communities and its nightlife. Many historical figures located to the city of light in search of inspiration, including Russian composer Stravinsky, American writer Hemingway and Spanish painters Picasso and Dalí.

View of Paris from the top of the Centre Pompidou with the Eiffel Tower a prominent landmark on the city skyline.
Photo Archibald Ballantine

France

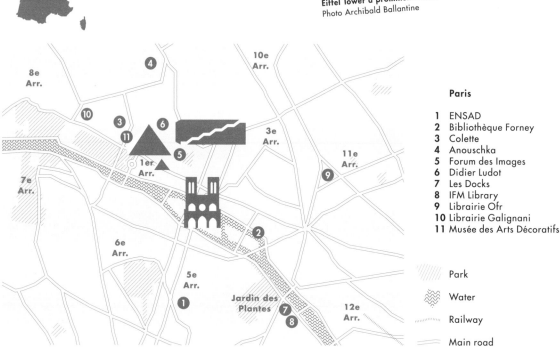

Paris

1 ENSAD
2 Bibliothèque Forney
3 Colette
4 Anouschka
5 Forum des Images
6 Didier Ludot
7 Les Docks
8 IFM Library
9 Librairie Ofr
10 Librairie Galignani
11 Musée des Arts Décoratifs

Park

Water

Railway

Main road

Course
Fashion Design

School
École nationale supérieure des Arts Décoratifs

City Facts

See more Paris City Facts on p.135

Bibliothèque Forney ②
The library has a large collection of works on art and architecture, with an extensive collection of books, brochures, posters, catalogues and periodicals on the graphic arts, printing and typography.
equipement.paris.fr/bibliotheque-forney-18

Colette ③
The Japanese-inspired concept store sells clothes, accessories, books, art, music and beauty products from renowned brands like Comme des Garçons, Lanvin and Marc Jacobs.
colette.fr

Anouschka ④
Back in the 1980s, Anouschka was a top model. She began to collect designer garments while she was modelling and now her vintage clothes store is a fashion world favourite.

Forum des Images ⑤
The Forum des Images, created 20 years ago as an audiovisual memory bank of Paris, is now a place for people to meet and discuss all aspects of the cinema. The festivals and events held at the Forum des Images celebrate the image in all its forms, through various works, encounters, analyses and debates.
forumdesimages.fr

Didier Ludot ⑥
Didier Ludot's boutique stocks second-hand haute couture garments and is also a place for the exchange of ideas and dialogue on the luxury, haute couture and vintage sectors.
didierludot.fr

Les Docks, Cité de la Mode et du Design ⑦
These former warehouses, which were refitted by architects Jakob and MacFarlane, house the IFM (Institut Français de la Mode), exhibition rooms, shops and dedicated areas for young fashion designers.
paris-docks-en-seine.fr

IFM Library ⑧
This reference library for the fashion, design and creative industries has collections of publications that are unique in Europe, covering the textiles, fashion and associated sectors.
ifm-paris.com

Librairie Ofr ⑨
This is a great bookshop for fashion and design. It stocks all the latest magazines, including *Vogue* and other fashion publications, and a wide range of art books. It is also an art gallery.
ofrsystem.com

Librairie Galignani ⑩
This bookshop stocks Anglo-American and French fine art books and has a wide selection of fashion books.
galignani.com

Musée des Arts Décoratifs ⑪
The museum has a large collection of textiles that comprises silks, embroidery, printed cotton, liturgical clothing, lace and tapestries. These collections (costumes, fashion accessories and pieces of textile) retrace the history of clothes, the development of innovations in textiles, and the history of Parisian couturiers.
lesartsdecoratifs.fr

Musée Galliera
Its collections of clothes and accessories present a history of dress codes and trends in France from the 18th century to the present day. The library specialises in the history of fashion and Western civil costume, from antiquity to today; these areas are only accessible to students, researchers, and professionals, by appointment only.
paris.fr/english/museums/municipal-museums

How to get around
Roissy-Charles-de-Gaulle airport takes the majority of international flights to and from Paris, and Orly is a host to mostly domestic and European airline companies. The former airfields of Issy-les-Moulineaux have become a heliport annex of Paris, and Le Bourget an airfield reserved for smaller aircrafts.
As far as national and European destinations are concerned, rail transport is beginning to outdistance air travel in both travel time and efficiency. Amsterdam, London, Brussels and Cologne can be reached within hours using the French high-speed TGV rail network which offers services more than 10 times a day.
A combination of traffic jams and the lack of parking spaces means that driving a car in the capital of France is not a very attractive prospect.
Besides 14 metro lines, 58 bus lines, 5 railway lines, some tramlines and one funicular (in Montmartre), Paris offers 20,000 bikes for rent.
In order to reach ENSAD, you can take metro lines 7 or 10, RER B or bus lines 21, 27, 47 and 38.

Arranging housing
Difficult

Housing support by school
No

Cost of room in the city
EUR 600 per month

Cost of campus housing
n/a

Edinburgh College of Art

The library collection consists of some 85,000 books and more than 350 periodical subscriptions.

Edinburgh College of Art (ECA)
74 Lauriston Place
Edinburgh EH3 9DF
United Kingdom

T +44 (0) 131 651 5800
eca@ed.ac.uk
ed.ac.uk/eca

The main building of Edinburgh College of Art is an elegant neoclassical structure in the beautiful historic city centre.

Course
Fashion Design

School
Edinburgh College of Art

Introduction

'We encourage our designers to create identities that are innovative and sustainable'

Mal Burkinshaw, programme director

When was the school founded, and how has it changed?
Founded in 1907, Edinburgh College of Art (ECA) can trace its origins back to the Academy of Arts established in 1760. In 2011, we officially merged with the University of Edinburgh, resulting in a new enlarged college with world class facilities in the disciplines of art, design, architecture, landscape architecture, history of art and music. This means that our students can take advantage of a vast array of opportunities for interdisciplinary study and creativity.

What is studying at this school all about?
We work across varying disciplines within the school to develop methods and approaches to people and culture that equip our students to design excellence into our lives.

What kind of teaching method is applied?
Most of our teaching and learning is through involvement in a range of experiential projects, in a studio environment. Conceptual, material and technical issues are explored through seminars, workshops, lectures, tutorials and critiques. Research, critical thinking and study of the visual, intellectual, social and professional contexts that shape creative design practice are regarded as essential to student development. This often involves participation in exhibitions, industry competitions and live projects.

What is the strength of this school?
The studio and workshop environment is unique. Our staff members are leading practitioners and theorists in their fields. We encourage our designers to create visions and identities that are both innovative and sustainable. We are educating not only problem-solvers but also opportunity-seekers. Our students will become the designers/ thinkers/makers who will positively shape the world we inhabit.

What is the most important thing for students to learn?
To be an originator of new ideas. Our vision is to develop students' ability to 'stand out from the crowd' by enriching their undergraduate abilities with further depth, understanding of materials, 3D creative cutting and diverse customer contexts.

What is the most vital skill for a fashion designer to acquire?
It is important to demonstrate a high aptitude in the full range of fashion design skills to truly become a 'master' in any subject. We believe that one skill does not dominate the others, as they are so intrinsically connected. The overall prerequisites are hard work, dedication, commitment and independent thinking.

Programme

We have developed a unique and cutting-edge MA/MFA Fashion Design programme with a strong emphasis on personal creative freedom and design innovation, ensuring that our students have the best chance of employment and career development upon graduation. Research is paramount to developing a unique design vision. The course also enables students to become independent thinkers with an advanced knowledge of the industry by offering a coherent and balanced teaching experience, symbiotically integrating technical, artistic and design based projects.

Our students also get to work alongside the MA/MFA Textile programme, exploring traditional and alternative approaches to textiles and materials. This is underpinned by an understanding of the breadth of contexts for textiles, driving innovation within the field.

We integrate practical studio work with theoretical and written studies, including professional practice elements to prepare you for employment in the industry, and a lecture/seminar series to examine the wider context of studies. In 2011, the programme launched the Edinburgh College of Art and All Walks Beyond the Catwalk Diversity Network. The network (the first in the UK) strives to work together with the fashion industry and education sectors to educate students, recognised as our future fashion designers and influencers, in the importance of developing a more responsible, diverse and emotionally considerate response to fashion design and fashion design communication.

ECA's modern Evolution House building.

Students have the opportunity to broaden their practical skills in all areas of fashion and textiles.

Programme
  Fashion Design

Leads to
  Master of Arts, Master of Fine Arts

Structure
  The MA Fashion Design programme is a 1-year full-time course of 180 credits, divided into three semesters (45 weeks in total). Students produce a body of work on an agreed proposed topic coupled with set projects within the programme curriculum. The programme is made up of a mix of design research,

research methods and design exposition. The MFA course is a 2-year programme of 240 credits over four semesters (60 weeks). Students produce an additional extended body of work on an agreed proposed topic.

Head of programme
  Mal Burkinshaw

Mentors and lecturers
  Claire Ferguson, Hazel Sharp, Sally-Ann Provan, Belinda Tippen, Elena Tsyplakova.

School Facts

Duration of study
1 year (MA)
2 years (MFA)

Full time
Yes (40 hours per week)

Part time
No

Female students
100%

Male students
0%

Local students
25%

Students from abroad
75%

Yearly enrolment
4

Tuition fee
- GBP 6050 per year for UK and EU citizens (approx. EUR 7080)
- GBP 16,550 per year for non-EU citizens on the MA programme (approx. EUR 19,363)
- GBP 13,700 per year for non-EU citizens on the MFA programme (approx. EUR 16,029)

Funding/scholarships
Yes, see ed.ac.uk/schools-departments/student-funding

Minimum requirements for entry
Bachelor's degree (UK 2:1 honours degree or its international equivalent) and/or appropriate professional experience, plus proven English language skills.

Language
English

Application procedure
Applications must be submitted online through the University of Edinburgh. The following documents must be submitted in order to complete the application:
- a copy of your qualifying degree, certified translation where necessary
- evidence of your English proficiency (IELTS or TOEFL tests)
- two references of which at least one must be academic
- a study proposal explaining in detail why you are applying
- your portfolio
- a writing sample. Shortlisted candidates will be interviewed.

Application details
ed.ac.uk/eca

Application date
All year round, with advised submission before 30 June

Graduation rate
100%

Job placement rate
High

Memberships/affiliations
The Colleges Council of the British Fashion Council and Graduate Fashion Week.

Accreditation
University of Edinburgh

Collaborations with
National Galleries of Scotland, Michael Kors New York, Mackintosh Scotland and H&M.

Facilities for students
Pattern-cutting and workrooms provision for technical garment production – includes industrial sewing machines, personal design desk provision, knitwear facilities, digital printing, rapid prototyping, library, art shop and reprographics facility, digital computer suites and student support.

City
Edinburgh

Country
United Kingdom

Student Work

Graduation Project (2012)
By Hannah Cumming

Sketches for Graduation Project (2012)
By Hannah Cumming

Sketches for the collection that was inspired by the designer's travels through South America.

A collection of womenswear that combines textures and fabrics to create new shapes and flowing forms.

Course
Fashion Design

School
Edinburgh College of Art

Urban Menswear (2012)
By Amber Hunter

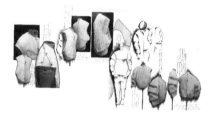

Graduation project of a menswear line that included the development of a casual jacket.

Floor-Hugging Garment (2012)
By Yushan Zou

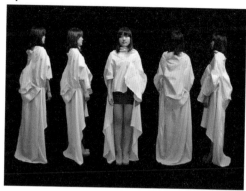

This project saw the development of a dress that hugged the ground at the back. The long and flowing design, was sculpted to have a shorter hemline at the front.

Sheer Overlap (2012)
By Linda Kim

The theme for this collection was traditional Korean architecture – not by the immediate outward appearance of such architecture but its innate essence, with a beauty that matures. Inspired by the subtle lines created by the overlap of porous rice paper, the womenswear collection was created based on the idea of layering of sheer fabrics. The aim for Kim was to make garments that mature with the wearers as seasons go by.

Versatility (2012)
By Yiyan Xie

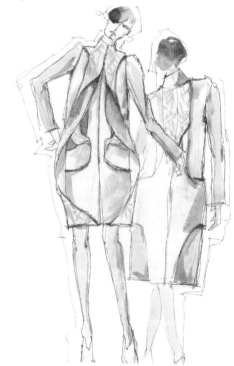

This collection was heavily inspired by the drawings from Karoline Bröckel, finding beauty in the chaotic lines and patterns. The aim was to create a confusing and complicated aesthetic, focusing on the structure of the garments, using twisting and folding to form a complex silhouette.

Alumna

Name Hannah Cumming
Residence Stockholm, Sweden
Year of birth 1988
Year of graduation 2012
Current job Designer at H&M

Why did you choose this school?
I chose ECA because it offered a general first year with the option to then specialise in a subject. This was great for me as I was still unsure what exactly it was that I wanted to do. I hadn't really thought about fashion and as soon as I had a taster of the department, I knew it was where I wanted to go. It's such a broad subject and we really got the opportunity to explore a lot of practices with sketching, pattern-cutting, sewing and life drawing and painting.

Are you still in contact with the school?
Yes, quite a lot. Since I left, the school has taken my work to show in Shanghai and I am also involved in the mentor scheme, advising new MA students. It was through the school that I learnt about the job I am presently in. The staff care about your progress, not just while you are studying but also when you leave, and they really help you to find the next step.

What was the most important thing you learned at ECA?
To have confidence in my own abilities and decision-making.

What are you doing now?
I moved to Stockholm in 2013 and work as an assistant designer at H&M.

How did the school prepare you for what you are doing now?
I don't think there's one particular thing, but it's more the way we were taught. So much is expected from you, at the time it can be very demanding but you appreciate it when you leave with a good portfolio and so many skills. I think the staff instill a hard work ethic in you and always encourage you to reach your potential.

What was your graduation project?
It was a study of colour and textures based on my travels, particularly in South America. It really focused on how colour, fabrics and garments affect the wearer and it looked at combining textures and fabrics in new ways.

Was the transition from graduation to working life a smooth one?
It was relatively smooth. I landed my job only a few months after graduating. I also worked in between as a visiting lecturer at Glasgow School of Art.

Cumming's graduation project was based on the colours and textures she experienced while travelling in South America.

Course
Fashion Design

School
Edinburgh College of Art

Current Students

'By following this course, I hope to understand and develop myself as a designer as opposed to somebody that designs. My master's at ECA has allowed me to develop myself as a brand.'

Amber Hunter

'As an international student, I think all the classes are valuable, because the teaching system is totally different from my undergraduate studies. I love the various tutorials and spending time in the studio. This is my dream school.'

Yunzi He

'My advice to future students is to make sure you have a good study proposal before you start at the university. You should have your own plans and goals about which direction you wish to go with your MA studies.'

Zou Yushan

'After completing my master's degree, I am going to return home and establish myself as a womenswear designer. I usually get inspiration from complex things and focus on the silhouette and the structure of the garments.'

Yiayan Xie

City Life

Edinburgh is the capital city of Scotland and the seat of the Scottish Parliament. The city was one of the historical major centres of the Scottish Enlightenment – the period in 18th century characterised by an outpouring of intellectual and scientific accomplishments, led by the University of Edinburgh – helping to earn it the nickname 'Athens of the north'. Edinburgh's economy today is overwhelmingly based on the service sector, which accounts for some 90 per cent of the city's employment, mainly in the fields of finance and tourism; in both sectors, Edinburgh is second only to London.

The Old Town together with the New Town districts of Edinburgh were listed as a UNESCO World Heritage Site in 1995 in recognition of the unique character of the medieval Old Town and the Georgian New Town, considered a masterpiece of city planning. New Town's most famous street is Princes Street, facing Edinburgh Castle. The city hosts the annual Edinburgh International Festival, a group of official and independent festivals held annually over about 4 weeks beginning in early August. The number of visitors attracted to Edinburgh for the festival is roughly equal to the settled population of the city (almost half a million).

Edinburgh has a large number of pubs, clubs and restaurants and is a popular destination to celebrate the New Year, or Hogmanay as it is called in Scotland. Stockbridge and the waterfront at Leith are increasingly fashionable areas.

United Kingdom

View from Calton Hill to Edinburgh Castle with the Dugald Stewart Monument in the foreground.
Photo The University of Edinburgh

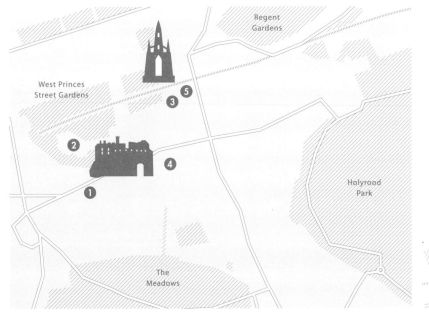

Regent Gardens

West Princes Street Gardens

Holyrood Park

The Meadows

Edinburgh

1 ECA
2 Edinburgh Castle
3 Mary King's Close
4 National Museums Scotland
5 Fruitmarket Gallery

///// Park

Railway

Main road

Course
Fashion Design

School
Edinburgh College of Art

City Facts

Edinburgh International Festival
A group of official and independent festivals held annually in August, which also encompasses the Edinburgh Festival Fringe – the world's largest performing arts festival. The number of visitors attracted to Edinburgh during this time is roughly equal to the settled population of the city.
edinburghfestivals.co.uk, edfringe.com

Edinburgh Castle ❷
Edinburgh Castle is a fortress which dominates the skyline of the city from its position atop the volcanic Castle Rock. The Royal Mile leads you all the way to the entrance.
edinburghcastle.gov.uk

Mary King's Close ❸
This spooky, subterranean labyrinth gives a fascinating insight into the historical daily life of Edinburgh. Costumed characters give tours through a 16th-century town house and the plague-stricken home of a 17th-century gravedigger.
realmarykingsclose.com

Loch Ness
A large, deep freshwater lake in the Scottish Highlands about 100 km from Edinburgh. Loch Ness is best known for the alleged sightings of the cryptozoological Loch Ness monster.
loch-ness-scotland.com

National Museums Scotland ❹
Explore the diversity of the natural world, world cultures, art and design, science and technology and Scottish history, all under one roof.
nms.ac.uk

Fruitmarket Gallery ❺
Originally built as a fruit and vegetable market in 1938, the building was renovated by Richard Murphy Architects in 1994. It has a cafe and a bookshop which stocks art, architecture, design and photography books and magazines.
fruitmarket.co.uk

Princes Street Gardens
A public park in the shadow of Edinburgh Castle. Sewage draining downhill from the Old Town for centuries probably made the park a fertile place for trees and flowers.
edinburgh.gov.uk

Flea Market
This huge car boot sale in the centre of the city takes place every Saturday and is a great place to observe the locals and find vintage treasures.

The Meadows
Originally a lake (Loch Burgh), the Meadows is now a stunning park. Many locals settle down here for lazy Sunday picnics. The Meadows is also one of the host venues for the Edinburgh Festival.

Shopping Malls
Edinburgh has six substantial retail developments outside the city centre: The Gyle, Hermiston Gait, Cameron Toll, Straiton Retail Park, Fort Kinnaird and Ocean Terminal.

How to get around
Edinburgh's International Airport (Turnhouse), located 13 km to the west of the city centre, is the principal international gateway to the city, as well as the busiest airport in Scotland. The airport serves a wide range of domestic and an expanding number of European and transatlantic destinations. Currently, the airport is connected to the city centre by a dedicated bus link operating from the main terminal building to Waverley Bridge. A new tram link from the airport to the city centre and Leith is currently under construction, and is due to commence operation in 2014.

Bus transportation is the principal means of public transport in Edinburgh, with an extensive bus network, covering all parts of the city, its suburbs and the surrounding region. Despite its many hills and cobbled streets, Edinburgh is also a cycle-friendly city. Since the campus is situated in the heart of the city, it can best be reached by foot, bike or bus, by car is not recommended.

Arranging housing
Quite easy

Housing support by school
Yes

Cost of room in the city
GBP 300 (approx. EUR 380) per month

Cost of campus housing
Between GBP 380 and GBP 530 per month (approx. EUR 480 to EUR 670)

ELISAVA School of Design and Engineering

ELISAVA is housed in a modern building on La Rambla in the heart of Barcelona.

ELISAVA Barcelona School of Design and Engineering
La Rambla 30–32
Barcelona 08002
Spain

T +34 (0)93 317 4715
elisava@elisava.net
elisava.net

The Enric Bricall Library supports research and teaching at the school.

Introduction

'We provide students with an in-depth outlook in all aspects of fashion'

Ramon Benedito Graells, dean of ELISAVA

What are the principles of this school?
Innovation, creativity and technology. For over half a century, these have been the guiding principles for ELISAVA Barcelona School of Design and Engineering in its domestic and international development, as well as in its relationship with companies and institutions.

How does the school approach its master's degree programmes?
ELISAVA is a cosmopolitan school that fosters debate and networking. It sees design work as multidisciplinary and cross-functional, anticipating the demands of society and adapting to different environments and projects. Promoting research and innovation is a pivotal element, with students having direct contact with companies and institutions in more than 100 real-life projects developed annually both domestically and abroad.

What is the scope of the school?
True to its roots as a pioneer in teaching design and engineering, ELISAVA's academic offer focuses on all necessary skills, ranging from the creative process to the technical details of project development. This comprehensive approach manages students' talent and skills through various official programmes from bachelor's degrees in design and industrial design engineering, all the way through to master's degrees and postgraduate courses, as well as summer schools, in which fashion design is just one area.

What is the focus of the fashion programme?
We provide students with an in-depth outlook in all aspects of fashion, including the culture of fashion design, textiles, smart textiles and materials research. All programmes are taught by highly qualified working professionals and include in-house internships in companies that facilitate job placement.

What is your teaching method?
Our methodology stresses the interaction between creativity, communication, science, technology, economics, research and social science, transcending the four walls of the classroom.

Programme

The MA Fashion Design degree programme is is split into two areas, the first being Fashion Design: Methods, Research and Creativity, and the second focusing on Branding Fashion Design: Collection and Brand. The first part is based on the educational paradigm of learning by doing, where theoretical knowledge and technical skills are integrated into practice. It is divided into different modules in relation to fashion design, textiles, smart textiles and material research, art and culture, creativity and innovation, interdisciplinarity and artistic direction, and interdisciplinary projects.

The second part enables students to create and experience all the stages of the fashion-collection professional design process, taking the current context into account. They will be able to create their own identity and to contextualise proposals in the new fashion system. Students design a collection inspired by a creative concept and study its production and commercial mechanism, basing their proposal on real practice in the current market. Both designers and communicators collaborate to create brand positioning and the strategy for a collection.

Students are encouraged to work on real-life projects.

Students have access to a wide range of resources.

Students outside the main entrance of the 11,000 m² ELISAVA building.

Programme
Fashion Design

Leads to
Master of Arts

Structure
The 1-year full-time course focuses on fashion design split into specific modules. The following blocks and subjects form the theory and practice of the course, which is based on the educational paradigm learning by doing, whereby theoretical knowledge and technical skills are integrated into practice. The programme fosters creativity and personal style in an interdisciplinary framework, providing students with the latest concepts and techniques in professional activity, integrating expertise in the context of the latest market trends. Students undertake design projects in which they explore creative identity while integrating textile research, material testing, art direction, innovation, trends, art and culture, branding, management principles, creative entrepreneurship and sustainability. This training helps to position them as professionals well-prepared for the future.

Head of programme
Beatriu Malaret

Mentors and lecturers
Bernard Arce, Jordi Ballús, Dorotea, David García Uslé, Teresa Helbig, Jan Iú Més, Enric Jaulent, Gloria Jover, Mariana Méndez, Txell Miras, Inés Monge, Charo Mora, Inmaculada Monters, Mariaelena Roqué, Chu Uroz, Mercedes Valdivieso and Sílvia Ventosa.

Notable alumni
Daniel Lierah, Laura Torroba, Flo Monti, Daniel Barros, Cristina Casasayas, Yuna Kono, Jolie Amado Vergara, Karina Rodríguez Canedo and Natalia Salgado.

School Facts

Duration of study
1 year

Full time
Yes

Part time
No

Female students
90%

Male students
10%

Local students
30%

Students from abroad
70%

Yearly enrolment
15

Tuition fee
EUR 8200 per year

Funding/scholarships
Yes, scholarships and financial aid
are available

Minimum requirements for entry
Bachelor's degree in fashion design,
design and fine arts, and/or
professionals with proven experience
in these different subject areas

Language
English and Spanish

Application procedure
Apply by submitting an online
application form and attaching
the following documents:
- your curriculum vitae
- a letter of expectation
- your portfolio
- a proof of payment of the EUR 300
  application fee.
  Successful candidates will be
  informed by email.

Application details
elisava.net

Application date
By 16 February for the March edition
By 8 September for the October edition

Graduation rate
100%

Job placement rate
80%

Memberships/affiliations
Platform of Catalonian Fashion
Schools

Collaborations with
Barcelona City Council, DHUB,
Museu del Disseny de Barcelona,
Museum of Textile and Attire,
CETEMMSA Technological Centre
Textil Santanderina and AITEX (Textile
Industry Research Association).

Facilities for students
Fashion workshop, library and
exhibition room.

Student Work

El Cortejo del Silencio (2012)
By Maider Perianes Somalo and Sayuri Villalba del Castillo

The silhouettes of the pieces making up this collection are based on the circle as simple geometrical form. 'Silence' is a fundamental part of the pieces and is captured in colour (beige) and textures (felt fabrics and cross-stitch). Finalist ModaFAD Awards 2012.
Photo Natalia Pereira

Versión Beta (2012)
By Pedro Rodríguez Capella, Elisabet Figueras Raurell and Agustina Castro Ferreira

This group of students created the brand Be Odd, with products that transmit an image of sophistication and style.
Photo Stefano Paddeu

Espejo de Tinta (2012)
By María del Villar and Natalia Salgado Rea

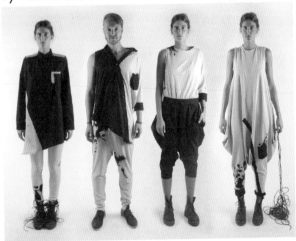

The brand Invertebrata mixes tradition with modernity, without losing the handcrafted principle.
Photo Antonella Vera

Big B (2012)
By Daniela Castilla and Andrés Manzano

Inspired by the Big Bang theory, Big B references urban tribes, space and royalty.

Kataezome (2012)
By Cristina Casasayas and Yuna Kono

Kataezome, the traditional Japanese technique of stamping, and *furoshiki*, Japanese wrapping techniques, underpin this project's theme.

The Second Chance (2012)
By students of the MA Fashion Design programme

This was a collection of jeans for homeless people, for the benefit of Fundació Arrels, an initiative organised by the City Council of Barcelona. The aim was to give a second chance to old jeans in good condition by customising them.

Biyü (2012)
By Erika Arelano Mc Beath and Francisca Julio Rosember

The designs of the brand Biyü are inspired by the environment and the femininity and elegance of classic shapes.
Photo Viviana Spaco and Marta Vinaixa

City
Barcelona

Country
Spain

91

Alumnus

Name Daniel Lierah
Residence Paris, France
Year of birth 1981
Year of graduation 2007
Current job Head designer at Martinez Lierah
Website martinezlierah.com

Why did you choose this school?
It showed an implicit modernity in its programme and its way of presenting itself. I wanted a school that gave attention to experimentation and innovation.

Are you still in contact with the school?
Yes, I gave some classes for the first time this course and it was a great experience.

What was the most important thing you learned here?
ELISAVA taught me how to be a contemporary designer and how different disciplines can improve and enrich my work and research.

What are you doing now?
I have my own fashion brand together with my associate Arturo Martinez. We are based in Paris and so far we have been lucky, with several sales points in Asia and America. We have also developed a shoe line that is very iconic to our brand and that sells well.

How did the school prepare you for what you are doing now?
It made me unafraid to experiment and not just stay only with one thought but to push the idea further....to make mistakes and to sometimes get to like the mistakes better that the expected result, or to be brave and say, no, let's go back and start again. But above all it taught me to develop my personality as a creative.

Was the transition from graduation to working life a smooth one?
No, it never is I think. First, I did some work for another company, and it was tough. But with time, you learn to use the skills you were taught in school and how to apply them efficiently. Now working for ourselves it really helps.

Any words of advice for future students at the college?
Work hard because it is a really amazing experience, and you only realise that sometimes when it's over! So enjoy the time you are there.

Since graduating, Lierah has founded the successful brand Martinez Lierah with Arturo Martinez.

Current Students

'I find the diversity of courses on offer, not only including the fashion process, of great importance. The school and the professors give you a great creative way to open your eyes and act consciously.'
Roxane Mercerat

'Through this course, I develop my creative skills so that I can confront any project in the future. I aim to now form the basis of my own work methodology and this is what makes my work unique and ensures the performance of my artistic creations at the highest level.'
Sara Lozano

'My advice to future students? Don't get crazy at school, and try to get to know Barcelona the best you can – it is a great city. You can't leave Barcelona before going to 'el búnker del Carmen'. Google it!'
Sofía Mattone

'I think the most valuable workshop is about conceptualisation. The complete fashion collection is made with created and proposed concepts related to personal experiences and influences more than fashion trends, obtaining a collection full of personal style and identity.'
Alma Victoria Palacios Marín

City Life

Barcelona is a cosmopolitan and open city offering its residents a high quality of life. This is one of the most attractive European cities to live in with excellent educational, cultural and leisure facilities its safety, efficient transport and health services, beautiful climate and natural attractions inviting people to enjoy the sea and mountain year-round. Barcelona is also known as a city that lives and breathes design. Design permeates the entire urban fabric, which is dotted with museums, art galleries, exhibition halls and showrooms, as well as restaurants, bookstores and establishments of all kinds which express their unique identity through their own furniture, lighting, commercial signs, etc. It is a real magnet for creative and designers from around the world. They are attracted by the city's display of latest trends and they know that the ecosystem surrounding them is also conducive to nurturing their creativity. All this makes Barcelona one of the best European destinations for design students. In fact, twelve percent of college students in the city come from abroad to this Mediterranean spot. Barcelona leads the quality of life ranking in Spain and is close to the top overall European ranking. The city blends together the artistic legacy of over two millennia with avant-garde architecture. Nowadays, Barcelona is a landmark in the world of fashion, art, design and new technologies.

Spain

Barcelona is known as a city that lives and breathes design.
Photo ELISAVA

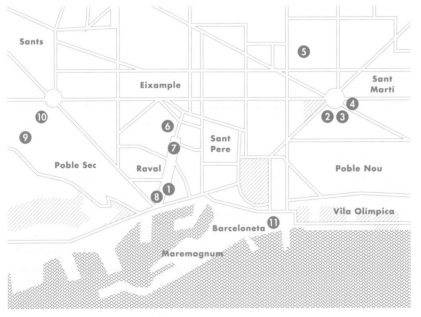

Barcelona

1 ELISAVA
2 DHUB Barcelona
3 Barcelona Design Week
4 Agbar Tower
5 La Sagrada Família
6 CCCB
7 La Rambla
8 Arts Santa Mònica
9 Sónar Festival
10 Mies van der Rohe Pavilion
11 Barcelona Beaches

Park

Water

Railway

Main road

Course
Fashion Design

School
ELISAVA School of Design and Engineering

City Facts

DHUB Barcelona (2)
The Disseny Hub Barcelona will be the reference space for design in Barcelona and the future site of the city's main design institutions. The DHUB includes collections of historical and contemporary decorative arts, ceramics, industrial design, textiles, clothing and graphic arts.
dhub-bcn.cat/en

Barcelona Design Week (3)
This international event focuses on design, innovation and business addressed to those companies and professionals in any industry or productive services that use knowledge and creativity as a driver of its business activity.
barcelonadesignweek.com

Agbar Tower (4)
Jean Nouvel's majestic Agbar Tower has stood in the Plaça de les Glòries since 2003. Its modern, louvered facade contrasts with the old flour mill, the Farinera del Clot, and the Mercat de Bellcaire, the city's flea market.
torreagbar.com

La Sagrada Família (5)
The expiatory church is in the centre of Barcelona and over the years it has become one of the most universal signs of identity of the city and the country.
sagradafamilia.cat

Centre de Cultura Contemporània de Barcelona (6)
The CCCB organises and produces exhibitions, debates, festivals and concerts, programmes film cycles, courses and lectures, and encourages creation using new technologies.
cccb.org

La Rambla (7)
Barcelona wouldn't be Barcelona without La Rambla. As you walk along, you'll see landmark buildings, such as the greatest theatre of Barcelona's opera, the Gran Teatre del Liceu, the Palau de la Virreina and the spectacular Boqueria Market.
laramblabcn.com

Arts Santa Mònica (8)
Arts Santa Mònica generates ideas, projects, research and materials that stimulate the dialogue between the local, and all it has to offer, and the global dimension of current society.
artssantamonica.cat

Sónar Festival (9)
Sónar is the International Festival of Advanced Music and New Media Art taking place in Barcelona for three days every June.
sonar.es/ca

Mies van der Rohe Pavilion (10)
Built from glass, steel and different kinds of marble, the pavilion was conceived to accommodate the official reception presided over by King Alphonso XIII of Spain along with the German authorities.
miesbcn.com

Barcelona Beaches (11)
All Barcelonan beaches are well communicated, maintained and equipped with all the services. By proximity, the most popular ones are those of Barceloneta, Sant Miquel and Sant Sebastià.
barcelonaturisme.com

How to get around
Barcelona and its metropolitan area have many options of public transport that allow reaching every spot in the city in an easy and comfortable way. Six lines of underground with a running frequency of between 2 and 3 minutes, an urban network of trains, a modern tram, more than a 1000 buses and a simple, practical and sustainable urban transport system based on the shared use of the bicycle, the Bicing.

Barcelona airport gets direct flights from the most important Spanish, European and world cities. Barcelona is also connected with Madrid by means of the AVE (high-speed train), apart from having other long-distance trains that connect it with other important cities of the country.

Arranging housing
Never a problem

Housing support by school
Yes

Cost of room in the city
EUR 300–475

Cost of campus housing
n/a

ESMOD
Berlin

Student facilities include a fully-equipped sewing studio.
Photo Natalie Toczek

**ESMOD Berlin International
University of Art for Fashion**
Görlitzerstrasse 51
10997 Berlin
Germany

T + 49 (0)30 611 2214
info@esmod.de
esmod.de

The school occupies one of the area's characterful old brick buildings.
Photo Natalie Toczek

Introduction

'Our students must clarify what they are the most passionate about in order to define their core values'

Friederike von Wedel-Parlow, course director

When was the school/course founded?
Historically, ESMOD Berlin has been in operation as a fashion school for almost 20 years. It is part of ESMOD International, comprising 21 fashion schools of which ESMOD Berlin was the first to be accredited as a university in 2011. That is the same year that the MA Sustainability in Fashion programme began.

Why should students choose this particular school?
The strength of the school and the master's programme is that is provides an intensive 1-year education with a practical, theoretical and critical approach to holistic design and fashion marketing. It is an exciting, professionally-engaged, innovative approach to specialised education, allowing students to be well poised and well connected to enter their professional working careers in sustainable fashion.

What is expected from the students?
They are expected to be fully engaged with the programme. The most challenging thing for students is to absorb and be exposed to as much information as they can about the area of sustainable fashion, and then to clarify what they are the most passionate about in order to define their core values as a designers and pursue their project with critical rigour and conviction.

What is the focus of your programme?
The brief of a fashion designer has undergone a shift in recent years. Rather than just the creation of collections, it also now involves taking responsibility for the context, services and processes associated with the entire life of the product. We also focus on the question of what happens to resources after they have been used, and how they can be fed back into the production cycle.

What is the most important skill to master?
The most important skill and challenge to designers is about finding the balance between creating a product which embodies the designer's core values – which is produced in an ethical and sustainable fashion, meeting the needs of the consumer – while still respecting the heart of fashion ideology.

What career paths do your graduates take?
Graduates from the master's programme pursue a variety of paths within the international fashion industry, such as designers, entrepreneurs, research, academia, education, etc.

Programme

The international programme for the MA Sustainability in Fashion course is unique in that it takes a holistic and interdisciplinary approach to design, positioning itself as an ecologically, ethically, socially and economically sustainable discipline. With a focus on innovation, the course unifies research, creative practise, professionalism and entrepreneurship to inspire students to create new solutions, to influence positive change and meet the requirements of a new consciousness in the international fashion industry.

The hands-on approach and dynamic working environment create a holistic educational framework encouraging students to explore the sustainable aspects of developing design strategies for the future, while providing them with access to innovative materials, technologies and production techniques.

International exchanges with academics and business partners provide students with an informed professionalism, while taking part in workshops, seminars and excursions informs a deeper understanding of the industry. The course maintains a highly professional and challenging curriculum supported by core lecturers, as well as discipline-specific guest speakers from the creative industries. Students are exposed to a variety of topics, current trends and best practices within sustainability in fashion, and individual tutorials with programme instructors provide critical support for the development and delivery of their master's degree projects.

President of ESMOD Berlin Silvia Kadolsky (left) presents awards at a graduate fashion show at the French Embassy in Berlin.

The MA Graduation Exhibition 2012 stressed the sustainability theme of the course.

The course takes a holistic approach, with an emphasis on the ecological context.
Photo Natalie Toczek

Programme
Sustainability in Fashion

Leads to
Master of Art

Structure
The 1-year full-time course is divided into two semesters (with a total of 60 credit points). The first includes modules that focus on the wide range of approaches to, and issues involved in, sustainable interaction within the textile industry. There are also short, hands-on workshops and visits from guest lecturers and critics who imbue the curriculum with the insights of real practising professionals.

The second semester (the master phase) is devoted to the individual students' final major projects.

Head of programme
Friederike von Wedel-Parlow

Lecturers
Rolf Heimann, Wickie Meier, Renate Stauss and Friederike von Wedel-Parlow.

Guest speakers
Miguel Adrover, Michael Braungart, Orsola de Castro, Franois Girbaud. Christoph Harrach, Magdelena Schaffrin and Mark Starmanns.

School Facts

Duration of study
1 year

Full time
Yes (25–35 hours a week)

Part time
No

Female students
90%

Male students
10%

Local students
15%

Students from abroad
85%

Yearly enrolment
18

Tuition fee
- EUR 11,500 for EU citizens
- EUR 14,500 for non-EU citizens

Funding/scholarships
Yes

Minimum requirements for entry
Bachelor's degree and/or
professional work experience

Language
English

Application procedure
Your application should include the
following:
- your personal and contact details
- your curriculum vitae
- application form
- portfolio
- education certificates
- letter of motivation.

Application details
master@esmod.de

Application date
Applications are accepted all
year round

Graduation rate
100%

Job placement rate
80%

Memberships/affiliations
Ethical Fashion Forum, Ethical
Fashion Show, Green Showroom and
Swiss Organic Fabrics.

Collaborations with
Esprit, Hessnatur, Institut Français de
la Mode Paris, Goethe Institut Paris,
Deutsch-Französisches Jugendwerk,
Swiss Organic Fabric, Mess Frankfurt
Lectra and Aveda.

Facilities for students
Industrial and domestic sewing and
over-locker machines, sewing and
pattern-making studios, print studio,
print machine and library.

City
Berlin

Country
Germany

Student Work

Save Nature, Stay in the City (2012)
By Anna Johannsen

The aim of this project was to create a long-lasting relationship between the product and the consumer through combining intelligent design with honest and clear communication. Cooperating with the German outdoor brand Vaude resulted in a multifunctional outdoor garment system.
Photo Tony Thomson

The Wuu Collection (2012)
By Daniela Franceschini

An expression of the traditional craftsmanship of the workers who make up the New Sadle NGO in Nepal, this fair-trade project meets the growing consumer demand for more sustainable, high-level design within the luxury market.
Photo Carlos Luque

Startklar (2012)
By Esther Bätschmann

This ready-to-wear collection is made from cradle-to-cradle certified fabrics, according to the design concept of the 'circular economy'. It proposes that our industries should function like an organism, in which material flows are of two types: biological or technical nutrients circulating in closed loops without losing raw materials. The female flight pioneers of the 1920s inspired the collection.
Photo Jürgen Herschelmann

Resgate (2012)
By Beatrice Melo

This project presents a timeless collection that showcases the delicate and colourful handmade lace and embroidery of Ceará, located in the North East of Brazil where Melo's family is from. This project aims to preserve the traditional craft of the region by translating it into luxury fashion.
Photo João Paglione

Course
Sustainability in Fashion

School
ESMOD Berlin

Clothes to Love (2012)
By Vida Ipektchi

As 20 per cent of the world's population is able to afford a simple H&M t-shirt, this market is essential to target for a greener fashion industry. This capsule collection explores how mass-market producers might approach sustainability. If consumers value their clothes more highly through knowledge and informed choices, they will start to accept more responsibility as fashion consumers.
Photo Linn Kuhlmann

Serial Upcycling Workshop (2012)
By Ralf Schuchmann

As part of their studies, the 2012 master's students completed an upcycling project with Hessnatur, which is recognised internationally as one of Europe's largest online distributors of eco-fashion. Students were given a range of dead stock from past seasons with the task of upcycling the clothes into new outfits, raising the level of design and extending the life cycle of the products.
Photo Jago Li

Heroine_Collection (2012)
By Bojana Drača

Inspired by the idea of revolutions (literal and metaphorical), this project turns simple two-dimensional shapes into sophisticated garments, which contrast sharp geometry with elegant drapery. This women's ready-to-wear collection uses Bluesign-certificated, recycled polyesters provided by cooperation partner Singtex, based in Taiwan. The collection is produced using a zero/low waste system of pattern making and with minimal haberdashery.
Photo Katja Žagar

Alumna

Name Stefanie Stolitzka
Residence Graz, Austria
Year of birth 1986
Year of graduation 2012
Current job Sustainable development manager at Legero Schuhfabrik
Website legero.at, superfit.at, thinkshoes.com

Why did you choose this school?
From my first call, they were attentive, friendly and interested. They immediately offered me the chance to visit Berlin to meet them and see the school.

What was the most important thing you learned here?
I learnt a lot of important things, especially since it is so hard to find good information about sustainable fashion. I think the most vital thing I learned is to keep asking people until you get the answer you are looking for. People or companies only tell you what they want to tell you about their sustainability, so if you need to go deep you have to be stubborn and keep asking. Otherwise, I would have never found out so much about conventional leather tanning and its risks for humans and nature.

What are you doing now?
After graduating, I started work straight away. I spent 2 months in Vietnam to experience conventional footwear production, then I started as a sustainable development manager for the Legero group. The trip to South East Asia helped me to understand where footwear production is now, and where it needs to go – it was a great experience. Currently I am developing sustainable and biological footwear collections for Superit (children's shoes), which should be launched in 2015.

How did the school prepare you for what you are doing now?
Through the school's connection to Hessnatur, I met a lot of amazing people from the sustainable leather and footwear industry.

What was your graduation project?
My MA project was a sustainable and biodegradable unisex footwear (sneaker) collection, inspired by Austrian tradition and its materials. It was important that all sourced materials would be from European or local suppliers, biodegradable and fair trade. The main materials were chamois tanned deer leather (from traditional Austrian tanneries), woollen Austrian Loden and a recyclable outsole which could be taken off at the end of the product's life. I tried to combine a contemporary object, the sneaker, with traditional materials, ornamentations and techniques to create an emotionally attractive and long-lasting unique product.

Was the transition from graduation to working life a smooth one?
As I had already developed and produced my MA footwear collection with Legero, it was a quite smooth one, even though I am now in charge of a whole new department, which is challenging but exciting and motivating.

Any words of advice for future students?
As the course is just 1 year, it can become quite tense and time-consuming – so it's important that you are happy and curious about what you are doing.

Stolitzka's graduation project on sustainable footwear led to her current job developing a sustainable shoe collection for Legero.

Current Students

'The classes are designed to cover all parts of the supply chain, which in my opinion is the most important thing in order to really understand sustainable fashion.'
Bojana Drača

'It is an intensive 1-year course, but there is also time for relaxation. My favourite places to hang out include Monbijou Park, Badeschiff pool/bar, Mein Huas am See bar, A2 bar and Friedrichshain.'
Anita Heiberg
Photo Natalie Toczek

'I learnt a lot from all the guest speakers. It is amazing to meet such successful people who are working with sustainability from different perspectives.'
Mayta Lara Garcia Leal
Photo Natalie Toczek

'The upcycling workshop was my favourite because it was so informative – just imagine the waste we are producing every year across the world.'
Ralf Schuchmann
Photo Natalie Toczek

'Future students can expect a mix of theoretical and practical work and to meet people from all over the world. I am from Sweden and we have students from Russia, Canada, Brazil, Germany and Iran. There is a nice cultural diversity and range of expertise in a group where we all want the same thing: to make a change!'
Sanne Lundblad
Photo Natalie Toczek

City Life

Germany is known internationally as a pioneer in environmentalism and Berlin is at the heart of eco fashion and sustainable design. The city is home to companies, networks and associations for whom sustainability is part of their core philosophy. ESMOD takes advantage of this through professional partnering with fairs and events such as the Ethical Fashion Show and Greenshow Room during Berlin Fashion Week.

The school itself is located in the heart of the cultural hotspot of Kreuzberg, the former home of punk, now one of Berlin's most exciting creative hubs, with many resident artists, designers and musicians. In a contemporary and historical sense, creativity and experimentation is interwoven into the very fabric of the city, making it an ideal study environment.

In terms of liveability, Berlin is the ideal student city. Finding an apartment here is easier and more affordable than in many other major European cities. The general cost of living in Berlin also suits the student budget.

Parallel to an exciting city lifestyle, more than a third of Berlin is composed of lakes and parks, so nature is easily accessed. Centrally located, Berlin also offers easy access to the rest of Europe.

Germany

The Fernsehturm (TV tower) was constructed at the height of the Cold War in 1969, and at 368 m it remains Berlin's tallest structure, visible from just about everywhere in the sprawling city.
Photo Katherine York

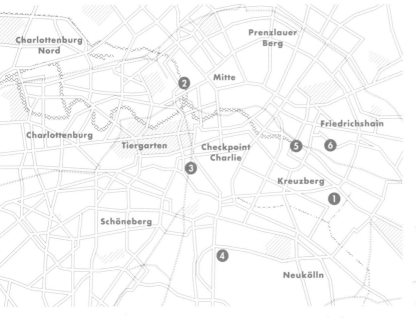

Berlin

1 ESMOD
2 Hamburger Banhof Museum
3 Martin-Gropius-Bau Museum
4 Flüghafen Tempelhof
5 Katerholzig Bar
6 Berghain

Park

Water

Railway

Main road

Course
Sustainability in Fashion

School
ESMOD Berlin

City Facts

Hamburger Banhof Museum ②
Set in a former rail station, this contemporary art museum features works by Andy Warhol, Cy Twombly, Roy Lichtenstein, amongst others, and also has visiting exhibitions of contemporary art.
hamburgerbahnhof.de

Martin-Gropius-Bau Museum ③
Originally built in 1881 as an arts and crafts museum, and now home to top travelling exhibitions of art and photography, the museum's building is a visual treasure in itself, designed by Martin Gropius (great uncle of Walter Gropius, the founder of the Bauhaus movement) along with Heino Schmieden.
berlin.de/orte/museum/martin-gropius-bau

Flüghafen Tempelhof ④
Until recently a functioning airport, these days the former Tempelhof terminal is a park – open to the public for a variety of events and activities.
tempelhoferfreiheit.de

Katerholzig Bar ⑤
A great Kreuzberg nightspot in an old soap factory, Katerholzig plays electronic dance music all night long.
katerholzig.de

Berghain Club ⑥
This legendary Berlin nightclub is named after its location near the border of Kreuzberg and Friedrichshain. It has been described as 'the world capital of techno'.
berghain.de

Berlin Fashion Week
Twice a year, Berlin becomes a magnet for international fashion enthusiasts, buyers, trade experts and the media, as Fashion Week presents hosts of shows and awards, exhibitions and off-site events. Eco-shows include Showfloor Berlin, Lavera Showfloor, the Greenshow Room and the Ethical Fashion Show.
fashion-week-berlin.com

Bread & Butter
The leading international trade fair for street and urban wear takes place in July, most recently at the former Tempelhof Airport. Around 600 exhibitors from the sectors of denim, sportswear, street fashion, functional wear and casual wear meet a host of buyers, retailers and press representatives from the textile industry.
breadandbutter.com

DMY Berlin
This annual International Design Festival presents established and young, experimental designers, new products, prototypes and projects. The exhibition is accompanied by a wide programme of symposia, designer talks and workshops.
dmy-berlin.com

Premium
Premium is a contemporary fashion trade platform for choice collections, international newcomers and exclusive trend products.
premiumexhibitions.com

How to get around
Berlin's public transport system will take you almost anywhere in the city and is easy and affordable to use. Taxis are readily available. The most popular way to commute for Berliners, however, is by bike. A network of bike paths makes cycling safe and simple. You can rent a bike for the day or buy a secondhand one from a market for a cheap, easy, efficient and sustainable way to get around the city.

Arranging housing
Average/quite easy

Housing support by school
No

Cost of room in the city
EUR 300 to EUR 450 per month

Cost of campus housing
n/a

HDK School of Design and Crafts at Steneby

Students work in the new printing workshop.

HDK School of Design and Crafts at Steneby
Hemslöjdsvägen 1
66010 Dals Långed
Sweden

T +46 (0)53171000
info@hdk.gu.se
hdk.gu.se

Students at Steneby enjoy a peaceful and green campus, which is literally amidst nature.

Introduction

'Our students develop their own individual methodology, material skills and contextual awareness'

Anna-lill Nilsson, director of studies

When was the school founded? and how has it changed?
The school was founded in 1938 and became a part of the University of Gothenburg in 2000. The master's programme began to include textiles in 2004. The school has changed enormously over the years, as has our master's degree education in applied art and design. There is one master's degree programme with three possible material directions, of which textiles is one. Although half of the students in the complete programme come from abroad, up until now, most textile students come from Sweden.

What is studying at this school all about?
Steneby is a learning environment for material-based artistic educations. Space and body are important issues at our school but also investigation, material and skill. Investigation in material is what differentiates this school from others. The students work very independently in their own field and have general classes in writing, theory and entrepreneurship together.

What kind of teaching method is is found to be important?
Learning by doing, as well as learning through writing, dialogue and reflection. We have recurrently arranged lectures but the main content of the programme is the students' individual work.

Why should students choose this school?
The strength is the learning environment: the workshops, the contemplative silence, and the closeness between students and teachers. The freedom to choose and formulate your own projects within the peacefulness of the surroundings, with an abundance of nature in close proximity.

What is expected from the students?
They are expected to work very independently. They should be able to manifest their work both in a material and in text. Finally, we want the students to develop and present an action plan of their future as professionals. We do this as a recurring assignment.

What do students learn during this course?
They learn to develop an individual methodology – material skills and contextual awareness – and to be prepared for a professional life outside school.

What is the most important skill to master?
An investigative approach to material, techniques, form and concepts. Plus, every student must know one's self and one's field. The student needs clear goals and big portion of energy and presence.

What career paths do your graduates follow?
They mainly run their own businesses with focus on galleries or public commissions as artists. Some work with scenography and costume, many of them teach as well.

Programme

The MFA Applied Arts undertaken at HDK Steneby of which the Textiles–Garments–Design programme is one of three streams. Steneby offers advanced opportunities for individual depth and investigative work within craft and design. The education includes time for process-based research work, with supervision in advanced theory and regular supervision meetings with professors within the subject area and visiting practitioners and teaching staff. The programme requires a high degree of autonomy, independence and personal motivation in order to achieve the aims and objectives of the education. The different specialisations generate interesting questions and discussions during the shared examinations, at which the different fields of specialisation will encounter each other.

The master's programme is international in its focus, and students and teachers will be from a variety of countries. The languages of tuition are English and Swedish, and supervisions and literature are available in both languages. Student presentations are preferably in English. Lectures will mainly be in English, whereas events and information not included in the programme will mainly be available in Swedish.

Our students have the opportunity to apply for exchanges with other schools during the second term of the first year. There will also be opportunities to participate in the activities of artists in residence, including both Swedish and international designers, artists and guest lecturers.

The school is well-equipped with textile labs and workshops.

Each master's student has a dedicated work station in the school.

Programme
Applied Arts

Leads to
Master of Fine Art

Structure
The 2-year full-time course is made up of workshop- and studio-based projects. Theory, entrepreneurship and writing are integrated in the project. Year 1 includes a workshop period of 6 weeks. Students will begin their projects developing them into spatial contexts. Later in the term, they participate in the entrepreneurship course, which involves developing their portfolio, and networking as they attend a number of lectures on the possibilities of 'living on your art'. Year 2 is primarily dedicated to the final degree project.

Head of programme
Anna-lill Nilsson

Lecturers
Alexander Grüner, Anna-lill Nilsson, Lina Selander, Karstein Solli, Pasi Välimaa and Sven-Olof Walenstein.

Notable alumni
Lisa Tagesson, amongst others.

Course
Applied Arts

School
HDK School of Design and Crafts at Steneby

School Facts

Duration of study
2 years

Full time
Yes (40 hours a week)

Part time
No

Female students
60%

Male students
40%

Local students
85%

Students from abroad
15%

Yearly enrolment
13

Tuition fee
- Free for EU citizens
- SEK 192,000 for non-EU citizens
  (approx. EUR 22,000)

Funding/scholarships
No

Minimum requirements for entry
Bachelor's degree in a related field

Language
English and Swedish

Application procedure
Your application should include the
following:
- your personal and contact details
- your curriculum vitae
- application form
- portfolio
- education certificates
- letter of motivation
- proof of language (if applicable).
Based on these documents, candidate
may be invited for an interview with
the programme director. Successful
applicants will be informed by email.

Application details
info@hdk.gu.se

Application date
By March

Graduation rate
81%

Job placement rate
High

Memberships/affiliations
ELIA, Cirrus and Cumulus.

Collaborations with
ADA Sweden, Karlstads Bostads,
Röhsska Design Museum, Rosendals
Trädgård, Dalsland Art Centre,
Dalspira Mejeri, Not Quite and
Ur Skog.

Facilities for students
In addition to several textile
workshops at Steneby, master's
students have a dedicated building
allocated where they have lectures,
place for sketching and writing,
bookable studio for larger workshops
and their own coffee room.

City
Dals Långed

Country
Sweden

109

Student Work

Spirituality (2010)
By Shadi Bokharaie

My personal interest in human's spiritualities, led me to investigate and create this study to reach a conceptual and emotional relation between the human and the artistic work.
Photo Marin Gustavsson

Work of Time, Light and Memory (2010)
Elin Jonsson

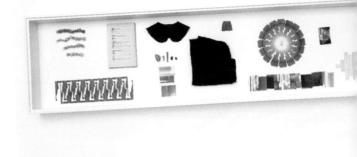

My work is about time and memories and based on a photograph. I have methodically broken down and then rebuilt the photograph in search of finding my own way to visualise time.
Photo Marin Gustavsson

Craft for Craft (2011)
By Pithalai Phoophat

This is a participatory art project reflecting the linkage between craft and inner life.
Photo Marin Gustavsson

Encapsulated (2011)
By Pia Ingemarsson

My work is dealing with the situation of being supressed into silence, and the feeling it creates within a person.
Photo Marin Gustavsson

Course
Applied Arts

School
HDK School of Design and Crafts at Steneby

Eet (2011)
By Anna Liljeholm

Formation (2011)
Cajsa Branchetti Hallberg

Inbetween states. Time disappears. In an undefined greyscale. Embraced by an uncomfortable sensation dissolving your thoughts. The compact, creeping, sweltering, humid movements. A void. An infinity of silence.
Photo Håkan Karlbrand

The amount of fabric is so vast that I cannot grasp it. The scissors come to my rescue. My lifeline, my companion. With the scissors I cut. Arrange in piles. Dye and starch.
Photo Håkan Karlbrand

Between Two Gardens (2013)
By Therese Carlsson

Övervakningsgrad 2 (2013)
By Emelie Rygfelt Vilander

I have chosen to examine a dump, not an established municipal recycling center, but one that lies at the side of individual settlements, or the edge of a village. The place is surrounded by forest but is clearly influenced by man. What defines what I call the place is all objects that have been placed there.
Photo Theo Rosengren

It is a part of my history, set in my childhood room. It is about emancipation. Emancipation within a confined system, a continuous and never-ending process.
Photo Theo Rosengren

Alumna

Name Lisa Tagesson
Residence Malmö, Sweden
Year of birth 1981
Year of graduation 2009
Current job Artist
Client Stockholm Sjukhem
Website lisatagesson.n.nu

Why did you choose this school?
I did my bachelor's degree at HDK Steneby. For me, the school has the perfect combination of art and craft, so I applied for the MFA degree in applied arts with specialisation in textiles, garments and design.

What was the most important thing you learned here?
One of them was to combine different techniques and ideas in process-based research work.

What was the most interesting project you did?
I studied for a semester in a guest studio at Goyang National Art Studio in Seoul, with a scholarship from National Museum Of Contemporary Art Korea. That opportunity gave me time to focus on my work and provided me with inspiration from international artists, contemporary art and traditional craft.

What do you wish you paid more attention to?
To learn more from professors and teaching staff and not to be so focused on my own things. It was sometimes hard to find a balance between staying focused on a project and being open to listening and trying new things.

Was there any class you found particularly difficult?
It was challenging – and interesting – during my master's degree to have art theory, art criticism and writing classes.

What was your graduation project?
It was an installation with five pieces of 5.75-m long lengths of embroideries, found garments and pleated fabrics shaped by stiches. The embroidery work included documentary presentations and materialised thoughts from people's daily lives. It connected the past, hidden history of traditions, with my present life.

Any words of advice for future students?
Think over your plan. It's you who can influence your own master terms.

Do you have any fond memories of studying here?
HDK Steneby is located amidst beautiful countryside; I loved being near the forest and the canal.

Was the transformation from graduation to working life a smooth one?
Since graduation, I have been doing different things, and I'm not sure if 'working life' will look the same further on. I was travelling and working as an 'artist in residence' for a couple of years after graduation. After that, I had my studio at Cirkulations Centralen in Malmö, had exhibitions, and then I got a commission work to do an artwork for the main entrance to the private hospital Stockholms Sjukhem.

Graduation work installation including the five lengths of embroideries, found garments and pleated fabrics shaped by stic

Current Students

'We have a great deal of independence and full access to wonderful workshops. Each student creates their own projects and gets tutoring both in groups and individually. The possibility of shaping your education according to your own needs is perhaps the best thing about this school.'
Annika Wahlstrom

'HDK at Steneby gives you time, space and opportunities. I did my bachelor's degree at Steneby and found that the more time you spend here, the easier it becomes to find peace here. Dals Långed is a cheap place to live, and I like to explore the surrounding beautiful nature. There is a moose-park nearby, a weird kiosk with the best mashed potatoes, a lovely art society with lots of activities, and I love going for swims in the Dalsland Canal.'
Funny Livdotter

'The location makes the school and course something special. If you want fantastic workshops and possibilities, time to focus and a very friendly, international study environment, HDK/Steneby is the place.'
Jokum Lind Jensen

'The most valuable part was the time I got to develop my own projects. I could decide myself what I want to focus on. This gave me the chance to find my own aesthetic and to boost my abilities.'
Lena Louisa Mayer

City Life

Steneby is located in Dals Långed, a small community located along the beautiful Dalsland canal with an abundance of natural surroundings. The town has almost 1500 inhabitants and is a popular destination for anyone seeking peace and quiet. There are shops, cafes, a library and the most important basic services available here.

Dals Långed is also culturally rich community with galleries and many working artists and artisans. At Steneby, students are able to focus on their work and enjoy the benefits of a creative and social environment. During the school year, there are numerous social activities and sports/dances classes organised, such as yoga, Thai boxing and lindy hop. There is also a well-equipped gym in Dals Långed and several trials for runners and hikers. A popular hang-out is Cafe Schucker, run by students and locals, where you can volunteer to help bake or participate in literature evenings and exhibitions.

Sweden

The Dalsland Canal is 250 km in lengthand enables ships to sail between Lake Vänern in the north and in the south.

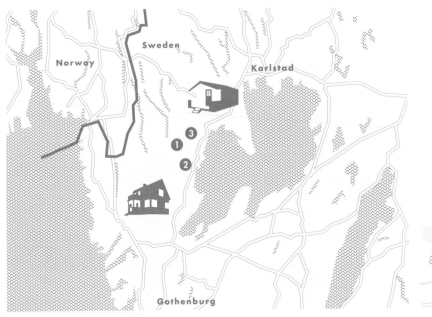

Norway

Sweden

Karlstad

Gothenburg

Dals Långed

1 HDK
2 Dalslands Konstmuseum
3 Not Quite

///// Park

Water

·········· Railway

Main road

Course
Applied Arts

School
HDK School of Design and Crafts at Steneby

City Facts

Dalslands Konstmuseum ②
This museum is home to the works of all other important Dalslandic artists, along with temporary arts and crafts exhibitions in its two galleries. There is also a permanent collection of craft, art, furniture, silver and everyday objects from old times in Dalsland.
dalslandskonstmuseum.se

Not Quite ③
A place and a network for artists, craftsmen and designers located in an old paper mill. There are work and exhibition spaces, a cafe and shop, where everyone can enjoy the vibrant creativity of the Dalsland forest.
notquite.se

Halmens Hus
A little to the north of Steneby in Bengtsfors, this museum explains to visitors the traditional crafts of the area. The name translates literally as 'house of straw', which was of such great importance here in Dalsland. It strives preserve the knowledge and the techniques of the craftmanship of straw, through exhibitions, courses, lectures, concerts and various other arrangements, in a setting which has fantastic views of the forests and lakes.
halmenshus.com

Skogsfesten
A festival set amongst nature with performances, acts musicians and artists from all over Sweden, held every May in the Dalsland forest.
skogfesten.se

Konstvandringen i Dalsland
An organisation who plans 'art walks' in the region. Artists and art craftsmen open their studios and workshops, giving a clear insight to the inspiration that can be found in the natural surroundings. Currently there are 47 artisans involved in the art walks programme in Dalsland.
konstvandring.nu

Dalsland Canoe Marathon
Not for a people who have a fear of water, the canoe marathon is a tough challenge for even the fittest sports men and women. It is Sweden's longest canoe race, held every year in Dalsland's lush forests and sparkling glacial lakes it.
vastsverige.com/en

Steneby Konsthall
This is the design and exhibition hub of the locality, with student exhibitions and other visitng exhibitions taking place here.

Dalslands Bokdagar
A Nordic literary event with writers' evenings and other activities – from author workshops to book clubs for young and old – held every year in October in the town of Åmål.
bokdagaridalsland.se

Baldersnäs
This is a classic mansion from 1912 which has a rich history and is popular with tourists. Located in beautiful parkland, it is well woth a visit or two.
baldersnas.eu

Håverud Aqueduct
The aqueduct in Håverud is the only place in Europe (as far as is understood) where boats, cars and trains can meet all in the same spot, at different levels. Here you will find exhibitions, a tourist agency, a restaurant and a smokehouse. A number of passenger boats depart from here, where you can book trips on the Dalsland Canal.

How to get around
HDK at Steneby is located 170 km to the north of Gothenburg. With car, from Gothenburg, it is very pleasant journey via Uddevalla and Bäckefors. The city of Karlstad is somewhat closer at 120 km distance. To drive from Oslo (ca. 200 km away), go via Halden and Ed. The local airport is Trollhättan-Vänersborgs and the nearest one with good international connections is Gothenburg airports, although Karlstad airport in Norway is somewhat closer (85 km).
If you go by local bus, or from Gothenburg, you will find time tables and prices at vasttrafik.se. The name of the bus stop closest to the school is Stenebyskolan. Travelling by train, it is advisable to go to either Åmål, Ed or Mellerud and then take a car, taxi or the bus to Steneby (timetables and prices at www.sj.se).
In the town itself, students usually walk or cycle, as everywhere is close to hand. Buses are also a popular mode of transport.

Arranging housing
Never a problem

Housing support by school
Yes

Cost of room in the city
SEK 2000 per month (approx. EUR 230)

Cost of campus housing
SEK 3000 per month (approx. EUR 350), incl. lunch and breakfast Monday to Friday

Heriot-Watt University School of Textiles & Design

The school is housed in an old textile mill in the Scottish Borders.

**Heriot-Watt University
School of Textiles & Design**
Scottish Borders Campus,
Nether Road
Galashiels TD1 3HF
United Kingdom

T +44 (0)1896 892133
enquiries@tex.hw.ac.uk
tex.hw.ac.uk

Students have access to great facilities, including textile labs and weaving workshops.

Introduction

'One of the main areas of study is the interface where design and technology meet'

Britta Kalkreuter, postgraduate programme director

When was the school founded and how has it changed?
The school was founded in 1883 – making it one of the oldest textiles schools in Europe – to service the needs of a global textile industry. Based in the Scottish Borders, the school has a great history but has evolved constantly over the last 130 years so that we now deliver both cutting-edge research and industry-relevant practice.

What is studying here about?
One of the main areas of study is the interface where design and technology meet. We encourage students to collaborate with academics in other academic fields in the university, such as the School of Engineering and Physical Sciences. There are always synergies to be found in unexpected areas which makes the master's degree programme very exciting and dynamic.

What kind of teaching method is applied?
The master's programme is centred around student-defined project work, but always with an emphasis on collaboration with others, to allow each student to reach their full potential.

Why should students choose this school?
The facilities are outstanding and leading designers, such as honorary graduate Dame Vivienne Westwood, declared that they are the best facilities in the United Kingdom. As the number of master's students is relatively small, our students form a close-knit community and have easy access to staff. The school is located in the heart of the Scottish Borders' global luxury textiles industry and students benefit from close links with this local industry through project collaborations.

What is expected from the students?
Initiative and willingness to collaborate are both essential to thrive in an environment that demands students to be passionately driven in their area.

When did you start offering the master's degree course in fashion/textile design?
We have been running ever evolving master's programmes since the 1990s.

What is the most important thing for students to learn during this course?
By the end of the programme, students should have discovered how best to use their talents and skills, and what their place in the fashion and textile industry might be.

What is the most important skill to master for a fashion/textile designer?
To be a successful designer, just learning how to design a frock is not enough. Our students will also learn how to read and determine the evolving needs of society through their designs.

Programme

The MA Fashion and Textiles Design programme challenges traditional and contemporary uses of fashion and textiles, as well as creating the opportunity, through well-resourced workshops, to promote new approaches and processes in fashion and textiles. Students concentrate on an appropriate area of study to acquire knowledge and expertise in an area of fashion and textiles that is conducive to their individual project intentions. Staff knowledge and expertise span the full spectrum from design to manufacture, context to management, technology to creativity and practice to theory.

The design of the programme also encourages interdisciplinary projects reflecting the school's strategy of creative collaborations between subject areas to foster design innovation. Students are assessed through a combination of practical and written course work, examinations and the master's project. Emphasis is placed on rigorous academic standards as well as acquiring and developing a range of transferable industry skills and individual creative development.

The school has developed an enhanced postgraduate programme designed to respond to the needs of local and global textile industries, utilising our unique combination of traditional and contemporary expertise in science, technology and creativity. The benefits of our location within Scotland's manufacturing centre of high-end cashmere and textile production and design, are extended and maintained through international links in fashion and textiles. Studying within a school that reflects such high-quality collaborations, research and teaching, positions our graduates highly within these rapidly evolving sectors.

Screen printing in the in the school's textiles workshop.

Students have 24/7 access to cutting-edge textile laboratories.

The facilities at the school include purpose-built accommodation on campus.

Programme
Fashion and Textiles Design

Leads to
Master of Arts

Structure
The 1-year full-time course is divided into three semesters and allows students to coordinate an area of study to acquire knowledge and expertise in an area of fashion and textiles which will support their individual project intended outcome. The first two semesters include eight modules in total, covering everything from design context and creative thinking, to fashion and textile practice and expertise. The final semester is dedicated to the master's project and all students will produce a design collection.

Head of programme
Britta Kalkreuter

Mentors and lecturers
Andrew Grieve, Britta Kalkreuter, Lisa Macintyre, Alison Harley, Fiona Pankhurst, Mark Parker, Emily Quinn, Pam Schenk, George Stylios, Danmei Sun, Christine Taylor, Colin Turnbull, Sara Keith, Angela Cassidy and Fiona Jardine.

Notable alumni
Hamish and Sheila-Mary Carruthers, Rosy Eribe and Tammy Kane.

Course
Fashion and Textiles Design

School
Heriot-Watt University School of Textiles & Design

School Facts

Duration of study
1 year

Full time
Yes

Part time
No

Female students
70%

Male students
30%

Local students
50%

Students from abroad
50%

Yearly enrolment
10

Tuition fee
- GBP 5440 per year for EU citizens (approx. EUR 6400)
- GBP 11,950 Per year for non-EU citizens (approx. EUR 14,000)

Funding/scholarships
Yes

Minimum requirements for entry
Bachelor's degree

Language
English

Application procedure
The following documents are required:
- application form
- copy of degree certificate/academic transcripts
- design portfolio
- your curriculum vitae
- a personal statement of interest
- letters of recommendation
- a copy of your passport
- proof of language (if applicable). Successful candidates will be informed by email.

Application details
r.paterson@hw.ac.uk

Application date
By 15 August

Graduation rate
High

Job placement rate
High

Memberships/affiliations
The Textile Institute, the Society of Dyers and Colourists, Scottish Academy of Fashion, Cumulus and IFFTI.

Collaborations with
Scottish Textiles Academic Group, National Institute of Design (India), Philadelphia University (United States), Turku University (Finland) and School of Textiles at the University of Borås (Sweden).

Facilities for students
Library, integrated learning facilities, computer suites, specialised workshops, spacious studios, gallery, knit and weave studios, the longest screen-print table in Europe, textile archive, fully-equipped clothing workshops, spacious studios with individual workspace, technical workshops and laboratories, state-of-the art production equipment and CAD suites. There is also a new creative hub which offers state-of-the-art studio and workshop space for textile, fashion designers and visual artists which master's students have access to.

Student Work

Printed Fashion (2012)
By Caroline Bell

Meticulous research and experiments in the print room and the clothing workshops prepared the realisation of this luxurious womenswear collection. The individual pieces take into account the effect of drape and body shape on the two-dimensional medium of digital print.

Fashion Knit Collection (2012)
By Rachel Wilson

Combining knitwear and digital print with sharp tailoring has enabled the creation of a womenswear collection that is contemporary and desirable as well as edgy – optical illusions create unexpected silhouettes.

Shima Collection (2012)
By Deborah Garner

This collection of Shima knitted garments was realised in collaboration with a leading luxury knitwear company. It explores the challenges and opportunities of placing design in the hands of technology.

Devoree Scarf (2012)
By Piotr Skibinski

This project was inspired by materials and process, as Skibinski immortalises his muse on silver-printed silk and devored velvet. His unsettling images transcend the categories of meaningful fashion and textile art.

My Mother's Garden (2012)
By Johanna Fleming

The meticulously drawn landscapes adorning Fleming's scarves are inhabited by giant creatures and magical plants which turn the personal memory of her mother's garden into luxurious decoration and engaging narratives at the same time.

Dress Fronts (2012)
By Xin Guo

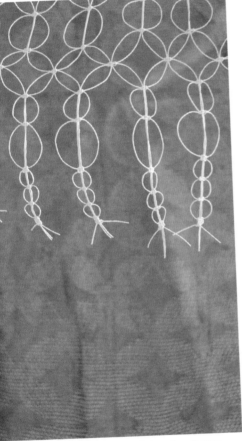

By reworking ancient craft techniques from Eastern and Western traditions in smart materials and new technologies, this project explores the balance between tradition and innovation in fashion.

Double Coth Pieces (2012)
By Liz Turton

Elaborate mark-making from built interventions in the natural environment, provide Turton with the visual material to be translated into precious double-cloth pieces that address sustainability by being multifunctional and luxurious.

Alumna

Name Ekta Khokhar Kaul
Residence London, United Kingdom
Year of birth 1977
Year of graduation 2006
Current job Textile designer
Website ektakaul.com

Why did you choose this school?
The deciding factor was the school's world-class textile design and production facilities. Being a fashion graduate, I was looking for a school that would enable me to explore textiles by offering access to a wide range of processes like screen printing, weaving and dyeing. The school has fantastic state-of-the-art facilities, for digital printing and laser cutting as well as CAD suites. Apart from these, the school's excellent faculty and links with local Scottish mills were the reasons I chose the school.

What was the most important thing you learned here?
To develop a focus, making it laser sharp.

What are you doing now?
I am a designer maker and own a small business specialising in luxurious handmade textile accessories. My work combines a love of bold colour and graphic pattern. Using traditional techniques of printing and embroidery I create handmade textile products for home and fashion.

What was your graduation project?
I investigated how traditional textile processes done by hand could be combined with modern technology in new ways to develop textiles. I explored combining traditional craft techniques like needle punching, and developed a range of textiles with distressed textures and graphic patterns for fashion and interiors.

How did the school prepare you for what you are doing now?
The school gave me the time and space to reflect on the kind of practice I wanted to build and enabled me to hone my fashion and textile skills which I continue to use every day.

Was the transition from graduation to working life a smooth one?
Yes, I think so. My plan was to set up my own creative business after graduating. I did tonnes of research into setting this while still at university, as well as looked at practices of designers and artists whose work I admired. While studying for my master's degree, I won a Creative Futures Award, which gave me 2 weeks of business mentoring from professionals at CIDA (UK) and from professors at the Indian Institute of Management in Bangalore. I got a lot of practical advice, connected with other creative practitioners and refined my ideas further, so by the time I graduated I had a pretty clear idea of what I wanted to do.

Any words of advice for future students?
You have to get out there and make things happen for yourself. Believe in your dreams and work your hardest to make them come true. And you'll see that they do!

Recent work from Kaul's studio has include fashion accessories employing traditional techniques of printing and embroidery.

Course
Fashion and Textiles Design

School
Heriot-Watt University School of Textiles & Design

Current Students

'I wanted to study textiles, especially weaving. I chose this school because it has excellent facilities and technical support. Also, the school is located close to many famous textile companies, which offers more opportunities to get involved in the industry.'

Wanfei Hu

'Future students can expect fantastic facilities and knowledgeable technicians. There is a lot of independent learning especially when it comes to the last semester. The school is a bit secluded, despite having fantastic bus links to the surrounding cities, so if you like small-town living in beautiful countryside, this is the place for you!'

Sophie Adamson

'I thought the most valuable course was Design Technologies and Textiles Futures. It provided lectures from a variety of professionals in the fashion and textiles field. The learning was supported by their engaging answers and availability for one on one discussion.'

Kaitlynn Smith

'The course is structured in a way that people from different backgrounds can build their projects around their expertise. It also gives the flexibility of a career either in the design side of a fashion house or as merchandiser/buyer. Overall, this course offers important ingredients for everyone in the field of fashion and textiles.'

Navneet Kumar

City Life

The School of Textiles and Design is located on the Scottish Borders Campus in the town of Galashiels. A free university shuttle bus school to Heriot-Watt's Edinburgh Campus twice daily, and it takes less than an hour to get to Edinburgh by car. Newcastle and Carlisle are also within easy reach, and the surrounding countryside is famous for walking, horse-riding and unspoilt coastline.

Galashiels offers a lively community with a compact campus that makes it easy to access all facilities. The campus recently underwent a multi-million pound refurbishment to create an inspiring learning environment and centre for excellence. The campus offers a range of support services for students and has a lively Students' Association with strong links to its partner on our Edinburgh Campus.

Southern Upland Way is a scenic, long-distance walking trail that run through the market town of Galashiels.
Photo Andrew Bowden

United Kingdom

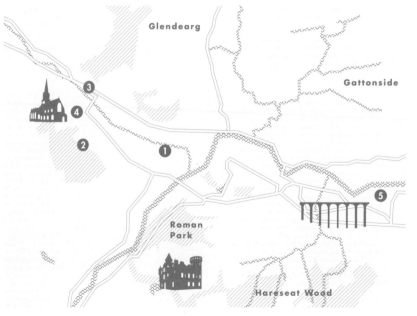

Galashiels

1 HWU campus
2 Braw Lads Gathering
3 Pavilion Cinema
4 Old Gala House
5 Borders Book Festival

Glendearg

Gattonside

Roman Park

Haréseat Wood

Park

Water

Main road

Course
Fashion and Textiles Design

School
Heriot-Watt University School of Textiles & Design

City Facts

Tartan Trail
Galashiels has been the centre of the tartan, tweed and woollen industries since medieval times and is still a global centre of the luxury textile market. As one of the largest towns in the Scottish Borders, it is a major commercial centre but offers easy access to unspoilt countryside. The iconic Eildon Hills are visible from town.

Braw Lads Gathering ❷
The town has a thriving cultural life and in late June is this focal point of the local calendar, involving traditional pipe bands and horseback riding down the high street and out onto the hills.

Pavilion Cinema ❸
If you are a film buff, this is a great hang-out in the town centre. It has four screens and shows the latest films, with cheap tickets for students on Tuesdays.

Old Gala House ❹
The home of the Lairds of Gala for several centuries, and inspiration for the St Trinian's televison and film series, is now a museum and art gallery set in landscaped gardens.

Borders Book Festival ❺
Nearby Melrose hosts an annual literary festival, with speakers including Booker prize winner Hilary Mantel.
bordersbookfestival.org

Gala Aisle
The site of historical significance, this has been the burial place for the Lairds of Gala since the 17th century and has recently been restored.

Southern Upland Way
One of the wildest and most scenic of long-distance walking trails, the Southern Upland Way runs through Galashiels – on route from Traquair to Lauder – and the town is a popular base for outdoor enthusiasts.
southernuplandway.gov.uk

How to get around
There are safe cycle routes to the Scottish Borders Campus from the town centre and surrounding area. There is also shuttle minibus runs between the Edinburgh Campus (main reception) and the Scottish Borders Campus (High Mill car park), twice daily on weekdays.
There is a well-developed network of local buses, an hourly bus service to Edinburgh and a daily service to Newcastle and Glasgow. Public bus services around the town and to nearby cities are provided by First Buses and Munro's of Jedburgh. Although there is no train station in Galashiels, there are stations at Edinburgh Waverley, Berwick-upon-Tweed and Carlisle that have connecting bus services to the school campus. Air links are good with three international airports within 2 hours of travel.

Arranging housing
Average

Housing support by school
Yes

Cost of room in the city
GBP 400 per month (EUR 465 per month)

Cost of campus housing
GBP 500 per month (EUR 580 per month)

Institut Français de la Mode

Programme director Hans de Foer leads the discussion in one of the fashion workshops.

Institut Français de la Mode
36 Quai d'Austerlitz
75013 Paris
France

T +33 (0)1 70 38 89 89
ifm@ifm-paris.com
ifm-paris.com

IFM is located right in the heart of Paris, positioned on the banks of the river Seine.
Photo Alexandre Tabaste

Introduction

'We break down barriers between management and design in an industry focused on products, brands, culture and design'

Hans de Foer, postgraduate design programme director

oto Isabelle Hedou-Beaufort

When was the school founded and how has it changed?
Institut Français de la Mode (IFM) was founded in 1986 by professionals in the sector fashion/luxury with support from the French Ministry of Industry, and remains under the ministry's tutelage. IFM has progressively widened its scope and has added fashion design to its original specialty, which is teaching fashion management.

What is the full offering in the master's level programme at IFM?
Our fashion design postgraduate programme was founded in 2000, offering three majors – garment, accessory and image – with a new 'image and media' major included from 2013.

What is studying at this school all about?
Professions in the fashion, design and luxury industries have diversified considerably in recent years. Marketing, retail, logistics and communication have developed as the industry has become more complex and requires more and more executives trained to an increasingly high-level. The managers and designers trained at IFM are known for their ability to fulfil these expectations by combining creativity and good management.

How are your courses focused?
The IFM enables postgraduate students to follow high-level professionalising programmes in both management and design. Students then take their training in both dimensions to work in companies where creativity is a major source of added value or alternatively develop their own business. The end result is the breaking down of barriers between management and design in an industry focused on products, brands, culture and design.

What kind of teaching method is applied?
The courses provided by IFM benefit from the expertise and research carried out by the institute's multidisciplinary teams. The teaching emphasises the involvement of companies at all levels: the programmes are designed according to the needs expressed by our professional partners. Major players from the sector and high-level contributors come in to talk to the students throughout the year.

What is expected from the students?
IFM recruits its students for their strong personality, creativity and willingness to develop concrete projects in direct partnership with reputable fashion houses and companies.

What is the most important thing for students to learn during this course?
The purpose of the programme is to link international designers with the know-how of the French fashion industry. Students work under pressure, exactly as in a professional context. At IFM, students learn how to work with other designers, with managers and with technical experts.

Programme

IFM fashion design students rely on the best technical savoir-faire. During the course of the year, they work together during classes and workshops to help them understand the industry, and they make prototypes with IFM's partner companies (mostly reputable French fashion houses and manufacturers).

This collaboration with 40 companies leads to prototypes of garments, bags, glasses and shoes being made each year with an exceptional abundance of creative ideas. Brands like Ballin, Berluti, Chanel, Dior, Cosmoparis, Hermès, JM Weston, Louis Vuitton, Nina Ricci or Tila March, and high-end manufacturers like Grandis, La Ferté Confection, Marty, Pollux/La Couture du Cuir, Production Simon Fonlupt or StylCouture actively participate in the creation of prototypes and welcome IFM designers in their workshops during the development. Following the year of classes, students undertake a 3 to 6 month internship in a company before they can graduate with their degree.

Group discussion and evaluation during one of the fashion workshops.

Facilities at the school include state-of-the-art lecture theatres.

Programme
Fashion Design

Leads to
Master of Arts (equivalent)

Structure
The course can last up to 18 months: 1 year of classes followed by a 3 to 6 month internship in a company. The programme has three sessions for enrolment (March, April and June). The classes are taught in English by professionals. During their studies, students are put in touch with companies and their recruiting departments, and benefit from a personalised coaching system that is designed to facilitate their future professional journey.

Head of programme
Hans de Foer

Mentors and lecturers
Jean-Michel Bertrand, Benoît Heilbrunn, Bénédicte Fabien, Marion Lavaine, Laurent Raoul, Patricia Romatet, Samia Buchan, Anne Corbiere, Maylis Duvivier, Daniel Henry, Valerie Praquin, Nathalie Ruelle, Josephus Thimister, Benoît Béthume, Eric Bauduin, Angelo Ciremele, David Hermann, Alice Litscher, Eduardo Dente, Luca Marchetti, Isabelle Hedou-Beaufort, Karine Piotraut, and more.

Notable alumni
Guillaume Henry, Wisharawish Akarasantisook, Christine Phung, Esther Perbandt, Steffie Christians, Arturo Martinez and Daniel Lierah.

Course
Fashion Design

School
Institut Français de la Mode

School Facts

Duration of study
1.5 year (plus internship)

Full time
Yes

Part time
No

Female students
60%

Male students
40%

Local students
20%

Students from abroad
80%

Yearly enrolment
20–30

Tuition fee
EUR 10,000 per year

Funding/scholarships
Yes

Minimum requirements for entry
Bachelor's degree in fashion, design or visual arts

Language
English

Application procedure
The following documents must be submitted as a presentation of your creative universe:
- your curriculum vitae
- your portfolio
- a statement outlining your achievements, previous experience, professional objectives and motivations
- creative project video (maximum 15 minutes)
- proof of language proficiency (if appropriate)
- letters of recommendation. Application is free. The admission jury is composed of members of the IFM teaching staff and industry professionals make the evaluation and final admissions decision regarding each candidate. Upon selection an initial fee of EUR 1500 must be paid on registration and is non-refundable.

Application details
creation@ifm-paris.com

Application date
By 15 January for March session

Graduation rate
100%

Job placement rate
90%

Memberships/affiliations
Conférence des Grandes Écoles and International Foundation of Fashion Institutes.

Collaborations with
With several actors of the luxury business and various members of the Cercle IFM: Armand Thierry SAS, Chanel, Chloé International, Christian Dior Couture, Disneyland Paris, Fondation Pierre Bergé-Yves Saint-Laurent, Fondation d'entreprise Hermès, Galeries Lafayette, Group Etam, Kenzo, L'Oréal Luxe, Louis Vuitton, Printemps, Vivarte and Yves Saint-Laurent.

Facilities for students
Classrooms, amphitheatre, computer room, library, labs and workshops.

City
Paris

Country
France

Student Work

Visual Optimism (2013)
By Aleksandra Ziravac

Assume that designing is like cooking and every good cake is baked in the mould of visual optimism. Be simple and bold with surprises. Believe that most precious things are hidden.
Photo Sol Sanchez

Question Your Perception (2013)
By Marie Curtin

This collection looks at a familiar but strange world. Question your perception. Find interest in moments of unusual clarity. Speak of stories, universes and landscapes coloured by mysterious presences. Motivate exploration through emotion and use imagery to guide the hand. Find colour and texture.
Photo Sol Sanchez

Extraordinary (2013)
By Kris Berden

See the world from a different perspective, where the ordinary becomes extraordinary. Deconstruct reality to create your own. Mix the sensitive with the structured. Contrast delicacy and bold geometry. Value quality, empathy, aesthetics and characteristics.
Photo Sol Sanchez

Oversized Volumes (2013)
By Luis Manteiga

The work involves designing oversized volumes using rich details alongside sensitive and precise lines. Create a contrast between the masculine and the feminine. Design for a contemporary individual with future perspectives and a vanguard spirit.
Photo Sol Sanchez

Brazility (2013)
By Natalia Assis Baptista

Use Brazility in its mysticism, optimism and naturality. Be inspired by authentic and spontaneous individuals. Abolish the beautiful and the ugly. Prefer the unique. Propose contrasts in organic but urban design. Foment communication between garments and body to find shape. Mix and match unexpected elements, colours, prints, textures and technologies.
Photo Sol Sanchez

Express Stories (2013)
By Stéfanie Salzmann

Express stories, be inspired by landscapes and geometrical patterns, catch hairy, airy and cold materials, create space around the body, imagine clothes to hide in, mix new technologies with handcrafts and add contrast.
Photo Sol Sanchez

uitful Fashion (2013)
y Deborah Jin

et to understand the kaleidoscopic attitudes m women. Be inspired by urban structures d nature in city landscapes, women's haviour and global trends. Observe dinary life and transform the experience o precious, fruitful fashion reflecting fine ts and design.
oto Sol Sanchez

Curiosity (2013)
By Juliette Leca

Be hard-headed, subtle, delicate and clear-sighted, curious, daring, demanding, precise and willing. Observe, discover, select, create and insist to obtain soft-structured or sharp neo-modern beauty. Apply a discreet twist and a touch of edgy know-how.
Photo Sol Sanchez

Delicate Sensibility (2013)
By Laura Geddes

Evoke natural femininity and lightness. Bring to products a narrative and delicate sensibility. Explore volume through soft curves and delicate lines. Search inspiration in the details. Draw with nature as an open source. Believe that happiness is found in little moments of pleasure and effortless perfection.
Photo Sol Sanchez

Alumna

Name Christine Phung
Residence Paris, France
Year of birth 1978
Year of graduation 2002
Current job Fashion designer
Clients Chloé, Dior, Lacoste, Vanessa Bruno, etc.
Website christinephung.com

Why did you choose this school?

I chose this school because I wanted to learn how to combine creativity and business in fashion. I wanted to experience the marketing and the management aspects linked with a strong creative direction.

What was the most important thing you learned here?

I learned how to do a business plan and financial forecast, then I realised how expensive it would be to launch a brand. That's why I decided to wait until I was ready. I waited 8 years… I learned how to be patient and strategic, conscious. You have to do the right thing at the right moment, otherwise you lose the energy.

What was the most interesting project you did?

We had the chance to work on a shoe development project with big fashion houses, such as Chanel and Vuitton. We visited a lot of factories and discovered all about the shoe creation process at first-hand – it was a fascinating experience.

Was there any class you found particularly difficult?

The business plan class was very difficult for me, because I have a creative brain and mathematics appeared so complex to me, like another language entirely!

Are you still in contact with the school?

Yes, I am still in contact with IFM because I love the spirit of this school. I'm regularly in touch with the academic team, sharing my news and keeping up-to-date with things there.

Do you have any fond memories about the city?

The school was next to the beautiful Avenue Montaigne and the Grand Palais, so it was amazing to walk on this beautiful street every day, to see all this luxurious world. It fascinated me, because it was so beautiful, very precise – almost like it was another world.

Where are you living now?

I am still living in Paris. I love my city, with its strong culture, history and open-minded spirit.

What was your favourite place to hang out as a student?

Not that you get a lot of time to hang out, but I used to like visiting an exhibition at the Pompidou Center, then going up to the Le Georges restaurant to have a drink with an amazing view of Paris.

Any words of advice for future students?

Be patient, persevere, work hard, stay very creative but understand the constraints. Go further than you ever have done before and keep dreaming of creation but be conscious.

Phung's Fall-Winter 13/14 collection encapsulated tension and release, between straight lines and curves.
Photo Grégoire Alexandre

School
Institut Français de la Mode

Current Students

'I found the Toile workshop very valuable because you deepen and perfect your knowledge in this area. I also really enjoyed the workshop where we worked jointly with management students to create a brand.'
Aleksandra Ziravac

'The thing I like about IFM is that it is a step between an art school and the professional world of fashion design. For me, it was the right choice to make considering where I want to go in the future.'
Kris Berden

'I chose this school because of the high-level reputation of its accessory master's programme and the fact that the students work on projects in partnership with brands.'
Ludivine Huteau

'I think the most valuable workshop was during the process of creating our personal collection. I had the opportunity to understand how the technical aspects of the garment can serve creativity. Also, how important it is to be able to express your vision with the right tools and knowledge.'
Flavien Juan Nunez

City Life

With an estimated population of over 2.2 million inhabitants, Paris is the capital and largest city of France. The river Seine divides the city in two parts.

Paris is today one of the world's leading business and cultural centres, and its influences on politics, education, entertainment, media, fashion, science and the arts all contribute to its status as one of the world's major global cities. It hosts the headquarters of many international organisations, such as UNESCO, OECD, the International Chamber of Commerce and the European Space Agency. Paris is considered to be one of the greenest and most liveable cities in Europe. It is also one of the most expensive. Three of the most famous Parisian landmarks are the 12th-century cathedral Notre Dame de Paris on the Île de la Cité, the Napoleonic Arc de Triomphe and the 19th-century Eiffel Tower.

Ever since the beginning of the 20th century, Paris has been famous for its cultural and artistic communities and its nightlife. Many historical figures located to the city of light in search of inspiration, including Russian composer Stravinsky, American writer Hemingway and Spanish painters Picasso and Dalí.

View of Paris from the top of the Centre Pompidou with the Eiffel Tower a prominent landmark on the city skyline.
Photo Archibald Ballantine

France

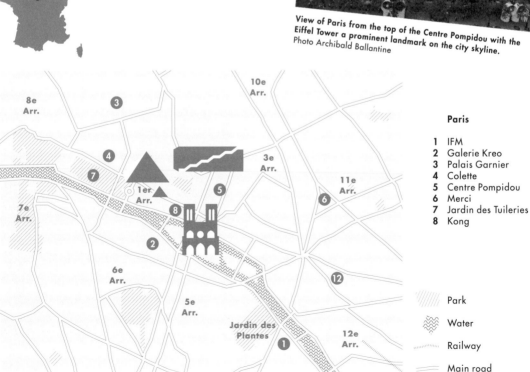

Paris

1 IFM
2 Galerie Kreo
3 Palais Garnier
4 Colette
5 Centre Pompidou
6 Merci
7 Jardin des Tuileries
8 Kong

////// Park

〜〜〜 Water

········· Railway

‒ ‒ ‒ Main road

Course
Fashion Design

School
Institut Français de la Mode

City Facts

See more Paris City Facts on p.75

IFM Library ①
The reference library at IFM is open to the public, including fashion, design and creative industries and has publications that are unique in Europe, covering the textiles, fashion and associated sectors.
ifm-paris.com

Galerie Kreo ②
Galerie Kreo is dedicated to artistic exploration in contemporary design, and has exclusive international rights to remarkable limited edition pieces by such luminaries as Ronan & Erwan Bouroullec, Hella Jongerius and Jasper Morrison.
galeriekreo.fr

Palais Garnier ③
The city's original opera house does not only show stunning theatre, but is also the most intimate and glamorous building in Paris.
opera-de-paris.fr

Colette ④
This Japanese-inspired concept store sells clothes, accessories, books, art, music and beauty products from renowned brands like Comme des Garçons, Lanvin and Marc Jacobs.
colette.fr

Centre Pompidou ⑤
A remarkable building by Renzo Piano, Richard Rogers and Gianfranco Franchini that houses a public library, the Musée National d'Art Moderne, IRCAM, a centre for music and acoustic research, and Le Georges restaurant and the panoramic terrace on level 6.
centrepompidou.fr

Merci ⑥
By the owners of Colette, Merci is a unique multi-storey concept store. Housed in a former factory, it stocks furniture, fashion items and much more, but customers can also have a coffee in the café. All profits go to a children's charity in Madagascar.
Merci-Merci.com

Jardin des Tuileries ⑦
Formerly known as the most fashionable spot in Paris for parading about in one's finery; today the garden is a favourite of all Parisians and forms part of the Banks of the Seine World Heritage Site listed by UNESCO in 1991.

Kong ⑧
This Philippe Starck-designed bar is carefully perched upon the Kenzo building opposite the Pont Neuf, the oldest standing bridge across the river Seine. An impressive interior by a great designer on a perfect location.
kong.fr

Père-Lachaise Cemetery
The largest cemetery of Paris with many beautifully-designed tombs attracts hundreds of thousands of visitors annually to the graves of such famous people as Jim Morrison, Édith Piaf and Oscar Wilde
pere-lachaise.com

Château de Versailles
This splendid and enormous palace was built in the mid-17th century during the reign of Louis XIV – the Roi Soleil (Sun King) – reflects his taste for profligate luxury and his boundless appetite for self-glorification.
chateauversailles.fr

How to get around
Roissy-Charles-de-Gaulle airport takes the majority of international flights to and from Paris, and Orly is a host to mostly domestic and European airline companies.
　　As far as national and European destinations are concerned, rail transport is beginning to outdistance air travel in both travel time and efficiency. Amsterdam, London, Brussels and Cologne can be reached within hours using the French high-speed TGV rail network which offers services more than 10 times a day. A combination of traffic jams and the lack of parking spaces means that

driving a car in the capital of France is not a very attractive prospect. Besides 14 metro lines, 58 bus lines, 5 railway lines, some tramlines and one funicular (in Montmartre), Paris offers 20,000 bikes for rent at very low rates.
　　In order to reach IFM, you can take metro lines 1, 5, 10 and 12, or bus lines 24, 57, 61, 63, 89 and 91.

Arranging housing
Average

Housing support by school
No

Cost of room in the city
Varied

Cost of campus housing
n/a

London College of Fashion, UAL

A student shapes a design on a mannequin at LCF's Golden Lane site in East London.

London College of Fashion, UAL
20 John Prince's Street
London W1G 0BJ
United Kingdom

T +44 (0)20 7514 7736
enquiries@fashion.arts.ac.uk
fashion.arts.ac.uk

LCF's John Prince's Street building is just off Oxford Street, in the heart of London's main shopping area.

Introduction

'We believe that fashion education needs to be responsive to fashion's changing culture'

Wendy Malem, dean of the Graduate School
at London College of Fashion

When was the school founded and how has it developed?
The Graduate School at London College of Fashion (LCF) was founded in 2003. Over the last 10 years, our portfolio has expanded to encompass 18 master's degrees, three postgraduate certificates, and three graduate diplomas across three core clusters: design and technology, media and communications; and business and management. LCF is part of the University of the Arts London, a creative community made up of world-leading colleges specialising in art, design, fashion, communication and performance.

What is studying at this school all about?
We believe that fashion education needs to be attuned and responsive to fashion's changing culture and this is reflected in our progressive range of courses that aim to fuel, inspire and lead all areas of the fashion industry, from management through to communication and design. Our curricula are relevant, innovative and student-centred.

What teaching methods do you use?
Students investigate their own practice to define design methodologies that encompass key concepts of fabric, cut and silhouette. Based on rigorous research and analytical thinking, the course encourages fresh perspectives in design. Using diverse production techniques – from couture craftsmanship to futuristic experimentation – students are able to explore their own perspectives to form the basis of their their final collection.

What is the strength of this school?
Over the last decade, we have established a reputation for quality fashion design that is innovative and well crafted. Traditional techniques are revered alongside innovative manufacturing and digital technologies.

What is expected of students here?
Students are expected to focus on their own research and direction, to develop their existing body of specific skills and knowledge and apply them to the discipline and craft of fashion design. They should also be creative, committed, resourceful and enthusiastic.

What skills does a fashion designer need?
Balance is key, both in the context of garments as individual designs but also the delicate balance of planning a collection that will work together.

What careers do students go on to pursue?
Some have set up their own design labels or businesses, others have gone on to work as designers in fashion houses or companies. A few individuals choose to carry on to an academic career in design.

Programme

The MA Fashion Design Technology (Menswear and Womenswear) programme spans a range of disciplines that place innovative design and production at the heart of various contexts, including both performance and sustainability. The 21st century studio is a cross between the couturier's atelier and a scientific laboratory where new forms and fashions are explored and tested, and where garment engineering is practised in parallel with traditional decorative techniques and draping on the stand.

Our dynamic menswear course has an international reputation for challenging the conventions of fashion design, nurturing and refining talent to produce some of the most forward thinking creatives in menswear design today. Meanwhile, the MA Fashion Design Technology, Womenswear course develops directional womenswear designers whose cutting-edge fashion influences the future of the industry.

Our entire fashion programme looks to find fresh responses and bold, radical solutions to the questions and demands that drive the industry. In the design and technology remit, LCF also offers the following master's degree courses (there is some crossover of classes for all the programmes): MA Fashion Artefact, MA Fashion Footwear, MA Fashion and the Environment and MA Costume Design for Performance.

Students craft their designs in LCF's East London workshop at Curtain Road.

The study room at John Prince's Street.

The canteen at John Prince's Street.

Programme
Fashion Design Technology: Menswear
Fashion Design Technology: Womenswear

Leads to
Master of Arts

Structure
The 15-month full-time course is divided into four terms (180 credits in total). The different units of each term include: Master's Project Proposal (20 credits), Contextual Studies (20 credits); Creative And Technical Development (40 credits); Research, Development and Professional Links (40 credits), Master's Project Planning and Master's Project (60 credits). It is possible to undertake a part-time course over 27 months and seven terms.

Course directors
Darren Cabon (Menswear) and Nigel Luck (Womenswear).

Notable alumni
Joseph Turvey, Baartmans and Siegal, Matteo Molinari, Domingo Rodriguez, Charlotte Simpson, Hana Cha, Manjit Deu and Hassan Hejazi.

School Facts

Duration of study
  1.25 years

Full time
  Yes (15 months)

Part time
  Yes (27 months)

Female students
  87%

Male students
  13%

Local students
  45%

Students from abroad
  55%

Yearly enrolment
  44

Tuition fee
- GBP 7500* per year for EU citizens (approx. EUR 8700)
- GBP 13,800* per year for non-EU citizens (approx. EUR 16,375)
  *Subject to change

Funding/scholarships
  Yes

Minimum requirements for entry
  Bachelor's degree in a related subject at 2:1 or above, or equivalent qualifications

Language
  English

Application procedure
  Your application should include the following:
- your personal and contact details
- personal statement
- study proposal and/or essay
- references
- application form
- portfolio
- proof of language (if applicable).
  Successful applicants will be informed by email. There will be a portfolio review and interview stage.

Application details
  enquiries@fashion.arts.ac.uk

Application date
  By 1 March

Graduation rate
  High

Job placement rate
  High

Memberships/affiliations
  n/a

Collaborations with
  n/a

Facilities for students
  Fully-equipped studios, digital textile printing, fashion and textile labs, 3D printing and LCF library.

Student Work

London Fashion Week Show (2013)
By Na Di

Fashion Menswear.
Photo Alex Maguire

London Fashion Week Show (2013)
By Octo Yan Yu Cheung

Fashion Menswear.
Photo Alex Maguire

London Fashion Week Show (2013)
By Gina Xin Sun

Menswear collection.
Photo Katy Davies

Power and Beauty Collection (2013)
By Na Di

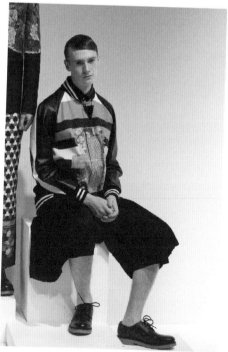

Menswear collection.
Photo Katy Davies

Course
Fashion Design Technology

School
London College of Fashion, UAL

Master's Final Collection (2013)
By Octo Yan Yu Cheung

Menswear collection.
Photo Katy Davies

London Fashion Week Show (2013)
By Sian Davies

Womenswear collection.
Photo Alex Maguire

Master's Final Collection (2013)
By Yi Xie

Womenswear collection.
Photo Katy Davies

London Fashion Week Show (2013)
By Maddelene Mangiaalavori

Fashion Womenswear.
Photo Alex Maguire

London Fashion Week Show (2013)
By Keiko Nishiyama

Womenswear collection.
Photo Alex Maguire

Alumna

Name Charlotte Simpson
Residence London, United Kingdom
Year of birth 1987
Year of graduation 2012
Current job Designer/director of own label
Website charlottesimpson.co.uk

Why did you choose this school?
I chose London College of Fashion because it has a reputation for being one of the best design schools in the United Kingdom.

What was the most important thing you learned here?
The course focused on establishing and thoroughly investigating our design methodologies whilst encouraging us to develop our collections as close to the industry processes as possible. We were required to collaborate with an industry partner to create our product which is where my involvement with hand embroiderers in India began. Building contacts whilst also the experiencing the pitfalls of working with resources abroad was a helpful experience for how I work now.

What was your graduation project?
As part of the course, we each produced a 10-piece collection. I focused on hand embroidery techniques that were inspired by electron microscopy imagery.

Are you still in contact with the school?
Yes I am, from time to time.

What are you doing now?
I set up my own label Charlotte Simpson after graduating in 2012. I am currently working on my third season which I will be showcasing during Paris Fashion Week.

Was the transition from graduation to working life a smooth one?
It has been a steep learning curve, as I am involved in every area of running my business, not just the designing. It has been made easier by accessing the support systems available young designer's in London, specifically the Centre for Fashion Enterprise which is supported by LCF.

How did your masters course prepare you for what you are doing now?
It allowed me to enhance my design and garment development skills whilst I was still refining my design aesthetic.

Any advice for future students?
Make the most of your time to experiment and take a few risks with your designs, It will help you to define your personal approach to design.

Hand embroidery techniques were incorporated into the graduate collection.
Photo Christopher Moore, Catwalking.com

Current Students

'The most valuable part of the course is the Design Process module, including the various tutorials on design development and production. It is inspiring to learn about the processes from design concept to actual creation, through discussions with tutors, design practice and manufacture.'
Seksarit Thanpransittikul

'Future students can expect to be challenged in their personal and professional development. They will develop an innovative approach to design through technology. Furthermore, part of the programme is to professionalise methodologies of research, sourcing, working with industrial partners and developing an industrial network.'
Anna Bezgubenko

'I decided to study at LCF for my master's degree because the offer of specialisations is impressive. There aren't many institutions specialising in so many different disciplines, and the course for Fashion Design Technology Menswear was exactly what I had been looking for.'
Sophie Skach

City Life

London is one of the world's fashion and cultural capitals. World-class museums and renowned commercial galleries sit comfortably next to small artist-run exhibition spaces that feature experimental work. International landmarks and major department stores are only around the corner from hidden markets, small boutiques and designer studios.

A multicultural and diverse city, London draws on its long-standing history to shape the future of fashion by combining urban innovation with British tradition and quirky originality. A fantastic range of international voices and visions inform London's position as a beacon of innovation. This is where new designers are raised and superstar designers are made.

LCF's John Prince's campus is situated in the heart of London's fashion retail hub, just off Oxford Street. Soho, Marylebone, and Saville Row are all a short walk away. The college takes full advantage of its position at the heart of Britain's fashion industry to offer young designers career-making professional opportunities, internships and connections. London College of Fashion also has campuses and connections in London's fashionable East End.

United Kingdom

The 30 St Mary Axe, designed by Norman Foster and Arup engineers, has become an iconic symbol of London.
Photo Dave Wilkie

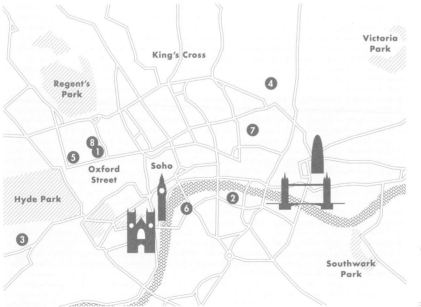

London

1 London College of Fashion
2 Tate Modern
3 Victoria and Albert Museum
4 Brick Lane and Shoreditch
5 Selfridges
6 The Southbank Centre
7 The Barbican
8 Fashion Space Gallery

Park

Water

Main road

Course
Fashion Design Technology

School
London College of Fashion, UAL

City Facts

See also more London City Facts on p.225

Tate Modern ②
This London art gallery houses the largest English collection of modern and contemporary art from 1900 to the present day, and hosts special exhibitions and events.
tate.org.uk/visit/tate-modern

Victoria and Albert Museum ③
The V&A's archive of fashion and textiles, and the museum's contemporary fashion exhibitions, are must-visits.
vam.ac.uk

Brick Lane and Shoreditch ④
The markets and pop-up shops of East London's Brick Lane and Shoreditch are places where students can find both cutting-edge urban design and classic vintage pieces.

Selfridges ⑤
This department store houses leading British and international fashion labels, as do the designer boutiques of surrounding West London.
selfridges.com

The Southbank Centre ⑥
The Southbank Centre is an art complex encompassing the Royal Festival Hall, Queen Elizabeth Hall, Purcell Room, Hayward Gallery, National Film Theatre and the Poetry Library.
sbc.org.uk

The Barbican ⑦
Europe's largest multi-arts and conference venue, includes the Barbican Theatre and the Pit, with a year-round programme of art, music, film and theatre.
barbican.org.uk

Fashion Space Gallery ⑧
London College of Fashion's gallery near Oxford Circus hosts a changing series of exhibitions focusing on Global fashion, design, photography and illustration.
fashionspacegallery.com

London Fashion Week
Twice a year, London hosts Fashion Week, attracting leaders of the fashion world, including London College of Fashion's students and alumni.
londonfashionweek.co.uk

British Fashion Awards
The annual ceremony which recognises outstanding British design.
britishfashionawards.com

How to get around
With four airports (Heathrow, City, Stansted and Gatwick), London has the largest city airspace in the world. From London, you can fly directly to almost every destination in the world. Transportation around the city centre is either underground or over-ground by bus, tram or bike. Car travel is common only in the suburbs. The London Underground – dating from 1863 – is the oldest underground railway network in the world and has 270 stations. London's bus network is also one of the largest in the world, running 24-hours a day, with 8000 buses, 700 bus routes, and over 6 million passenger journeys made every weekday. The distinctive red double-decker buses are internationally recognised, and are a trademark of London transport along with black cabs and the underground. Cycling in London has enjoyed a renaissance since the turn of the millennium. Cyclists enjoy a cheaper, and often quicker, way around town than those using public transport or car, and the launch of the Barclays Cycle Hire scheme in July 2010 has been successful and well-received.

Arranging housing
Average

Housing support by school
Yes

Cost of room in the city
GBP 600 per month (approx. EUR 740)

Cost of campus housing
Between GBP 400 and GBP 1000 per month (approx. EUR 500 to EUR 1250)

Massey University

In 2013, the fashion design students took charge of their final end of year exhibition to organise and perform an alternative catwalk experience that revealed the 'back stage' of the fashion world.

Massey University, School of Design
College of Creative Arts
Buckle Street, Museum Building
PO Box 756
Wellington 6041
New Zealand

T +64 (0)6350 5701
contact@massey.ac.nz
massey.ac.nz

The school's studios are in a state-of-the-art building called Te Ara Hihiko, dedicated to new teaching and learning practices.

Course
Fashion Design

School
Massey University

Introduction

'Massey fashion designers have been exploring what it means to design fashion in a post-consumerist world'

Julieanna Preston, College of Creative Arts
postgraduate coordinator design

When was the school founded?
The College of Creative Arts at Massey traces its origins back to 1886. The School of Design was incorporated in 2002, one of two schools within the college. Its strong postgraduate programmes have an emphasis on creative practice-led research, including a Master of Design (MDes) and a Master of Fine Art (MFA), both with the option of specialising in fashion design.

What is studying at this school all about?
Fashion designers studying at master's level undertake independent research projects that explore contemporary topics, such as questioning gender values, alternative aesthetics, new applications of digital software for grading draped designs and fuller sizing, integrated sustainable design and business models, zero-waste design and pattern work and design's role in mitigating cultural differences.

What is the strength of this school?
We offer bespoke postgraduate programmes that afford students the opportunity to build a strong personal relationship with their academic mentors and other students in a warm and supportive learning environment. We have some of the finest facilities, and our supervision is complemented by the encouragement to experiment and speculate. Additionally, we are the only design school in Australasia to be ranked by Red Dot, and we have the highest number of internationally-ranked design researchers, according to the New Zealand government.

What is the biggest challenge for students?
The biggest challenge for students on the Master of Design is the fact that it is only 1 year. This time frame demands that students use the year wisely, starting with a well-defined proposal.

What is the most important thing for students to learn during this course?
The value of fashion design thinking and processes in the context of interdisciplinary and collaborative design practise.

What is the most important skill for a fashion designer to acquire?
To question aesthetics and meaning and provide new expression in fashion design.

What jobs do your graduates end up doing?
A high number have excelled in their own design businesses internationally or are employed by successful companies, such as Bendon, Ice Breaker, Nike, Karen Walker, NomD, Zambesi and Paul Smith, as well as in the design workshops of Weta Film Studios.

City
Wellington

Country
New Zealand

147

Programme

Massey University College of Creative Arts offers two programmes for those seeking to study at a master's level: a 1-year Master of Design which focuses on applied design research practice often carried out with an industry partner and a 2-year Master of Fine Arts, a trans-disciplinary-oriented programme intended for designers and fine artists seeking to expand the boundaries of their creative practice through exploration and experimentation. Both programmes benefit from a high-calibre team of internationally recognised research academics who serve as supervisors, mentors and critics in independent and self-motivated study to achieve professional and creative mastery in a specific discipline or across disciplines. These learning experiences place emphasis on design excellence and critical reflection relative to the questions and concerns facing contemporary culture. Practical and theoretical skills develop simultaneously via workshops, seminars, masterclasses, studio work, symposia, field trips, social events and lectures.

Students in fashion design have access to facilities specific to all phases of the design process, including pattern-cutting, tailoring, sewing, sampling and fitting.

Every year is marked by the spectacle of a fashion show that explodes with colour, texture, accessories and drama for an audience of some of New Zealand's famous designers and fashion experts.

Programme
Fashion Design

Leads to
Master of Design, Master of Fine Arts

Structure
The Master of Design thesis consists of a body of advanced design work, an exegesis that contextualises and critically reflects on the project, a final exhibition and an examination presentation. Students link to a network of industry specialists and scholars to realise design's power to respond to or solve significant social, environmental, political or spatial problems. Students in both the 1-year MDes and 2-year MFA engage in a study that is self-motivated, experimental, sometimes interdisciplinary and often geared towards linking with an industry partner on a specific design research and development project (120 credits). Students develop their projects under the guidance of supervisors and in the context of a studio environment with other design and art postgraduates.

Head of programme
Julieanna Preston

Mentors and lecturers
Deb Cumming, Holly McQuillan, Jennifer Whitty, Catherine Bagnall, Sue Prescott, Janet Webster and Lillian Mutsaers.

School Facts

Duration of study
1 year (MDes)
2 year (MFA)

Full time
Yes (35–40 hours a week)

Part time
Possible

Female students
100%

Male students
0%

Local students
90%

Students from abroad
10%

Yearly enrolment
22

Tuition fee
- NZD 5500 per year for domestic students (approx. EUR 3500)
- NZD 28,000 per year for international students (approx. EUR 16,715)

Funding/scholarships
Opportunities for industry-based scholarships linked to study as well as various scholarshipsfrom Thailand, Vietnam or Indonesia.

Minimum requirements for entry
Bachelor's degree (honours) or by permission of Head of School with practice or degree equivalence. Proof of English proficiency (IELTS or TOEFL).

Language
English

Application procedure
Applications are made directly to the university. The following documents must be submitted in order to complete the application:
- application form
- verified copies (translated where necessary) of all academic transcripts and graduation certificates
- a research proposal of approx. 1000 words
- verified copy of passport or birth certificate (birth certificates should be translated where necessary)
- portfolio of recent design work
- example of recent written essay or research report
- proof of English proficiency (IELTS or TOEFL language scores).
There is no application fee charged. Applications will be reviewed shortly after 1 September and 1 December deadlines for study in the following year. Successful applicants will be sent an offer, including details of the

Massey enrolment procedures and information about how to apply for university-managed accommodation.

Application details
j.preston@massey.ac.nz

Application date
Applications can be sent throughout the year

Graduation rate
100%

Job placement rate
85–90%

Memberships/affiliations
IDSA

Collaborations with
Research design collaborations with other international universities in the UK, USA, Canada, Denmark, Australia, plus international student exchanges.

Facilities for students
Workshops and labs: woodworking, plastics, metal, welding, resin, digital fabrication, photography, audio studio, green screen, animation; high-end computer labs; print, textile print, print studio; fashion lab; and access with permission to other labs across the three campuses at Massey and some of its industry partners including the Wellington Fab Lab.

Student Work

In-Use Clothing (2013)
By Nina Preston

This research focuses on the durability and longevity of products, both physically and emotionally. It explores the idea that consumption patterns can be slowed if we are able to create a bond to the clothing we own. An emotional attachment to the product will change the value we associate with them. In this project, the consumer–garment relationship works on a repair-and-modify basis and supplies a visual record of garment maturation and individualisation, all contributing to the consumer's sense of self.

ReFashion ReDunn (2008)
By Janet Dunn

This study developed terminology and methods for fashion made with recycled materials. Based on the proverb 'waste not, want not', the aim was to develop an ethos for ReFashion and a design process for ReDunn. A collection of prototypes demonstrates the potential for transforming recycled garments using various techniques. The tableaux depicts urban ruin, drought and flood scenes with outfits styled from the collection.

Maintaining Design Aesthetics (2011)
By Michelle Freeth

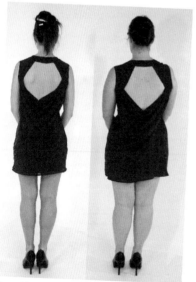

Fit problems continue to plague the women's fashion design industry, for those whose bodies are not the standard size or shape. In this investigation, complex shape-based grading was successfully developed and tested. This mode and process of grading and fitting intricate designs to a variety of body shapes is sensitive to line, shape and form and ultimately reveals the potential to cater to a wider garment-wearing audience.

Course
Fashion Design

School
Massey University

Garment for the Upper Body (2011)
By Julia Lumsden

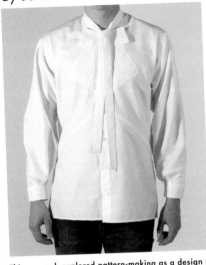

This research explored pattern-making as a design tool with the design process led by a goal of developing zero-waste patterns. When designing the shirts, it was important to maintain a minimalist tailored design aesthetic with the challenge of creating zero-waste patterns, leading to subtle quirky design details in the finished garments.

The (Co)re-creation of Self (2008)
By Jenny Deonarain

Researching through design, this thesis explored the implementation of an online kit as a means through which the postmodern individual could participate in the creative processes of home sewing. It encouraged the liberation of the consumer from the restrictions of traditional sewing processes through the introduction of adaptable alternatives, processes of re-creation and co-creation.

Mao & Me (2012)
By Aihua Wei

This narrative project was a journey though a process of practice-led design research while re-evaluating and reflecting upon Chinese culture in New Zealand. 'One people, one voice, one nation' became the overarching stimulus that referenced Mao Zedong's jacket, which represents a strict ideology that sought to unify a nation
Photo Mandi Lynn

Alumna

Name Claire Hacon
Residence Gold Coast, Australia
Year of birth 1956
Year of graduation 2011
Current job Fashion designer, lecturer
Website aicdedu.com.au

Why did you choose this school?
The balance in the curricula between the provision of industry production and design skills.

Are you still in contact with the school?
Yes, via various people who work there.

What was the most important thing you learned here?
To trust the design process. Research is the fundamental starting point for any collection; it inspires and opens up new ideas.

What are you doing now?
I'm a full-time fashion lecturer and a freelance designer, collaborating with two other local fashion designers in a shared design studio.

How did the school prepare you for what you are doing now?
It provided me with a balanced set of knowledge and skills, both theoretical and practical.

Tell us about your graduation project.
I argued that the business suit typically worn by female professionals was disempowering because it functions as a reductive version of male power dressing and denies its wearer any opportunity to express her individuality. It was a practice-led research project which involved re-figuring the woman's business suit. As tailoring is the central discipline of my practice, I utilised these skills to offer women multiple suit forms to challenge stereotypes of feminine representation in professional organisations.

Was the transition from graduation to working life a smooth one?
I had peer tutored during my study, therefore I transitioned into teaching without any difficulty after graduation.

Any words of advice for future students on this course?
Research and develop fantastic ideas but realise from that point on that the design process becomes more practical and less abstract. It is really important to understand the technicalities of pattern cutting, garment construction and the possibilities of fabric. Also, fashion design is a collaborative process, and it is important to be able to work within a team of individualists who assist, share and extend your creative ideas.

Hacon's graduate project looked at women's professional suiting from a new and subversive angle.

Course
Fashion Design

School
Massey University

Current Students

'Wellington is a really easy city to live in while you are a student. It is compact enough to be able to walk most places; otherwise the bus system is really well connected and easy to navigate. Recently I got a bike and really enjoy riding around the city, which is good for you too, as there are a few hills around which require a bit of work!'
Alex Barton

'My advice for future students – don't stress it if you get lost; the path will turn up eventually. Getting lost is the fun part!'
Monica Buchan-Ng

'The aspect of the course I find most valuable is that it is a combination of seminar and studio work, which make it stimulating. A focus on conceptual ideas and experimentation generates a highly creative environment.'
Katie Collier

City Life

Wellington, with a total of 393,400 residents, is the capital and second most populous urban area of New Zealand. It is situated at the south-western tip of the North Island, between Cook Strait and the Rimutaka Range. In 2011, Lonely Planet Best in Travel 2011 named Wellington as fourth in its top cities to visit, referring to the New Zealand capital as the coolest little capital in the world.

Wellington's compact city centre supports an arts scene, cafe culture and nightlife much larger than many cities of a similar size and it is an important centre of New Zealand's film and theatre industry. The Te Papa Tongarewa (the Museum of New Zealand), the New Zealand Symphony Orchestra, the Royal New Zealand Ballet, Museum of Wellington City & Sea and the biennial New Zealand International Arts Festival are all sited there. Wellington's cafe culture is prominent. The city has more cafes per capita than New York City.

View of Wellington Harbour, one of the city's many bays that are great for water sports or people-watching from one of the many terraces.

New Zealand

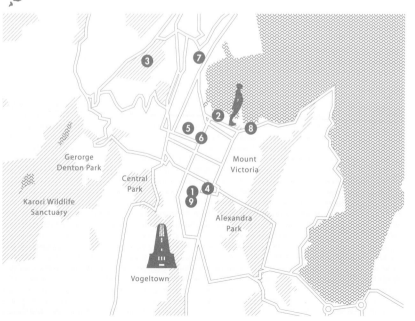

Wellington

1 Massey University
2 Te Papa Tongarewa
3 Wellington Botanic Gardens
4 Havana Coffee Works
5 Matterhorn
6 Mediaplex
7 Arbitrageur Wine Room & Restaurant
8 Oriental Parade
9 Tussock Bar and Cafe

George Denton Park

Central Park

Karori Wildlife Sanctuary

Mount Victoria

Alexandra Park

Vogeltown

Park

Water

Main road

Course
Fashion Design

School
Massey University

City Facts

Te Papa Tongarewa (the Museum of New Zealand) ②
New Zealand's national museum is renowned for being bicultural, scholarly, innovative and fun. The collections span five areas: Art, History, Pacific, Māori and Natural Environment.
tepapa.govt.nz

Wellington Botanic Gardens ③
A short walk from downtown Wellington are the beautiful 25-hectare gardens with views over the city and a little cafe.
wellington.govt.nz

Havana Coffee Works ④
Just 2 minutes' walk from the school, students can get their caffeine shot at Havana Coffee Works, where the beans are roasted on-site.
havana.co.nz

Makara Peak Mountain Bike Park
A mountain bike park surrounds Makara Peak. In the past 14 years, volunteers have built around 40 km of track, with a variety of degrees of difficulty.
makarapeak.org.nz

Matterhorn ⑤
On the menu are over 300 wines, 200 spirits and cocktails with some of the ingredients brewed in-house. Drinks can be enjoyed after a good meal, while listening to a live jazz jam-session or some DJ tunes.
matterhorn.co.nz

International Comedy Festival
Held simultaneously over 3 weeks in Auckland and Wellington during April and May, the festival then takes to the road with the comedy convoy, touring to regional cities across New Zealand.
comedyfestival.co.nz

Mediaplex ⑥
The Film Archive is the home of New Zealand's moving image history with over 150,000 titles spanning feature films, documentaries, short films, home movies, newsreels, TV programmes and advertisements.
filmarchive.org.nz

Arbitrageur Wine Room & Restaurant ⑦
Serving up food from the wine growing areas of the world, each dish has been specifically matched carefully selected wines from their extensive collection.
arbitrageur.co.nz

Oriental Parade ⑧
Running along the Oriental Bay, the Parade is bustling with life. Many restaurants and cafes line the way which is perfect for a walk.

Chocolate Fish Cafe
You couldn't really get more Kiwi than sitting on a beanbag in the grass, eating a freshly made BBQ fish sandwich, with a fresh ocean breeze blowing through your hair.
chocolatefishcafe.co.nz

Tussock Bar and Cafe ⑨
Located on campus terrain this is the student's watering hole, offering a wide range of great value food and beverages. The bar operates from 12.00 and is fully licensed with a happy hour from 16.00.
creativehospitality.co.nz

How to get around
Wellington International Airport is in Rongotai, about 5 km from the central city. It is a major transit point for domestic travellers. There are frequent flights to Auckland, Christchurch, Palmerston North, Rotorua, Hamilton, Nelson, Blenheim and many other destinations. International flights from Australia (Sydney, Melbourne, Brisbane) arrive about twice daily.

The fact that Wellington is not that crowded is proved by the simplicity of the infrastructure. There are only two major roads into Wellington (State Highways 1 and 2) and there is only one train service between Wellington and Auckland.

It is easy to get around the central city on foot, as it is very compact and pedestrian-friendly. In addition, New Zealand's best public transit network with buses, commuter trains and suburban ferries is available to take you farther afield. Massey University is surrounded by Central Park and Alexandra Park and can be assessed using at least 12 local bus stops.

Arranging housing
Average

Housing support by school
Yes

Cost of room in the city
n/a

Cost of campus housing
Between NZD 700 and NZD 1000 per month (approx. EUR 450 to EUR 650)

NABA/Nuova Accademia di Belle Arti Milano

The landmark architecture of NABA's campus, which occupies a newly-renovated industrial complex.

NABA/Nuova Accademia di Belle Arti Milano
20 Via C. Darwin
Milan 20143
Italy

T +39 02 973 721
info@naba.it
naba.it

NABA courses are generally led by well-known designers.

Introduction

'We expect students to challenge both current views and the boundaries between disciplines'

Nicoletta Morozzi, fashion area leader

What is studying at this school all about?
For 30 years, NABA has been refining its proven method, which encompasses a wide variety of learning experiences: team and individual work, lectures and tutoring, free experimentation and workshops with companies on real briefs, conceptual research and manual practice. All these experiential practices are meant to foster the capacity of students to face the complexity of the contemporary world.

When did this master's programme begin and what is your approach?
The original course began in 1997 with the current format of the MA Fashion and Textile Design course being established in 2011. Our approach is reflected in our main values, such as experimentation, innovation and research. We place students at the centre of an educational process based on direct participation in the everyday practice of the faculty.

What kind of teaching method do you employ?
An interdisciplinary didactic methodology centred around the students. This approach is the result of a strong propensity towards innovation, research and connections with artistic and professional contexts, promoted by a faculty of excellence which combines teaching and profession in a continuous dialogue.

What do you expect from your students?
We expect them to be open-minded and ready to challenge both current views and the boundaries between disciplines. Our students go on to learn how to become self-confident, and to be able to find their own role within the fashion system.

What is the most important skill to master?
To be aware of ongoing global developments, to respond in real time to the market's requests, and to anticipate new possibilities for the future. The connection with art is an important aspect of the professional quality of our students and their job prospects, rather than simply being a creative side of design.

What kind of jobs do your students go on to do?
They become fashion designers, textile designers, fashion journalists, creative consultants in companies, entrepreneurs with their own company, pattern designers and accessory designers. Companies they work for include Costume National, Gianni Versace, Gucci, Jil Sander Italia, Kenzo, Missoni, Ratti Group, Tirelli Costumi, Trussardi and Valentino Fashion Group.

City
Milan

Country
Italy

157

Programme

The main subjects of the MA Fashion and Textile Design programme, taught by Romeo Gigli and Angela Missoni, give a strong degree of lab experience, alongside the great names of Italian fashion design. While in most schools teachers of this calibre have the role of visiting professors, in our programme they guide the full design experience, interpreting and enhancing the students' individual skills. The same goes for accessories design, where courses are led by Federica Moretti (hats) and Giancarlo Montebello (jewellery). In the communication and critical side too, we have Mariuccia Casadio (art editor *Vogue Italia*), and Stefania Seoni (Diane Pernet's correspondent in Italy).

Collaborations with companies on special projects occur throughout the two year course, with the students working in small, selected groups for each project. Students are constantly monitored, with the aim of defining each one's particular skills. In their graduation thesis, students can deepen their skills in the professional field they are most interested in: fashion design, textile design, art direction, visuals or communication.

The programme runs as a sort of permanent lab in which the students play a central role. The lab recreates the atmosphere of an atelier-greenhouse in which the connection between cultural content and real-life application is the source of creative output. The programme embraces theoretical and practical lectures, as well as internships that allow students to experience the creative realities that make the Milan area an international fashion centre.

Students busy with their projects in the NABA Fashion Lab.

Projects on display and under discussion in NABA's Great Hall.

The library has over 4000 books and magazines on relevant topics.

Programme
Fashion and Textile Design

Leads to
Master of Arts

Structure
The 2-year full-time course is divided into semesters. First-year subjects include: computer graphics, materials culture, projects methodology, visual design, history of applied arts, textile design I, fashion design I, design management and accessories. Second-year subjects include: fashion design II, textile design II, textile and new materials technology, concept planning, decoration, art direction and fashion setting. Students also undertake a final thesis, portfolio, internship, professional development and study abroad.

Head of programme
Nicoletta Morozzi

Mentors and lecturers
Romeo Gigli, Angela Missoni, Cinzia Ruggeri, Mariuccia Casadio, Alessandra Galasso, Colomba Leddi, Stefania Seoni, Ivo Bisignano, Angarad Rixon, Marina Nelli, Federica Moretti and Manuela Porta.

Course
Fashion and Textile Design

School
NABA/Nuova Accademia di Belle Arti Milano

School Facts

Duration of study
2 years

Full time
Yes (30 hours a week)

Part time
No

Female students
76%

Male students
24%

Local students
41%

Students from abroad
59%

Yearly enrolment
34

Tuition fee
- EUR 9490 per year for EU citizens
- EUR 12,590 per year for non-EU citizens

Funding/scholarships
Yes

Minimum requirements for entry
Bachelor's degree in fashion design, design or architecture

Language
English

Application procedure
Please apply digitally through our online application service with:
- your personal and contact details
- your curriculum vitae
- application form
- portfolio
- motivation letter
- references
- project proposal
- transcripts
- proof of English proficiency if required.
Successful individuals will be informed by email. All admissions are based on a personal evaluation by the course director.

Application details
int.info@naba.it

Application date
Before 30 November

Graduation rate
30%

Job placement rate
100%

Memberships/affiliations
Industrial Design Association, European League of Institutes of the Arts and Laureate International Universities.

Collaborations with
Fondazione La Triennale di Milano, The Swatch Group, Giorgio Armani, Pininfarina Extra, Provincia di Milano, Armando Testa, Publicis, Arnoldo Mondadori Editore, Editrice Abitare Segesta, McCann Erikson, Lorenzo Riva and Saatchi & Saatchi.

Facilities for students
Design Lab with band saw, bench drill, milling cutter, lathe machine, paint spray booth, polystyrene cutting machine, etc., 3D Design Lab equipped with 3D printer laser-cutting machine, thermoforming and blender machine, Fashion Lab equipped with industrial sewing machines, presses, irons and standers, Textile Design and Knitting Labs with looms and dye tanks, and Library with over 4000 books and magazines.

Student Work

Hair Dress (2012)
By Ali Karami

Project developed during the MA fashion course of Professors Romeo Gigli and Claudia Nesi.
Photo G Giannini

Menswear Collection (2012)
By Miao Ran

Project developed during the MA fashion course of Professors Romeo Gigli and Claudia Nesi.
Photo Ramona Tabita

Dress (2012)
By Gay Di

Project developed during the MA fashion course of Professors Romeo Gigli and Claudia Nesi.
Photo G Giannini

Dresses (2012)
By Teresa Maccapani Missoni

Project developed during the MA fashion course of Professors Romeo Gigli and Claudia Nesi.
Photo G Giannini

Course
Fashion and Textile Design

School
NABA/Nuova Accademia di Belle Arti Milano

Stills from Video Unhurried (2012)
By Marzia Bia, Sandra Okune, Martina Padrin, Teresa Ribeiro, Deepa Xaxa, Elisabetta Sapia, Carla Rudloff and Gizem Yucelen

Project developed during the MA experimental tailoring course of Professor Manuela Porta, directed by Alex Avella Sara Cardillo.

Hat (2012)
By Gizem Yucelen

Project developed during the MA fashion course of Professors Romeo Gigli and Claudia Nesi.
Photo Moretti

Hat (2012)
By Sandra Okune

Project developed during the MA millinery course of Professor Federica Moretti.
Photo Moretti

Plastic Dress (2012)
By Ramona Tabita

Project developed during the MA fashion course of Professors Romeo Gigli and Claudia Nesi.
Photo Ramona Tabita

Alumna

person, to wake up early in the morning, to have serious tasks to do, to be part of a team that has to work!

Any words of advice for future students?
Just enjoy being a student. Try to experiment, feel free and have fun – that's the most important thing!

Name Ladina Steinegger
Residence Milan, Italy
Year of birth 1987
Year of graduation 2013
Current job Intern at Ufficio Stile Ratti Spa
Clients Aldo Coppola, QYZ Design, oppa, Gamma&Bross, Francesco Librizzi Studio
Website ladinasteinegger.com

Why did you choose this school?
After visiting other fashion schools, I choose this one because I felt an affinity with its artistic approach. It's not just about fashion, it's also about art and design. I really like this mix of different creative people studying and working together.

Are you still in contact with the school?
I'm still in contact with some of my teachers who are still available to help and give me advice and support in the creative process.

What was the most important thing you learned here?
I learned a lot about materials, fibres and printing techniques which are helping me a lot now in my work for a textiles company.

What are you doing now?
After graduating I started an internship at a famous textile factory in Como. Ratti Spa is one of the biggest printing factories in Europe. I am working in the men's design office for clients such as Givenchy, Louis Vuitton and YSL.

What was your graduation project?
I created my own brand, called Lady Na. As part of that, I designed a small collection of textile patterns which I used for making the dresses and accessories.

Was life post-graduation smooth?
Yes, it was actually quite smooth. The hardest thing is to switch to being a professional

Steinegger's graduation project involved making a collection of fabric patterns to highlight her own brand, Lady Na.

Course
Fashion and Textile Design

School
NABA/Nuova Accademia di Belle Arti Milano

Current Students

'I chose NABA because the master's course offered the possibility of a deeper contact with fabrics while still working with fashion.'
Teresa Ribeiro

'We have great instruments here for a lot of experimentation. I loved the textile design workshop with Bonapace where we found our way around the project with a philosophical approach.'
Martina Padrin

'It's actually quite easy to find a house in Milan, All over the NABA campus, you can find walls full of student advertisement looking for a room.'
Ramona Tabita

'Future students should always try to think what you are. If you want to do something, just go to the place!'
Mina Kanemura

'NABA for me is not just a university, It is the centre of fusion in the world of fashion design for creating the modern future.'
Ali Karami

'To work and study with all these masterful professors is an opportunity of lifetime. That's how you improve your aesthetic vision.'
Miao Ran

'I like that the course is more practical than theory. I really enjoyed the courses about patterns and natural dyes.'
Elisabetta Sapia

City Life

Milan, with a population of 1.3 million, is not only Italy's capital but also its creative heart of design and fashion. All the important furniture factories are located in Lombardy, the area around Milan. The major design and fashion events worldwide take place in Milan every year, with the pinnacle being the Salone del Mobile with its Fuorisalone events. This is why you can live design and fashion 24/7 in Milan better than in any other city all over the globe. The city combines this with ancient arts and history, as well as looking to the future. The Duomo di Milano ❸, the Sforzesco castle ❽, numerous ancient churches and the Last Supper by Leonardo Da Vinci are important traces of the past, while Milan is welcoming future talent by creating the new fashion district, and planning the 2015 Universal Exposition. The most important design and art galleries are located in the Ventura Lambrate area and all the fancy fashion shops can be found in the golden triangle. Students that attend NABA will find themselves in a thriving metropolis with an international dimension.

Italy

Milano Centrale, the main railway station in Milan, was originally opened in 1854 and was designed by the French architect Louis-Jules Bouchot.
Photo Jeremy Hunsinger

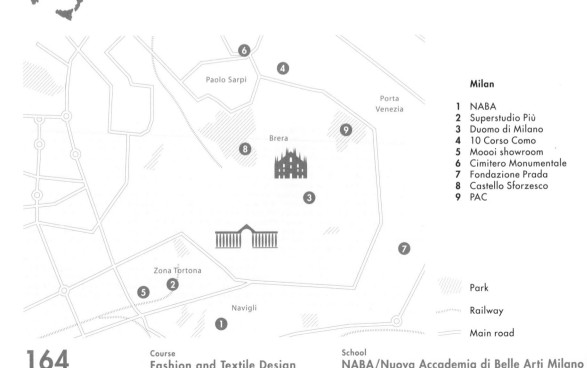

Paolo Sarpi

Porta Venezia

Brera

Zona Tortona

Navigli

Milan

1 NABA
2 Superstudio Più
3 Duomo di Milano
4 10 Corso Como
5 Moooi showroom
6 Cimitero Monumentale
7 Fondazione Prada
8 Castello Sforzesco
9 PAC

Park

Railway

Main road

Course
Fashion and Textile Design

School
NABA/Nuova Accademia di Belle Arti Milano

City Facts

See more Milan City Facts on p.65

Superstudio Più
Representing an alternative to the Milan Fair and hosting permanent or temporary art and fair exhibitions, Superstudio Più ❷ houses the most important and cutting-edge fashion, art and design brands.
superstudiogroup.com

Duomo di Milano ❸
This Gothic cathedral, officially inaugurated in 1965, took nearly 6 centuries to complete. It is the fourth largest cathedral in the world.
duomomilano.it

10 Corso Como ❹
A gallery, a bookshop, a store, a cafe, a restaurant, a journal, a small hotel, a roof terrace, an outlet and a space for events – 10 Corso Como has it all. The slow shopping concept invites visitors to participate in a succession of social and cultural activities.
10corsocomo.com

Moooi showroom ❺
The Moooi showroom, located in a building by Matteo Thun, opened its doors in the heart of Zona Tortona in April 2010. It remains a permanent showroom, accessible by appointment only.
moooi.com/showrooms/milano

Cimitero Monumentale ❻
Designed by architect Carlo Maciachini, the cemetery has been filled with contemporary and classical Italian sculptures, as well as Greek temples, elaborate obelisks and other original works such as a scaled-down version of Trajan's Column.
monumentale.net

Fondazione Prada ❼
A non-profit organisation that is generated by a shared passion for contemporary art. Architect Rem Koolhaas was recently commissioned to design a new building for this foundation by Miuccia Prada and Patrizio Bertelli.
fondazioneprada.org

Quadrilatero della moda
The quadrilateral of fashion is a high-class shopping district in the centre of Milan, characterised by the presence of numerous boutiques and related retail outlets which represent most of the world's major fashion houses.

Castello Sforzesco ❽
The Sforzesco castle was demolished, then rebuilt several times, embellished and restored to become a symbol of both happy and dramatic events that are to be found in the historical background of the city.
milanocastello.it

PAC ❾
This Contemporary Art Pavilion (PAC) is one of the earliest examples of architecture in Italy designed expressly for modern and contemporary art, similar to the European Kunsthalle, and conceived as a lean exhibiting venue.
comune.milano.it

How to get around
Milan has an extensive internal transport network and is also an important transportation junction in Italy, being one of the country's biggest hubs for air, rail and road networks.

The city is served by three major airports: Malpensa Airport (60 km from the city centre), the biggest in northern Italy; Linate Airport (6 km from the city centre), mainly used for domestic traffic; and Orio al Serio Airport (50 km from the city centre), used mainly by low-cost airlines. Due to its position, Milan is also the main gateway for international passenger traffic to Europe.

The internal public transport network includes the metro, suburban railway, tram and bus networks, as well as taxi, car and bike sharing services. NABA is surrounded by many tram stops. The nearest metro stop is Romolo, accessible with Linea 2.

Arranging housing
Quite easy

Housing support by school
Yes

Cost of room in the city
Between EUR 300 and EUR 600 per month

Cost of campus housing
n/a

NC State University College of Textiles

The College of Textiles has state-of-the-art facilities that are available to students 24/7.

Students in the CAD/CAM studio.

**NC State University
College of Textiles**
1000 Main Campus Drive
Raleigh, NC 27695
United States

T +1 (0)919 515 1858
graduate-school@ncsu.edu
tx.ncsu.edu/tatm

Introduction

'Our students acquire design and marketing skills, plus knowledge of the entire textile supply chain'

Karen Leonas, head of the department

When was the school founded and how has it changed?
NC State University (NCSU) was founded in 1887 and the first textile course was taught from 1899. The college definitely evolved since the first day, as has our graduate programme.

What is studying at this school all about?
We offer students hands-on experience with the latest technology in the field whilst collaborating across disciplines, including technical textiles, apparel design and product development, textile design, management and entrepreneurship. Students work with industry practitioners and build their professional portfolio, whilst perfecting their research skills. We strive for them to reach their personal and professional goals and become leaders in the field.

What kind of teaching method is applied?
In addition to delivering knowledge foundation through lectures, faculty members work closely with each individual graduate student on their projects. Students are provided hands-on experience and also opportunities to work on industry sponsored projects.

Why should students choose this school?
Our college is the worldwide leader in the education and research in the field of textiles. Under the same roof, the college houses facilities and expertise covering the whole supply chain of the textile industry, from fibre to final consumers. Not only providing this excellent access to the facility and expertise internally, the college also embraces great connections with the industry, hence providing a variety of opportunities for students to work on industry-sponsored projects.

What is the focus of your programme?
Our master's programme in textiles has a technical and analytical focus, with our students acquiring the skills needed for the design and marketing of new products gaining a detailed knowledge of all aspects of the textile supply chain.

What is expected from the students?
Students are challenged to perform their best during the programme.

What is the most important thing for students to learn during this course?
Consumer oriented approach for design, product development and brand management.

In what industries do your graduates end up?
In the textile and apparel/fashion industries, as well as retail and government agencies. Specific jobs include product managers, personal stylists, material specialists, footwear and apparel designers, textile specialists in government offices, textile designers the automotive industry, CAD specialists, etc.

Programme

The objective of the Master of Science in Textiles programme is to develop our students' potential for research and the technical and analytical skills required for the design and marketing of new products, processes and for careers in the textile industry. Our students gain knowledge of the full sector and can go on to work in the textile supply chain, marketing organisations, design and development programmes, research laboratories, government agencies and in higher education.

The degree is taught in the Department of Textile and Apparel, Technology and Management which has a focus in the following areas: textile design, fashion design, retail and brand management, and textile technology. Students can decide on the tracks they follow, which include exploring issues in new product development, direct digital printing and computer-aided design (CAD), as well as consumer behaviour, entrepreneurship, and global brand management in textiles and apparel. Medical textiles, industrial fabrics, 3D textile structures, aerospace applications, technical textiles and smart materials are examples of new areas for textile technology.

A whole range of textile facilities in the various labs and workshops are at the disposal of master's students.

Creativity abounds among the fashion and textile students at NCSU.

A highlight at the end of each year is the NCSU fashion show.

Programme
Textiles

Leads to
Master of Science

Structure
The 2-year full-time course is divided into semesters. The master's degree is a thesis-based 36-credit-hour programme (12–15 where students conduct independent investigation). Students may conduct research in the following areas: brand management and marketing, fashion and textile design, textile supply chain and textile technology.

Head of programme
Karen Leonas

Mentors and lecturers
Katherine Carroll, Nancy Cassill, Genessa Devine, A Blanton Godfrey, William Harazin, Helmut Hergeth, Cynthia L Istook, Traci Lamar, Hoon Joo Lee, Karen Leonas, Trevor J Little, Marguerite Moore, Lisa Parrillo-Chapman, Erin Powell, Nancy Powell, Lori Rothenberg, Abdel-Fattah Seyam, Moon W Suh, Kristin Thoney-Barletta, Andre West and Yingjiao Xu.

Notable alumni
Unknown

Course
Textiles

School
NC State University College of Textiles

School Facts

Duration of study
2 years

Full time
Yes

Part time
No

Female students
67%

Male students
33%

Local students
80%

Students from abroad
20%

Yearly enrolment
50

Tuition fee
- USD 4676 per year for North Carolina residents (approx. EUR 3500)
- USD 10,845 per year for all other citizens (approx. EUR 8125)

Funding/scholarships
Yes

Minimum requirements for entry
Bachelor's degree and/or relevant experience

Language
English

Application procedure
The following documents are required:
- application form
- copy of degree certificate/college transcripts
- your curriculum vitae
- statement of purpose
- letters of recommendation
- a copy of your passport
- proof of language (if applicable). Some candidates may be contacted for interview. International applicants are not required to have an in-person interview. Successful candidates will be informed by email.

Application details
graduate-school@ncsu.edu

Application date
by 1 March (applicants) or 15 July (US applicants)

Graduation rate
98%

Job placement rate
High

Memberships/affiliations
International Textile and Apparel Association, International Foundation of Fashion Technology Institutes, AATCC, SDC and the Textile Insitute.

Collaborations with
Universities such as Donghua University (China) and Seoul National University (Korea), as well as industry: Polo Ralph Lauren, VF, Hanes, Eastman, Cotton Inc., etc.

Facilities for students
Studio spaces, CAD/CAM and laboratory facilities with specialised software, a hand-weaving lab; a printing/dyeing lab, library, computer labs and materials labs.

Student Work

Tranquility (2012)
By Kathleen Kelly

This project included a digitally-printed and pleated fabric which comprises a knitted jersey structure with a cotton core wrapped multifilament yarn. Coloration was applied by digitally printing the cotton surface and fabric texture was created by a permanent heat-set pleat.
Photo Lisa Chapman

Ruffle Frenzy (2012)
By Anthony Wilson

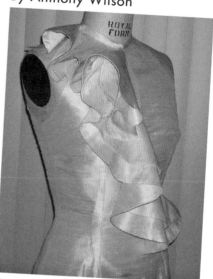

The outcome of this project was a sleeveless Dupioni silk sheath dress which incorporated a dramatic explosion of ruffles at the neckline.
Photo Anthony Wilson

Automotive Knit Design (2009)
By Jenna Eason

This project was an investigation into textile designs that could be applied to automotive interiors. Inspiration came from patterns in nature and applied in this knit design project.
Photo Nancy Powell

Egyptian Elegance (2013)
By Anthony Wilson

This Egyptian inspired matte jersey gown has low sides and back, asymmetrical hemline and leather neckline detail.
Photo Anthony Wilson

Dreams (2010)
By Kelly Roth

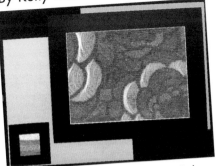

The focus of this project were jacquard acoustical fabrics, designed from a technical perspective.
Photo Nancy Powell

Samurai Chic (2011)
By Emily Wzszak

These fabrics and the tabi were inspired by Samurai warrior costume and the patterns of modern kimonos. The fabrics were designed in a CAD system and knitted on the electronic jacquard knitting machine.
Photo Traci Lamar

Strata (2013)
By John Knox

The knitted jacquard fabric shown is made using a process of four colour jacquard knitting, pushing the four yarn machine set-up by using CAD to create patterns with varying percentages of colour that could be filled into closed shapes in the compositional design.
Photo Lisa Chapman

Mariposa (2010)
By Claire Stanhope

These fabrics were inspired by the wings of a butterfly, textures and patterns. The fabrics are jacquard woven with chenille yarns.
Photo Lisa Chapman

Alumna

Name Caroline Cockerham
Residence Ventura, United States
Year of birth 1987
Year of graduation 2012
Current job Materials developer for technical knits at Patagonia
Website patagonia.com

Why did you choose this school?
I chose NC State because of the prestige and expertise in the realm of textile design and research. I wanted a programme that would offer real-world, industry-applicable experience. I'm a hands-on person and at NC State you have the most state-of-the-art equipment for textile development, right at your fingertips.

What was the most important thing you learned here?
I found that one of the best ways to learn is to mess up! I did plenty of that during graduate school. Learning from mistakes is much easier when you have strong support and guidance. I learned to be flexible, to be open and accepting of change and opportunities, and to not get too attached to one certain outcome.

What was the most interesting project you did/or the most fun?
I worked in Lima, Peru in a vertical textile mill for 6 weeks and at a design agency for 3 months. I learned some incredible lessons and it helped me grow as person. During my time at the design agency, I worked one-on-one with Peruvian artisans, manufacturers, hand knitters and weavers to help elevate and export their crafts. For one project, I hiked deep into the Ucayali jungle to lead a design workshop with basket weavers. It was one of the most creative and dynamic experiences I've ever had.

What was your graduation project?
I wrote a thesis on textile digital library systems for product development. Though this might sound super boring, it actually had the potential to really help the preproduction efficiency of textile mills. My main focus during grad school was sustainable design for textiles and I found that implementing systems which support design and production was a wonderful way to improve the sustainability of a product. I conducted my research and piloted this system while working in Peru.

Was the transformation from graduation to working life a smooth one?
They are too different to compare. I love that the working day ends at 18.00 whereas the grad school day lasts through the weekends and into the early morning hours. However, decisions seem to carry more weight in the working world – which can be stressful – but at least you're getting paid.

Any words of advice for future students?
Mould your experience. Make it exactly what you want it to be. Take risks, travel, get involved with your school and allow it to work for you. Graduate school is an amazing way to gain exposure – whether it be with influential people, major brands, technology, or ground breaking research. Use it!

Cockerham's womenswear designs are eye-catching with flamboyant and dramatic silhouettes.
Photo Keith Papke

172

Course
Textiles

School
NC State University College of Textiles

Current Students

'Interacting with the industry is very important for me, so I found the most valuable class to be Global Textile Brand Management and Marketing. It provides an understanding of the global market environment, brand management and market strategies.'

Jinzhao Lu

'The staff members are professional, helpful and really want you to excel in the industry once you graduate, so my advice for future students would be: don't be afraid to ask for help. The connections available between the College of Textiles and the industry are endless – make the most of this!'

Katelynn Suggs

'I chose NCSU's College of Textiles because of the school's reputation for a thorough and well-rounded study of textiles, the hands-on learning and applications to industry, and the highly knowledgeable professors. I completed my undergraduate degree here, so graduate school was a natural progression.'

Shelley Cernel

'At the end of this course, I hope to have learnt how to experiment with new design techniques and to have increased my knowledge of the world of textile design.'

Allison Tate

City Life

Raleigh is the capital of North Carolina, the fastest growing city in the United States and one of three adjacent cities that make up the Research Triangle. The Triangle is home to NCSU, University of NC/Chapel Hill and Duke University, with students moving freely among the three institutions for courses and cultural events. Research Triangle Park, a commercial and government partnership, is an international centre for technological research and innovation with internship and employment opportunities for NCSU students.

Raleigh is 2 hours from the coast, 3 hours from the mountains, and short flights to Washington and New York. The city is known for its extensive green space and public park system, pleasant year-round climate, and gentle hospitality. It is home to three state museums, a children's museum with an Omnimax theatre, and a collection of galleries and arts events, including monthly gallery walks. A downtown amphitheatre hosts outdoor concerts and festivals and the city's cafes, restaurants and bars support an active nightlife. Nearby Chapel Hill is a centre for independent music.

NCSU operates a downtown studio in a second floor walk-up; a student-run gallery in the middle of the city; and the Contemporary Art Museum as the centrepiece of the arts warehouse district. The university's research campus is located on over 1000 acres within the city and includes a lake, golf course and bike trails surrounding university buildings with leased spaces and labs for commercial research partners.

United States

The bell tower on the vast NCSU campus is as recognisable on the skyline of Raleigh as the city's skyscrapers.

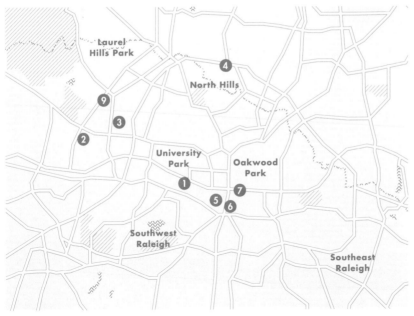

Raleigh

1 NCSU
2 PNC Arena
3 NC Museum of Art
4 Farmers' Market
5 Contemporary Art Museum
6 Red Hat Amphitheatre
7 NC Museum of Natural History

/// Park

=== Main road

Course
Textiles

School
NC State University College of Textiles

City Facts

PNC Arena ②
Since it was opened in 1999, the PNC Arena has held over 1500 events for audiences of all ages. From NCAA Basketball Tournaments to NHL Stanley Cup Finals and from Disney on Ice to Taylor Swift.
thepncarena.com

NC Museum of Art ③
The 164-acre museum park is home to more than a dozen monumental works of art, with artists actively involved in the restoration of the park's landscape and the integration of art into its natural systems.
ncartmuseum.org

Farmers' Market ④
Raleigh's farmers' market is dedicated to providing the community access to healthful food options, as well as educational opportunities to learn about sustainable farming methods and food systems.
midtownraleighfarmersmarket.com

Contemporary Art Museum ⑤
The CAM in Raleigh seeks to curate the most contemporary works of art and design possible – those still emerging, growing and living.
camraleigh.org

Red Hat Amphitheatre ⑥
This is a great venue for live concerts, festivals and events, set in the heart of downtown Raleigh.
redhatamphitheater.com

NC Museum of Natural History ⑦
Through its exhibits, programmes and field experiences, the museum provides visitors with opportunities to get up-close and personal with science and nature.
naturalsciences.org

NC State Fair
Featuring the famous Dorton Area by architect Matthew Nowicki, the NC State Fair is an annual agricultural exposition held in Raleigh which attracts visitors from far and wide.
ncstatefair.org

Institute for Emerging Issues
The Institute for Emerging Issues at NCSU is a public policy think-and-do tank concerned about the future of North Carolina. Past speakers include former President Bill Clinton, *New York Times* columnist Tom Friedman, Steve Forbes, and many others.
iei.ncsu.edu

First Friday Gallery Walks
Local art galleries, art studios, alternative art venues, and museums stay open late on the first Friday of every month to welcome thousands of art-seeking enthusiasts downtown.
godowntownraleigh.com/first-friday-raleigh

American Dance Festival
Since 1934, ADF has remained committed to serving the needs of dance, dancers, choreographers and professionals in dance-related fields in nearby Durham. The programme includes performances, education, awards, community outreach, humanities and media projects, and national and international initiatives.
americandancefestival.org

How to get around
Only a 15-minute journey by car from the city centre is Raleigh-Durham International Airport, the region's primary airport. It is the second-largest in North Carolina, located northwest of downtown Raleigh and serves the city and greater Research Triangle metropolitan region, as well as much of eastern North Carolina. Within the area, the Capital Area Transit, Cary Transit, R-Line and Wolfline bus systems provide riders with an extensive network of local routes, and campus is also served by the Triangle Transit Authority bus service. If you want to visit the coast, the Amtrak train will take you there. If you want to get around in the city centre or the campus, the free campus bus, walking or cycling are the best options.

Arranging housing
Never a problem

Housing support by school
No

Cost of room in the city
Various

Cost of campus housing
Starts at USD 3000 per term for single occupancy (approx. EUR 2280)

Oslo National Academy of The Arts

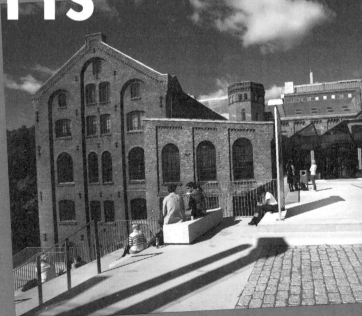

During the course, students take part in many fashion workshops like this one.
Photo Kirsti Bræin/Oslo National Academy of the Arts

Kunsthøgskolens i Oslo
Fossveien 24
0551 Oslo
Norway

T +47 22 995 500
postmottak@khio.no
khio.no

The main entrance to the Oslo National Academy of The Arts.
Photo Lund Hagem architects/Søyland Architects

Introduction

'The idea of entrepreneurship and innovation within each subject field is important'

Maziar Raein, head of the master´s degree programme

oto Siri Østvold

What are the landmarks in this school's history?
It was founded in 1818 as the Royal Norwegian Drawing School. Later, it became a school of arts and crafts and in 1996 it merged with four other art schools to become Oslo National Academy of the Arts. In 2010, all the schools were moved to renovated, customised buildings on the Seilduken campus.

What is studying at this school all about?
Master's degree students at our school develop their own unique fashion project. The idea of entrepreneurship and innovation within each subject field is important. Our aim is to educate artists and designers to reflect on, and experiment in, their chosen field and make lasting contributions to the diversity of society.

What teaching methods do you favour?
The curriculum addresses theories of design, research-based design and contemporary practice. We facilitate interaction between students and professionals from the international fashion industry through workshops and projects. We also invite professionals for particular projects. The students get their own personal tutors within their chosen specialisation.

Why should students choose this school?
We have the best facilities of any art school in Northern Europe. Students choose us for our high-tech workshops and advanced sewing

and knitting machines. We also have a distinctive, interdisciplinary approach to design. Fashion students study alongside those studying graphics, furniture, etc., so interdisciplinary collaborations are possible.

What do you expect of students?
To develop from personal practitioners to independent professionals. The ability to experiment and find relevant methods is crucial.

What is the most important thing for students to learn during this course?
Design thinking plus entrepreneurship and collaboration. Students are expected to reflect on their role in society and develop a social, ethical and environmental awareness.

What is the most important skill for a fashion designer?
To be able to carry out original research, and implement it in your design work. You also need to be able to contextualise your design and communicate it to society and the professional target area. Another important skill is the ability to create a network of collaborators.

City
Oslo

Country
Norway

Programme

Students on the Master in Design programme get a unique chance to develop critical design-thinking methodology, integrating awareness of social, ethical and environmental issues as a natural part of the designer's consciousness. The design faculty has extensive links with cultural institutions within the fashion and design, and collaborations with production companies and the press. These valuable contacts lead to collaborations and help students get their work exposed and critiqued. Our students take part in the growing Oslo fashion scene, participating internationally in contests and shows.

Our target groups are graduate designers who are exceptionally dedicated, who desire to explore their work through research and practice, and emerging designers with sartorial sensitivity, who want to explore, take risks, challenge the existing, and make an impact on fashion for tomorrow. This programme offers the opportunity to study fashion design in a unique and inspiring environment with designers, artists and performers in different fields. The partly interdisciplinary course facilitates collaborations and results in a holistic and professional view of design.

The school offers numerous advanced workshops on different materials and techniques. Specifically, we have superb facilities for those who want to investigate knitting and knitwear in fashion, with our highly qualified technical staff and advanced computer knitting machines.

The students have a house by the river for social activities, such as this music festival in 2012.
Photo Oda Hveem/Jovialbiennalen

A stylish lounge space between the reception, library and print shop.
Photo Fin Serck-Hansen/KAELS

Programme
Fashion and Costume Design

Leads to
Master of Design

Structure
The 2-year full-time course (120 credits) leads to a Master of Design degree. It offers the following specialisations: fashion design and costume design, visual communication, interior architecture, and furniture design. The course is divided into four main areas: theory and method locating design practice within a critical framework of design knowledge; specialisation I, enabling students to explore nominated areas of design study; specialisation II, building upon the previous two areas and allowing in-depth study in a chosen direction; and a major project and thesis, allowing students to research, explore, create and develop a collection of objects/garments or processes of design, while reflecting upon them within a structured narrative.

Head of programme
Maziar Raein

Mentors and lecturers
Theo Barth, Kirsti Bræin, Admir Batlak, Christina Lindgren, Camilla Bruerberg, Annabeth Kolstø and Maziar Raein.

Notable alumni
Unknown

Course
Fashion and Costume Design

School
Oslo National Academy of The Arts

School Facts

Duration of study
2 years

Full time
Yes (40 hours a week)

Part time
No

Female students
73%

Male students
27%

Local students
89%

Students from abroad
11%

Yearly enrolment
6

Tuition fee
None

Funding/scholarships
Yes

Minimum requirements for entry
A bachelor's degree in design, fashion, arts, crafts, costume or textiles, or relevant professional experience

Language
English and Norwegian

Application procedure
Please apply digitally through our online application service with:
- your personal and contact details
- your curriculum vitae
- application form
- portfolio
- references
- project proposal
- transcripts
- proof of English proficiency (except from English speaking-countries, Sweden and Denmark) need to submit IELTS or TOEFL-test results. Successful individuals will be informed by email.

Application details
opptakdesign@khio.no

Application date
Before 1 February

Graduation rate
95%

Job placement rate
79%

Memberships/affiliations
Norwegian Centre for International Cooperation in Education, Cumulus, Nordplus and Erasmus.

Collaborations with
Central Saint Martins, Chelsea College of Art and Design and Goldsmiths College (United Kingdom), School of Design Copenhagen and The Royal Danish Academy of Fine Arts (Denmark), The Swedish School of Textiles and Umeå Institute of Design (Sweden), and the Institute Superiore de Artes Cultura (Mozambique).

Facilities for students
A well-facilitated workshop with advanced sewing machines, knitting workshop with Shima Seiki digital and Dubied handflat knitting machines, textile workshop with a digital embroidery machine and digital weaving machine, Nimaki Digital textile printer, textile dyeing workshop and equipment for silk screen printing, print shop with 3D printer and laser-cut printer, library, photography studio and a student house for social activities.

Student Work

Papa Need Milk (2013)
By Joachim Kvernstrøm

These individually-designed products have individual stories. Mostly street-wear for men, but the collection has the scope for any product where the idea is strong enough. Social situations are often Kvernstrøm's starting point.
Photo Jørn Nyseth Ranum/KHIO

Survival Box (2012)
By Linn Kristoffersen Kurås

The lightweight modular survival box is easily carried as a backpack. In just a few seconds, it transforms into a raft or a room shelter. Standing upright it serves as an observation post to keep you warm and protected from all kinds of weather.
Photo Linn Kristoffersen Kurås

Combination Babe (2013)
By Nilhan Durmusoglu

Inspired by contrasts and combinations through collages. Mixed with hip-hop slang, words, lyrics – anything goes really.
Photo Simon Skreddernes

Course
Fashion and Costume Design

School
Oslo National Academy of The Arts

Bedroom Project (2013)
By Ole Thomas Spæren

Centred around the theme of intimacy, this project explores the relationship between fashion and intimacy, and fashion as a public spectacle. It is about 'private life acted out in public' as Octavio Paz wrote, describing life in the 20th century.
Photo Marthe Næstby

Flettverk Initiative (2013)
By Elisabeth Stray Pedersen

Working with the technicians at the knitwear factory Dale of Norway, this project is inspired by Norwegian knit culture and Shima Seiki digital knit research. Processes include burying the garment to make a whole new connection with nature.
Photo Simon Skreddernes

Untitled (2013)
By Susanne Roti

Reinterpreting six menswear classics; the trench, duffle, blazer, shirt, shawl-collar jumper and quilted jacket. The boxy silhouette makes each piece resemble a canvas, consisting of both sewn and (printed ballpoint) drawn details.
Photo Roger Fosaas

Transparency and Layers of the Cocoon (2013)
By Signe Rode Rio

Natural materials such as alpaca, wool and cotton alternate with thin, transparent nylon in experimental materials techniques. Intense stitching gives subtle texture, while the padding in the jackets builds volume and strong silhouettes. The prints are based on the designer's own hair.
Photo Lasse Fløde

Nytelsen i det nære (2012)
By Karoline Sand Steen

This project invites the user to experience a knitted collection of dynamic garments handcrafted for longevity and practicality.
Photo Tanya Shoonraad Wallin

Alumna

Name Marthe Næstby
Residence Oslo
Year of birth 1977
Year of graduation 2012
Current job Self-employed
at Studio Fintfolk
Website studiofintfolk.com

Why did you choose this school?
Because of its excellent reputation as an arts and craft school. I had some friends who were studying here and I was attracted to the open and creative milieu at the campus. The interdisciplinary and research-orientated approach to design suited me.

Are you still in contact with the school?
I had the opportunity to stay as a designer in residence for one year after I graduated. It was great to have access to the school facilities during my start-up period as a freelancer. During that year I did some teaching and organisation, which was good experience.

What was the most important thing you learned here?
It sounds silly, but the most important thing I learned was to defy the fear of getting lost in my own project. I learned to keep focused and not be confused by all the advice from other people. I found my own identity as a designer, and I found confidence in my work.

What are you doing now?
I started my own business after I graduated. Mostly I do freelance jobs in teaching, fashion consulting and design services for different clients, such as working as a consultant for a newly-established Norwegian webshop called Just Fashion.

How did the school prepare you for what you are doing now?
The new collection I am working on now is a continuation of the work I did for my master's project. The business course was a good preparation for defining and communicating my own identity as a designer.

What was your graduation project?
Fintfolk was a conceptual fashion project about design in relation to people and their individual wardrobes. It was based on researching eccentric people. As a part of my research I started a blog (fintfolk.com) to celebrate eccentricity and to inspire people who don't want to go with the flow.

Was the transition from graduation to working life a smooth one?
I developed a business model and found my own design philosophy during the last year of the course, and I was ready to establish my own business right after graduation. I am still working on how to present myself as a professional.

Any words of advice for future students?
Don't try to do everything yourself! Ask for help from other students or professionals to handle tasks outside your area of skill. And don't be afraid to experiment and try out your crazy ideas!

Marthe Næstby's graduation project celebrated eccentricity.
Photo Tor Orset

Current Students

'I chose KHIO because of the wide variety of workshops and resources available. The school has a long tradition of arts and crafts, which can be reinterpreted, developed and taken into a contemporary setting.'
Ole Thomas Spæren

'My favourite workshop was collaborating with technicians in a knitwear factory in Norway. Through this course, I got to experience knitwear production from a different angle.'
Elisabeth Stray Pedersen

'My advice to future students? Use the facilities as much as you can. Try to get involved in various workshops to teach yourself about different machines and techniques. It opens up so many possibilities!'
Sahzene Nilhan Durmusoglu Johansen

'At KHIO, there is freedom to study exactly what you feel a natural interest in. It doesn't feel like you have to create an interesting profile just for the sake of it.'
Joachim Kvernstrøm

City Life

Oslo, the capital of Norway, was founded in 1048. The city is surrounded by nature, with forests and fjords close to the city centre. The school is located in Grünerløkka, a formerly industrial, now trendy district renowned for its vibrant local life. In this neighbourhood, there are independent galleries, design studios and bookshops, and nearby is Birkelunden park, with its weekend flea and farmer's markets.

Just a short walk away from the school, Olaf Ryes square is surrounded by cafes, galleries and unique bars and restaurants.

At the north end of the square is Parkteatret, which has recently evolved into one of the most interesting concert venues in Oslo. The city is famous for its cafe culture with many serving great coffee right across town.

KHIO is a part of a growing creative area beside River Akerselva. Our closest neighbour is the Oslo School of Architecture and Design. Not far down the river, there is another old industrial area called Vulkan which is now home to various cultural attractions.

Norway

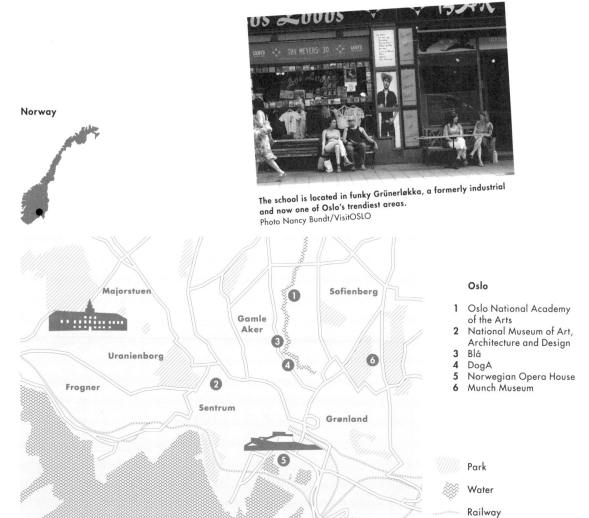

The school is located in funky Grünerløkka, a formerly industrial and now one of Oslo's trendiest areas.
Photo Nancy Bundt/VisitOSLO

Oslo

1 Oslo National Academy of the Arts
2 National Museum of Art, Architecture and Design
3 Blå
4 DogA
5 Norwegian Opera House
6 Munch Museum

Park

Water

Railway

Main road

Majorstuen

Gamle Aker

Sofienberg

Uranienborg

Frogner

Sentrum

Grønland

Course
Fashion and Costume Design

School
Oslo National Academy of The Arts

City Facts

National Museum of Art, Architecture and Design ②
This museum appears in four different locations in the centre, with a varied exhibition programme as well as permanent collections.
nasjonalmuseet.no

Blå ③
A dark and industrial jazz club known for booking some of the best jazz and electronica live acts in the world.
blaaoslo.no

DogA ④
The Norwegian Centre for Design and Architecture, housed in a cool industrial complex, is a lively meeting place hosting a variety of events and facilities.
doga.no

Norwegian Opera House ⑤
Dedicated to the life and work of the famous Norwegian artist Edvard Munch, with the world's largest collection of his paintings – including the iconic *Scream*.
munch.museum.no

Munch Museum ⑥
Dedicated to the life and work of the famous Norwegian artist Edvard Munch, with the world's largest collection of his paintings – including the iconic *Scream*.
munch.museum.no

Oslo Fashion Week
Annual celebration of Norwegian fashion and the country's biggest fashion event.
oslofashionweek.com

Up Design
Bi-annual fashion show for newly-established Norwegian fashion designers selected by a professional committee.
updesign.no

Dansens Hus
The national stage for contemporary dance, housed in a former industrial building.
dansenshus.com

Holmenkollen and Oslo Winter Park
Oslo's biggest ski resort, at Tryvann, is only 20 minutes by metro from the city's central station.
oslovinterpark.no

Mathallen
This is the place to go for anyone who appreciates high-quality food and drinks. The hall offers fish, meat, vegetables, baked goods and coffee. Everything from the best suppliers and distributors of Norway, as well as some imported products.
mathallenoslo.no

Astrup Fearnley Museum
A great private collection of contemporary art in a brand-new Renzo Piano building. Includes works by Damien Hirst, Matthew Barney, Cindy Sherman, Jeff Koons and Takashi Murakami.
afmuseet.no

How to get around
Oslo is not a very big city, which makes it easy to get around by foot and bicycle. However, there is good public transport provision, with trams, metro and bus. City Bikes are places all around the city, and around EUR 12.50 buys you a card to get access to these. The major train stations in Oslo, Central Station and National Theatre, are both about 3 km from the school. The nearest tram and bus stop are at Birkelunden, just a few blocks away from the school.

Arranging housing
Difficult

Housing support by school
No

Cost of room in the city
NOK 5500 per month (approx. EUR 700)

Cost of campus housing
From NOK 3000 to 3500 for housing from the student organisation (SIO) (approx. EUR 380 to 450)

Pearl
Academy

Student work presentation with guest lecturer and fashion designer Michele Michele Bohbot.

Pearl Academy delivers its programmes over its three campuses.

Pearl Academy
New Delhi 110028
India

T +91 (0)11 4980 7100
counsellor@pearlacademy.com
pearlacademy.com

Course
Design (Fashion and Textile)

School
Pearl Academy

Introduction

'The course hones creativity, initiative, innovation and judgment compatible with the fashion industry'

Usha Nehru Patel, course leader

When was the school founded and how has it changed?
Founded in 1993, Pearl Academy is India's largest private institution in fashion, design and related businesses. Since its inception, it has evolved into a globally-renowned institution of higher learning with a focus on internationalism, entrepreneurship and generating employability, while catering to the needs of the design, fashion and retail industries.

What is the school all about?
Pearl Academy delivers over 30 uniquely designed undergraduate, graduate and professional programmes over its three campuses in Delhi, Noida and Jaipur. Driven by a commitment to create adaptable and highly sought-after graduates, Pearl Academy is backed by the resources and expertise of a global network of renowned institutions, such as London College of Fashion, Nottingham Trent University, Domus Academy and NABA, amongst others.

What kind of teaching method is applied?
The academy's educational philosophy combines faculty teaching with independent learning by students. Students learn from interactions with industry, case studies, field trips and practical workshops. Projects, research papers and dissertations are interspersed with formal teaching to permit individual growth. Lectures, tutorials, study groups, case studies, seminars, workshops, project research, field trips, guest lectures by industry experts and industry internship are the teaching/learning methods.

Why should students choose this school?
Pearl Academy is one of the finest institutes nurturing best-in-class talent across the disciplines of design, art and business of fashion. Students are moulded into well-rounded professionals, equipped with contemporary skills and thorough knowledge of the industry.

What is expected from the students?
Pearl Academy has an emphasis on learning with an open mind and hands-on attitude. Students experiment under the guidance and supervision of our expert faculty members so that they can explore their hidden talents, creativity and innovation. Students are expected to keep evolving, learning and growing with every single step that they take towards achieving their goals.

What is the most important thing for students to learn during this course?
The course hones creativity, initiative, innovation and judgment along with intellectual and conceptual acumen compatible with the fashion industry. The various projects, exercises and sessions inculcate graduates with capacity for critical professional engagement and investigative attitude in the fashion business context.

City
New Delhi

Country
India

187

Programme

The MA Design (Fashion and Textile) programme provides design and lifestyle-related inputs arranged to generate and encourage specific design applications based on the self-chosen areas of the students. The principal aims of the MA programme are: to educate students to function as managers and specialists for the fashion industry in India and abroad; to hone creativity, initiative, innovation and judgement along with intellectual and conceptual acumen; to provide a capacity for critical professional engagement and investigative attitude in the context of the industry; and to ensure students work with self-direction, professionalism and originality to contribute to business and society at large through the domain of fashion.

Students are encouraged and expected to proactively participate in the organised seminars, guest lectures and field trips. They develop verbal and written presentation skills and the ability to analyse, express findings and clear conclusions. The academy emphasises hands-on learning and teaching, with students acquiring new techniques/methods by experiencing them directly. Creativity and skills are honed in this way alone.

During the first semester, students enhance their conceptualisation skills and the ability to identify individual needs for specialisation. The second semester is project-driven, with the presentation of a group project, based on design trend forecasting, analysis and interpretation; and an individual project that focuses on the development of options for creative application(s). The aim is to develop creative and practical abilities required for advanced design applications, which will be converted to actual prototype development in the final semester through the master's project. During the course, as well as undertaking an internship in industry, students are eligible to undertake freelance consultancy service or set up their own business alongside their studies.

Gaurav Gupta and Shefalee Vasudev presenting a seminar to fashion and business students.

British Council delegation speak to students.

Programme
Design (Fashion and Textile)

Leads to
Master of Arts

Structure
The 1.5-year full-time course is divided into three semesters, each lasting for 6 months. The semesters are divided into modules including design studies, product development and professional practice. In the final master's project, students must develop a brief for product development based on the findings stated in the individual research project during the second semester.

Head of programme
Seema Majahan

Mentors and lecturers
Seema Majahan, Usha Nehru Patel, Alam Pervez Khan, Tarun Panwar and Ambika Magotra.

Notable alumni
Unknown

Course
Design (Fashion and Textile)

School
Pearl Academy

School Facts

Duration of study
1.5 years

Full time
Yes

Part time
No

Female students
80%

Male students
20%

Local students
100%

Students from abroad
0%

Yearly enrolment
20

Tuition fee
- INR 420,000 per year for local students (approx. EUR 5000)
- INR 680,000 per year for international students (approx. EUR 8000)

Funding/scholarships
Yes

Minimum requirements for entry
Bachelor's degree or sufficient relevant experience in fashion/textile design

Language
English

Application procedure
The following documents are required:
- application form
- copy of degree certificate/college transcripts
- design portfolio
- your curriculum vitae
- statement of purpose
- letters of recommendation
- a copy of your passport
- proof of language (if applicable)
- proof of payment of the INR 30,000 registration and admission fee (approx. EUR 330).
  Some candidates may be contacted for interview. International applicants are not required to have an in-person interview. Successful candidates will be informed by email.

Application details
counsellor@pearlacademy.com

Application date
By 1 April

Graduation rate
High

Job placement rate
90%

Memberships/affiliations
IFFTI and the Fashion Design Council of India.

Collaborations with
Amsterdam Fashion Institute (the Netherlands), Berliner Technische Kunsthochschule (Germany), Nottingham Trent University, Birmingham Institute of Arts and Design, London College of Fashion and Manchester Metropolitan University (United Kingdom), Domus Academy and NABA (Italy), Fashion Institute of Design & Merchandising and Santa Fe University of Art & Design (United States), George Brown College (Canada) and National Institute of Design (India).

Facilities for students
Library, workshops, internet and wi-fi services, and hostel/accommodation facilities.

City
New Delhi

Country
India

Student Work

Using Khadi (2012)
By Pavan Parvath

This project used 'khadi' (hand spun yarn) for knitting. With extensive focus on ethics, climate change and environmental impact, this concept was aimed at reviewing khadi, with a view to reviving it as a handcrafted and eco-friendly fabric of India. The making of the fabric involves human intervention from farming to finished goods with the help of tools and simple machinery. The collection is created to initiate new trends and movements to khadi, incorporating a classic men's look and breaking the rules of the establishment. The range is for the young, sophisticated, eclectic and eco-aware consumer.

Fit For Fashion (2013)
Diksha Prabhakar

Aim of this project was to create a new line of active wear for women. The collection turns active wear garments into city attire with a modern and luxurious appeal. The garments combine tailoring with the design philosophy of eco-fashion, using bamboo fabric with digital prints that give the range a modern, contemporary and luxurious look. The design has been customised to best utilise the anti-bacterial, absorbent, deodorisation, smooth drape and insulating properties of the bamboo fabric.

Appliqué (2013)
By Purnima Sharma

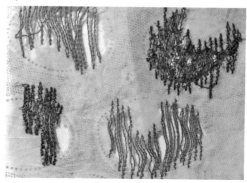

This project includes textile designs produced using techniques to recreate designs with a human touch. Surfaces feature an indigenous and inimical nature, connected to sentiments of religious aspects with a hereditary culture of handcrafted authentic designs and patterns. Using techniques in a timeless, sustainable, functional as well as in a manner of ornamentation, the products are not limited to fabric or garments – it is an eternal journey of surfaces.

Cotton Organdy (2013)
By Leesha Arora

Aromatic plants and spices were investigated to produce an assortment of home textiles, utilising the fabric Cotton Organdy. The bed linen and home textiles needed to be insect-repellent, with the products decorated with handcrafted ornamentation. The production utilised two techniques to get the desired appearance of the textiles, including high temperature narrowing of polyester yarn and Cotton Organdy.

Chirita (2013)
By Anuja Khandelwal

Chirita is a range of intricately-styled outwear garments and accessories that are hand knitted with exquisite Himalayan nettle yarn. The collection draws inspiration from the growth of organic plant life to realise products with detail and care. The artistry of nature has been used to produce wraps, collars, shrugs and accessories, in a perfect amalgamation of innovative designs and contemporary styling with traditional perspective.

Women at Work (2013)
By Swati Matta

There are regional differences in the way people dress for business in India. Clothing helps others identify who you are – one's educational background, occupation and social status. Following extensive research, a collection of business attire was produced that aims to present a global style, portraying corporate culture. Prints, collars, a combinations of knits and laces, plus neon colours were introduced to give a feminine and attractive look within the borders of formal dressing.

Twist & Drape (2013)
By Riti Bansal

 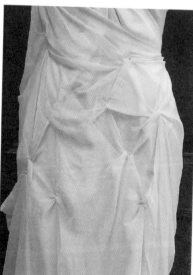 

This collection aimed to explore innovative silhouettes based on draping, with unique and subtle colour combinations. The collection incorporates innovative, modern scenarios creating interesting garments for women of India who are fashion forward, with an urban youth aesthetic that is very close to their feminine self. The garments include drapes with various placement and usage of knots and twists, whether it is decorative or functional with a soft touch of embellishment.

Alumna

Name Richa Sood
Residence New Delhi, India
Year of birth 1981
Year of graduation 2004
Current job Senior designer at Rohit Bal Designs

Why did you choose this school?
I wanted to pursue a master's in fashion, and this is the only school in India that offered an MA Fashion, in collaboration with Nottingham Trent University in the United Kingdom, with the best faculty pool. Which meant that I could pursue a master's programme, that was at par with international standards, while staying at home.

Are you still in contact with the school?
Yes. I do teaching assignments there now, which is a tremendously enriching experience. Especially the way the MA course is designed, by facilitating both the student and the mentor to develop a connection. Irrespective of my assignments, I have a deep regard for my mentors and share a life-long bond.

What was the most important thing you learnt here?
A creative mind is primarily intuitive and fluid. It's important to give a direction to this flow of ideas. The course was designed in a way where one is forced to discover this for yourself.

What was the most interesting project you did?
The individual research project was super fun. I worked on the concept of 'reflections'. It began with this whole series of photography, capturing the occurrence of reflection. I would be forever seen with a camera, and kept clicking like an alien tourist who had descended on earth. The next stage was to take forward the concept into material exploration. The drapes and silhouettes I explored during this project were most exciting.

What subject you wish you paid more attention to?
I would give more time to my final project. I wanted to find out what other designers had already created on the same theme. I would have loved to travel to other design schools outside India, and explore possibilities of ideas, material and technical execution.

Was there any class you found difficult?
Each assignment had a different challenge. The whole idea was to polish up research methods, and your conclusions should be derived from detailed research and personal interpretation. Every small idea must be backed with data.

What was your graduation project?
It was based on interactive design. The theme was based on the illusive perceptions of the mind related to its environment. A realm of the mind where objects around you are not perceived by logic. It is an amalgamation of the 'unreal' that weaves a story around itself. The idea is best expressed by fusing movement and the illusion into design.

Any word of advice for future students?
I would advise students to get a year or two industry work before embarking on a master's degree. This helps mature your reasoning and keeps your perspective real. A master's is an excellent opportunity to go wild with your creativity and challenge boundaries – follow your intuition.

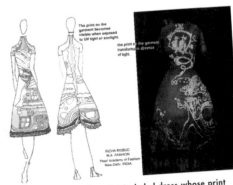

Sood's graduation work project included dress whose print only became visible when exposed to UV light.

Current Students

'Future students can expect to receive a good education in fashion and textiles. The facilities are great and the teachers are very helpful and friendly. After following this course, your depth of knowledge in your areas of interest will help you establish yourself as a designer after graduation.'
Ruchi Roy

'New students should definitely expect a huge amount of exposure and a lot of opportunities which the school gives its students in different areas.'
Neha Kasat

'My advice to future students? As a master's is more of a course which requires you to do a lot of self-study and explorations, make the most of it and ensure you work and give your heart and soul to it, because in the end it is your project and work that will help you prosper.'
Neeta Nandakumar Bhat

'I find the mentoring sessions to be very interesting because it gives a best option to explore yourself with your research area.'
Jay Gulati

'I want to work in the fashion field and this course has helped me be a driving force in it. The way we are being taught about research and coordinating with industry is quite awesome.'
Sankarshan Lodh

City Life

Delhi is a cosmopolitan city in northern India where people are open to embracing new ideas and lifestyles. There is a noticeable transition with the changing lifestyle and the influence of modern ideas in the lives of Delhites.

The city is cosmopolitan, mature and there is unity among the citizens from all caste and creed from across the country. This 'unity in diversity' can be seen in social and cultural gatherings where people from all communities can be seen on one platform sharing one common view. Be it Holi, Diwali, Id, Guru Purab or Buddha Purnima; you will find the same vigour and bliss among the people from different communities.

Launched in 1993, the Delhi campus of Pearl Academy has emerged as the preferred choice of students and industry alike, for the quality of its teaching and faculty. Located at

Naraina, an erstwhile garment manufacturing stronghold of the city, the Delhi Campus is spread across eight buildings and houses a plethora of facilities that provide the necessary infrastructure to deliver courses effectively. World-class facilities along with well-qualified faculty provide students with a holistic learning experience.

India Gate, designed by Sir Edwin Lutyens and unveiled in 1933, is a prominent landmark in the city.
Photo Arian Zwegers

India

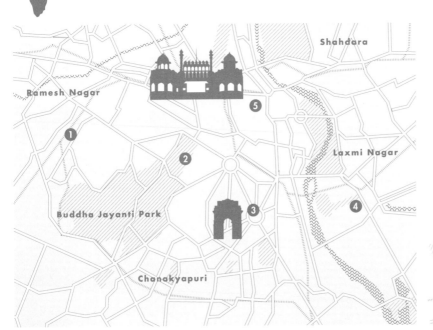

New Delhi

1 Pearl Academy
2 Birla Mandir
3 India Gate
4 Akshardham Temple
5 Red Fort

Park

Water

Railway

Main road

Course
Design (Fashion and Textile)

School
Pearl Academy

City Facts

Birla Mandir ②
Laxmi Narayan Temple, also known as Birla Mandir, is one of Delhi's major temples and a popular tourist attraction. Built by the industrialst GD Birla in 1938, this beautiful temple is located in the west of Connaught Place and is dedicated to Laxmi (the goddess of prosperity) and Narayana (the preserver). The temple was inaugurated by Mahatma Gandhi on the condition that people of all castes will be allowed to enter the temple.

India Gate ③
At the centre of New Delhi stands the 42-m high India Gate, an 'Arc-de-Triomphe'-like archway in the middle of a crossroad. Almost similar to its French counterpart, it commemorates the 70,000 Indian soldiers who lost their lives fighting for the British Army during the World War I.

Dilli Haat
Providing the ambience of a traditional Rural Haat or village market, but one suited for more contemporary needs, here one sees a synthesis of handicrafts, cuisine and cultural activity. A unique bazaar, in the heart of the city, it displays the richness of Indian culture on a permanent basis.

Akshardham Temple ④
This temple epitomises 10,000 years of Indian culture in all its breathtaking grandeur and beauty. It brilliantly showcases the essence of India's ancient architecture, traditions and timeless spiritual messages. The Akshardham experience is an enlightening journey through India's glorious art, values and contributions for the progress, happiness and harmony of mankind.

Red Fort ⑤
The Red sandstone walls of the massive Red Fort (Lal Qila) rise 33-m above the clamour of Old Delhi as a reminder of the magnificent power and pomp of the Mughal emperors. The walls, built in 1638, were designed to keep out invaders, now they mainly keep out the noise and confusion of the city.

Garden of Five Senses
This is not just a park, it is a space with a variety of activities, inviting public interaction and exploration. The 20-acre site, located in the south of the city at Said-Ul-Azaib village, close to the Mehrauli heritage area, is spectacular. Majestic rocks stand silhouetted against the sky, others lie strewn upon the ground in a casual yet alluring display of nature's sculptural genius.

Jama Masjid
This great mosque of Old Delhi is the largest in India, with a courtyard capable of holding 25,000 devotees. It was begun in 1644 and ended up being the final architectural extravagance of Shah Jahan, the Mughal emperor who built the Taj Mahal and the Red Fort.

Parliament House
The Parliament house is a circular colonnaded building. It also houses ministerial offices, numerous committee rooms and an excellent library. Conceived in the Imperial Style, the Parliament House consists of an open verandah with 144 columns. The domed circular central hall with oak-panelled walls and the three semicircular buildings are used for the Rajya Shabha and Lok Shabha meetings.

Qutab Minar
This is a soaring, 73 m-high tower of victory, built in 1193 by Qutab-ud-din Aibak immediately after the defeat of Delhi's last Hindu kingdom. The tower has five distinct storeys, each marked by a projecting balcony and tapers from a 15-m diameter at the base to just 2.5 m at the top. The first three storeys are made of red sandstone; the fourth and fifth storeys are of marble and sandstone.

How to get around
Delhi is well connected with domestic and international flights, to all the major cities within and outside India. Almost all the major airlines have flights operating from Indira Gandhi International Airport at New Delhi. The Domestic Airport connects Delhi to the major cities in India.
The railway network connects the city to many destinations across India. The three important railway stations are New Delhi Railway Station, Old Delhi Railway Station and Hazrat Nizamuddin Railway Station. There are three major bus stations across the city, Inter State at Kashmiri Gate, Sarai Kale-Khan and Anand Vihar, all with frequent bus services.

Arranging housing
Average

Housing support by school
Yes

Cost of room in the city
INR 000 to INR 8000 per month (approx. EUR 60 to 100)

Cost of campus housing
INR 180,000 per year (approx. EUR 2150)

Rhode Island School of Design in Providence offers its own vibrant art scene and is conveniently located between two the major cultural centres of Boston and New York.

Rhode Island School of Design

Rhode Island School of Design (RISD)
2 College Street
Providence, RI 02903
United States

T +1 (0)401 451 5848
admissions@risd.edu
risd.edu

Enjoying the wealth of resources in the Fleet Library.

Introduction

'Our students require a strong sense of focus and determination'

Brooks Hagan, acting head of department

What is your school's emphasis?
Since the turn of the millennium, Rhode Island School of Design (RISD) has expanded its emphasis on research and its advanced-level programmes in art and design. As a result, graduate student enrolment has more than doubled. Our students greatly influence the creative community here, with their energy, passion, focus and commitment.

What is your teaching method?
Although they spend long hours in the studio, RISD grad students are very much engaged in the world around them. There is a major goal of both articulating and synthesising the ideas behind their studio work and of contributing to the development of knowledge.

What is the school's main strength?
Graduate students are drawn to RISD by the faculty – professional artists and designers working at the top of their fields – and the calibre of fellow students. They want to make work that matters and be a part of a community dedicated to developing innovative and responsible approaches to art and design. Our programmes are challenging and demanding, requiring a strong sense of focus and determination. The sense of belonging and contributing to a creative community is exhilarating, and the intellectual and creative challenges inherent in graduate study at RISD make it a great place to be.

What is expected from the students?
Students develop their abilities in print, knit and/or weaving. This entails working by hand as well as learning advanced technologies, such as digital printing and Jacquard design. At the same time, they broaden their exposure to the field through seminars, trips and internships. The development of a context for their personal work is important throughout.

What is the most important thing students to learn during this course?
A working process, grounded in fine arts practice, that embraces hand techniques and advanced technology.

What is the most important skill for a textile designer?
Understanding the balance between originality and appropriateness of end use.

What kind of job do your graduates go on to do?
They become leaders in the textile industry, from the interiors market, to the apparel industry, to education and beyond. Jobs include designing for textile manufacturers and producers, working for well-know brands, and teaching at universities.

City
Providence

Country
United States

197

Programme

RISD's MFA Textiles programme focuses on woven, knit and print design of fabrics used for apparel and interior applications. Working from a foundation of solid technical skills and a proficient design process, students engage in individual research to gain an understanding of design as an expression of a continually evolving culture. Through this, they develop a strong personal vision and the problem-solving skills to respond to global human needs.

Geared towards those who have a background in textiles, along with experience in visual studies from an undergraduate programme or professional practice, the 2-year full-time course helps students to broaden and sharpen their skills, hone their artistic identity and become well versed in the technical and creative potential of their chosen medium and its context. It also emphasises studies in drawing and colour, along with participation in graduate seminars, as a means of building analytical and critical thinking skills.

The first year of the programme focuses on enriching students' creative background and expanding their skills, including the use of digital technology in design. The second year allows for more individual exploration of weaving, knitting or surface design, with the final semester culminating in a thesis project that entails both studio work and writing. Students are encouraged to create design collections that break new ground while also reflecting a depth of research and well-developed material and visual language.

Exchanging ideas at the graduate studios open night.

The painting studio exemplifies the fine art orientation of the textiles programme.

Programme
Textiles

Leads to
Master of Fine Arts

Structure
The 2-year full-time course is split into the fall and spring semesters (15 credits per semester), and the winter session. The programme is made up of seminars, studios and electives, with a thesis project taking up a major portion of the second year. During their two years in the programme, students are required to take three drawing or colour electives. For a semester in which a drawing or colour elective is taken, the graduate studio credits will be adjusted to bring the total programme for the semester to 15 credits.

Head of programme
Anais Missakian

Mentors and lecturers
Brooks Hagan, Mary Anne Friel, Maria Tulokas, Lisa Scull, Susan Sklarek, Harel Kedem, Joe Segal, Sally Barker, Liz Collins and Gina Gregario.

Notable alumni
Mark Pollack, Mary Murphy and Michael Koch.

School Facts

Duration of study
2 years

Full time
Yes (40+ hours a week)

Part time
No

Female students
90%

Male students
10%

Local students
76%

Students from abroad
24%

Yearly enrolment
12

Tuition fee
USD 41,332 (approx. EUR 31,500)

Funding/scholarships
Yes (see risd.edu/financial_aid)

Minimum requirements for entry
Bachelor's degree

Language
English

Application procedure
Apply by registering online
and sending an application file
containing:
- your personal and contact details
- your curriculum vitae
- application form
- official transcript
- statement of purpose
- portfolio
- three letters of recommendation
- TOEFL score (if English is not your
  native language)
- proof of application fee of USD 60
  (approx. EUR 45).
  For more on these requirements, visit:
  risd.edu/grad/apply

Application details
admissions@risd.edu

Application date
Before 10 February

Graduation rate
100%

Job placement rate
80%

Memberships/affiliations
Association of Independent Colleges
of Art and Design, National
Association of Schools of Art and
Design, and New England Association
of Schools and Colleges.

Collaborations with
Knoll, Designtex, Fabricut, Chilewich,
Grahame Fowler, Rubelli, Dashing
Tweeds, Gary Graham, Sheila Hicks
and Cornell University.

Facilities for students
Weaving, knitting and print studios,
computer lab, scanners and digital
projectors, plus dedicated space for
graduate students.

Student Work

Phase 3 (2013)
By Agustina Bello Decurnex

Mohair, poly, plastic, glue, hand knitted, coated with plaster and glue, and cracked.
Photo Andy Romer

Beginning's End (2013)
By Chase Taylor

Jacquard woven mohair, metallic, rayon, cotton. Sections cut away and hand embroidered.
Photo Ji Weo

Phase 7 (2013)
By Agustina Bello Decurnex

Untitled (2013)
By Maggie Barber

Mohair, dyed silk. Hand knitted and finished.

Mohair, poly, elastic, felt, modelled in rhino, laser cut, jacquard knitted and melted.
Photo Andy Romer

Horseplay (2013)
By Sarah Wertzberger

Jacquard woven wool, rayon, cotton.
Hand cut and reassembled.

Untitled (2013)
By Suruchi Kabra

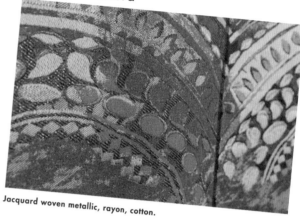

Jacquard woven metallic, rayon, cotton.

Untitled (2013)
By Jessica Bourque

Cotton, acrylic, dye. Hand printed and embellished,
appliqued, sewn and coated.

Swayed Space (2013)
By Chase Taylor

Jacquard woven mohair, metallic, rayon, cotton. Sections
brushed and embellished.
Photo Ji Weo

City
Providence

Country
United States

Alumna

Name Vedrana Hrsak
Residence Providence, United States
Year of birth 1976
Year of graduation 2011
Current job Material designer
at Converse
Website vedranahrsak.com

Why did you choose this school?
I was impressed that studio workspaces were open 24/7, and inspired by how RISD students literally spent day and night labouring on their projects. The idea of having unlimited access to facilities, being surrounded by like-minded people, and of working with a world-famous faculty sealed my decision. As a graduate student, I was looking to refine and focus my design skills by incorporating a fine arts perspective.

What was the most important thing you learned here?
I furthered my understanding of the principles of integrity, simplicity and consistency, reminding me to leave the literal behind, to break apart preconceptions, and to hone my findings with tireless vigour in the production and variation of samples.

What are you doing now?
I'm a materials designer at Converse. I work specifically with the team that focuses on skate, basketball and running shoes.

How did the school prepare you for what you are doing now?
RISD taught me to problem solve, to think critically and to apply the core knowledge of my field, while remaining agile and adaptable in the evolution of my working process.

What was your graduation project?
Through my graduate thesis work I sought to document and explore the contradictions inherent in the cityscape of Providence. How the sensations created by urban decay and restored architecture are redefined through a dialogue with human experience. By combining these elements into textile designs, my hope was to offer an individual and unique yet broad perspective on the 'here and now' and the 'there and then'.

Was the transition from graduation to working life a smooth one?
Since it happened so fast, work life really became and still is an extension of my education. I have learned so much over the past 2 years about the footwear industry. In turn, I have tried to contribute my experience and knowledge of textile design to realise materials fit for sneakers.

Any words of advice for future students at RISD?
Early on Merlin Szasz, my 3D professor at RISD, said something to the effect of, 'Work on what makes you uncomfortable, what you don't yet know, to reach new ground'.

Hrsak's graduation project translated local cityscapes into textile designs.

Course
Textiles

School
Rhode Island School of Design

Current Students

'I got so much out of each class that it is difficult to choose a favourite one, but I found my CAD in Textiles class (taught by Gina Gregorio) to be very valuable. As I came to RISD primarily to learn the skills I needed to translate my paintings into textile designs, this course taught me so much in that regard.'
Olivia Wendel
Photo Karen Cattan

'I was looking for a programme that would give me a comprehensive education in textiles, strengthen my fine art skills, and make me well prepared to enter the world as a textile designer. RISD's programme serves all of these areas tremendously well. I can't imagine having gone anywhere else.'
Allison Stocco

'I think future students can expect to gain an incredibly different outlook on making and creating, as well as new and innovative ways to learn while doing.'
Chase Taylor

'I love that Providence has a tight community. You get to meet very talented and amazing people at events and make friends in different departments that lead to great collaborations.'
Agustina Bello Decurnex

'RISD was introduced to me in my freshman year back in India. I had always wanted to study at a place that balanced a student's artistic endeavours with acquiring a skill set that would make us ready for the 'real' world.'
Suruchi Kabra

City Life

With its cobbled streets, ornate colonial-era architecture, spontaneous art installations, outdoor concerts and events, Providence is an engaging and exciting environment. The city has an interesting mix of buildings, culture, nightlife and other urban amenities. A place where colonial history meets the latest in contemporary design, it is home to seven colleges as well as to waterfront parks, ethnic restaurants, dance and theatre companies, and extraordinary historic architecture.

Providence is known for being unusually welcoming to artists and the arts, perhaps because so many RISD alumni choose to live in Rhode Island after graduating. The city's galleries welcome emerging artists and there are also opportunities to escape to the world of performing arts thanks to the presence of several theatres.

Since Providence is ideally situated between Boston (100 km) and New York (290 km), it's easy to travel north or south for the day or weekend to check out current exhibitions at major museums and galleries.

Providence is rich in colonial architecture, especially on Benefit Street.

United States

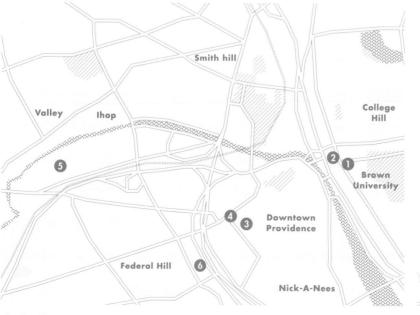

Providence

1 RISD
2 Museum of Art
3 Trinity Repertory Company
4 AS220
5 The Steel Yard
6 New Urban Arts

Park

Main road

Course
Textiles

School
Rhode Island School of Design

City Facts

RISD Museum of Art
On the school campus, Rhode Island School of Design's own museum has varied exhibitions of art and design representing diverse cultures from ancient times to the present.
risdmuseum.org

Trinity Repertory Company ❸
Trinity Rep is Providence's premier acting troupe, putting on an average of six productions a year – varying from contemporary to classic – in a beautiful theatre.
trinityrep.com

AS220 ❹
Notable among the city's creative outlets is AS220, a thriving non-profit arts organisation that supports gallery spaces, live/work studios, a performance space, a community darkroom and a bar/restaurant.
as220.org

The Steel Yard ❺
An industrial arts space run by a number of RISD alumni and other community arts advocates and occupying one of the city's many former factories and mills.
thesteelyard.org

New Urban Arts ❻
New Urban Arts is a nationally-recognised community arts studio for students and emerging artists in Providence. Its mission is to build a vital community that empowers young people as artists and leaders to develop a creative practice.
newurbanarts.org

Benefit Street
One of the highest concentrations of colonial buildings in the country makes this street the place to experience old Providence.
rihs.org

WaterFire
Worthy of medieval Venice, the centrepiece of the WaterFire spectacle is a line of 100 braziers, afloat on the water. Music also helps to light up the night.
waterfire.org

Gallery Night
On the third Thursday of every month, many of Providence's art galleries stay open late for the popular Gallery Night.
gallerynight.info

How to get around
The nearest international airport is just 19 km away. This is the award-winning TF Green Airport (in Warwick) is just 10 minutes away. Public transit is managed by Rhode Island Public Transit Authority (RIPTA). Kennedy Plaza, in downtown Providence, serves as a transportation hub for local public transit as well as a departure point for Peter Pan and Greyhound bus lines.

Providence Station, located between the Rhode Island State House and the downtown district, is served by Amtrak and MBTA Commuter Rail services. Approximately 2400 passengers daily pass through the station. It offers a commuter rail route running north to Boston and south to the airport. There are three bus stops near RISD (S Main at County Court, Tunnel NS S Main and Memorial FS Westminster).

The entire city is easily navigable by bike, bus or car. RISD's downtown hillside campus and the neighbourhood that houses it are also especially welcoming to foot traffic.

Arranging housing
Never a problem

Housing support by school
Yes

Cost of room in the city
Varies

Cost of campus housing
Between USD 6820 and 11,934 per semester (approx. EUR 5203 to 9104)

RMIT University

This is the newest building on campus – an innovative space will house new state-of-the-art studios, technology and learning facilities giving students a creative arena to push the boundaries of design.

RMIT's campuses are filled with a combination of organic, traditional and cutting-edge architecture – like this building which houses the design studios.

RMIT University
25 Dawson Street
Brunswick, Victoria
Melbourne 3056
Australia

T +61 (0)3 9925 2000
fashionandtextiles@rmit.edu.au
rmit.edu.au

Introduction

'RMIT offers project collaborations that capture shifts in design thinking'

Olga Troynikov, programme director,
and Karen Webster, deputy head of school

What is the background of RMIT?

It was one of the first Australian institutes to develop courses in textile design, sewing and illustration early last century and today it is Australia's largest education and research leader in the fashion and textiles domain. In 2000, RMIT Fashion was listed by *Wallpaper* magazine as one of the top six innovative fashion programmes globally.

What is studying at this school all about?

The school is an academic community dedicated to transforming the landscape of fashion and textiles through the scholarship of change and active industry engagement, with a reputation as a leading global player in education, research and consultancy.

What is the educational approach?

There is a strong sense of community within the school, which adopts a personal teaching experience with small class sizes and considerable opportunity for feedback and review. The school's diverse offerings can provide individuals with academic mapping that enables mobility, flexibility and personalised study paths.

What is the strength of this school?

We have extensive networks across aligned industry sectors driving research initiatives and project collaborations that capture shifts in design thinking, advanced technologies and with total supply chain expertise.

What is expected of students?

A significant commitment to be active and engaged participants within their own educational development. Students are required to have a focus on self-directed learning combined with industry and class engagement.

What is the most important thing that students learn on this programme?

Knowledge and understanding of global supply chains, international fashion business and product management, plus knowledge of how trend forecasting, fashion product development and fashion styling work within the business and management structures of companies. Graduates acquire knowledge and skills during the programme which will develop their entrepreneurial and business expertise to lead an organisation efficiently and effectively.

Olga Troynikov (left) and Karen Webster

Programme

The Master of Fashion and Textiles programme has a focus that is unique in the fashion and textiles industry. It provides opportunities for students to develop skills and knowledge in business strategy and analysis by including courses such as global business management, product and merchandising management, and e-retail. We also combine this with specific industry and product understanding, such as sustainable fashion product design and development, trend forecasting, and fashion styling. Students have the opportunity to apply these skills in industry situations and contexts, providing them with in-depth and balanced and balanced expertise for their future careers.

The programme set up is one of face-to-face delivery and hands-on industry involvement to reinforce academic learning. As with any graduate programme, there is a significant element of self-directed, independent learning under the supervision of academics. RMIT's programme offers students quite a unique blend of strategic business understanding, along with the specific skills to prepare students for the competitive rigours of the global fashion industry.

Advanced centres for learning, like the fashion production studio, provide quality-integrated learning environments.

The Design Hub by architecture alumnus Sean Godsell is the first centre of its kind in the country.

Programme
Fashion and Textiles

Leads to
Master of Fashion and Textiles

Structure
The 2-year full-time programme is divided per semester (48 credit points each) into eight core courses (total of 120 credit points) and selection of electives (total of 72 credit points). Core courses include: Advanced Case Studies in Fashion and Textiles; Fashion and Textiles Product Management; Global Business Issues in Fashion and Textiles; Leadership and Management; Research Methods (Fashion and Textile); and Sustainable Product Design and Development for Fashion and Textiles. Electives range from Fashion Styling and Visual Merchandising to Sportswear and Performance Textiles. All candidates undertake a major project. Candidates with an undergraduate degree in the discipline of fashion and textiles are eligible for the 1.5 year (144 credit points) duration of the programme.

Head of programme
Olga Troynikov

Mentors and lecturers
Joanne Drysdale, Karen Lurati, Olga Gavrilenko and Chris Watson.

Course
Fashion and Textiles

School
RMIT University

School Facts

Duration of study
2 years

Full time
Yes (40 hours per week)

Part time
Yes

Female students
80%

Male students
20%

Local students
40%

Students from abroad
60%

Yearly enrolment
100+

Tuition fee
- AUD 20,160 per year for domestic students (approx. EUR 13,570)
- AUD 23,040 per year for international students (approx. EUR 16,000)

Funding/scholarships
Yes

Minimum requirements for entry
Bachelor's degree or significant professional practice

Language
English

Application procedure
Complete and submit your application online with the following:
- your personal and contact details
- your curriculum vitae
- application form
- portfolio
- references
- project proposal
- transcripts
- proof of English proficiency if required.
An application fee may apply. Successful candidates will be informed by email.

Application details
nicholas.maggio@rmit.edu.au

Application date
Before April

Graduation rate
100%

Job placement rate
70%

Memberships/affiliations
Strong industry links with a wide range of organisations and associations, including the Design Institute of Australia, the Council of Textile & Fashion Industries of Australia and the International Foundation of Fashion Technology Institutes.

Collaborations with
AMFI Amsterdam (the Netherlands), Fashion institute of Technology, LIM and Parsons New School of Design (United States), Hong Kong Polytechnic University (Hong Kong), London College of Fashion, Nottingham Trent University and Salford University (United Kingdom), Paris American Academy (France), Royal Academy of Fine Arts Antwerp (Belgium), Ryerson University (Canada), and Technical University of Munich and RWTH Aachen University (Germany).

Facilities for students
Student facilities include a campus library, cafeteria, spacious outdoor facilities, free wi-fi on campus and comprehensive IT facilities, such as a dedicated computer lab and use of relevant specialised software. In addition, there are a number of testing labs and studios.

City
Melbourne

Country
Australia

Student Work

PM Wear Range (2012)
By Kristy Wijesekera, Diana Eau
and Grishma Sha

Strategic new fashion range development for spring/summer with
iconic phraseology attracting customers, such as 'Field of Dreams'
and 'See the Light'.

Neon (2012)
By Linsey Mackay

A CAD project for a collection of bright and vibrant clothes for spring/summer 2012. Neons were used as the next focus for the season to express excitement, with sheer silk and cotton fabrics.

Radical Cubic (2012)
By Sunhye Kim

A CAD project for a range of fashion womenswear. A palette of murky neutral hues signals a return to sturdy materials, such as leather, wool and tweed. Raven grey and purple develop dark and reliable bases while gold is an essential metallic tone running through the collection.

Alumna

Name Neha Kulkarni
Residence Heidelberg, Germany
Year of birth 1986
Year of graduation 2012
Current job 2010

Any words of advice for future students at the college?
RMIT is an amazing place to study. All the lecturers and professors are industry professionals. They come with a vast amount of experience and knowledge. This is the core of the course and helps immensely in real-life work. Make the best use of their knowledge!

Why did you choose this school?
Because it provided the best combination in terms of courses. I had done my bachelor's degree in garment manufacturing. The course at RMIT provided a perspective from the other sides of the fashion business, including the buying side.

What was the most important thing you learned here?
The global experience. I met students from Australia, but from many other countries as well which was a bonus. This sharing of experiences and cultures is what I really treasured.

How did the school prepare you for what you are doing now?
The exchange of cultures and ideas gives a good foundation with respect to dealing with others in the fashion world, as the industry is so global. Also, with regard to my most recent work (as an auditor in ethical compliance), we had various lectures, discussions and projects on the importance of being ethical in trading and the fashion business.

What was your graduation project?
I did my graduation with Myer, a major Australian retailer. The project was about re-positioning and re-defining Kenji, one of Myer's in-house youth brands.

Kulkarni's graduation project aimed at defining and re-positioning a retail brand for a specific fashion season.

Course
Fashion and Textiles

School
RMIT University

Current Students

'I chose the fashion course at RMIT because it has a good reputation both locally and abroad. Coming from a design background, I was particularly interested in the business aspect of the fashion industry that the program is focused on.'
Yawen Chang

'I find the Textile Product Development and Engineering to be the most valuable workshop. I enjoyed discovering the specifics of textiles by investigating the product technically, seen from the perspective of both the buyers and manufacturers.'
Hery Setianingsih

'Future students can expect 100 per cent dedication from the faculty, and the same is also expected in return. Any student studying at the RMIT is well prepared to take on the challenges in their profession.'
Pavna Mehta

'I like to hang out on Flinders Lane for its cute little cafes. Brown Alley has really cool gigs and Victoria market is always a good place to go, especially the night markets with food from all over the world, always a treat!'
Thamalee Palansuriya

'The course gives you a business-oriented knowledge of fashion and textiles. I learnt how to apply my experience in a more methodical way which will give me a better position in the industry.'
Kanishka Chathuranga Jayasundara

City Life

Melbourne, the capital of the state of Victoria, Australia, is one of the world's most liveable cities, with a multicultural environment and a well-developed infrastructure. The city embodies a creative ethos that positions it as an innovative hub attracting students from around the world. Across many design disciplines, Melbourne leads and challenges original thinking and as a result its independent designers, established businesses and educational institutes benchmark with top tier peer organisations across the globe.

Melbourne embraces fresh ideas and is known for both its contemporary fashion chains and the multitude of small to medium businesses that are unique and pioneering. As an international cultural centre, Melbourne hosts major events and festivals in most of the arts and is also home to the National Gallery of Victoria, Australia's oldest and largest public art museum.

RMIT University has three main campuses around Melbourne: City, Brunswick and Bundoora. RMIT City campus has been an integral part of Melbourne's character for more than 100 years and unlike other university campuses, it isn't closed off or surrounded by walls.

The Brunswick campus, which is home to the School of Fashion and Textiles, is just a few minutes away from Sydney Road, a vibrant, multicultural area with a variety of shops, restaurants, bars and markets.

Melbourne is renowned as the cultural capital of Australia, with a vibrant arts and creative scene.

Australia

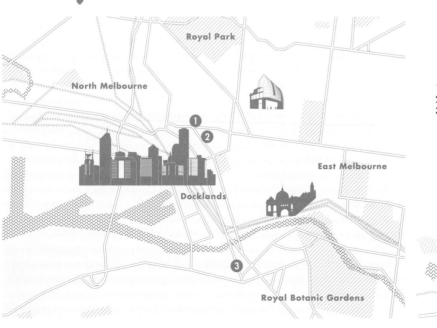

Melbourne

1 RMIT and Gallery
2 State Library of Victoria
3 National Gallery of Victoria

Royal Park

North Melbourne

East Melbourne

Docklands

Royal Botanic Gardens

Park

Water

Railway

Main road

Course
Fashion and Textiles

School
RMIT University

City Facts

RMIT and Gallery ❶
The campus of RMIT also accommodates a public art gallery that presents Australian and international exhibitions of design, craft, architecture, technology, new media and fine art.
rmit.com/rmitgallery

State Library of Victoria ❷
Among the world's great libraries, with a range of services, exhibitions and cultural programmes.
slv.vic.gov.au

National Gallery of Victoria ❸
Australia's oldest public art gallery contains over 68,000 works of art displayed at two locations, one devoted to Australian and one devoted to international works.
ngv.vic.gov.au

Heide Museum of Modern Art
A unique combination of art, architecture and landscape to the east of the city, including a sculpture park and meadow plus three dedicated exhibition spaces.
heide.com.au

L'Oréal Melbourne Fashion Festival
LMFF is an annual celebration of fashion, design, business and creative endeavour held every March.
lmff.com.au

Agideas International Design Forum
Melbourne's annual showcase of design, covering graphics, industrial design, fashion and much more.
agideas.net

International Film Festival
An iconic Melbourne event hosting films from over 50 countries for over two weeks. Started in 1952, it is one of the oldest film festivals in the world.
miff.com.au

Food and Wine Festival
Over 250 events that attract the world's biggest culinary and wine personalities and Victoria's own celebrated chefs, restaurateurs, winemakers, sommeliers, producers and artisans. Every March.
melbournefoodandwine.com.au

Melbourne Festival
One of the world's leading arts festivals, showcasing a wide variety of theatre, dance, music, visual arts, film and outdoor events that takes place in Melbourne each October.
melbournefestival.com.au

How to get around
Melbourne's trains, trams and buses are easy ways to get around. The train network includes over 17 lines linking up all five major stations in the city loop. City Circle Tram is a free service around Melbourne's city centre.
Tourist Shuttle is the free bus service with stops at all key tourist destinations in the city. To travel on all other Melbourne public transport you will need a Myki card (can be purchased at close to 800 retailers, from Myki machines located at all train stations and major tram and bus interchanges).

Train and tram services run between 05.00 and midnight, Monday to Thursday, with extended hours at the weekend. On Sunday, trains and trams run from 07.00 to 23.00. Many of Melbourne's bus routes run from 06.00, later at weekends. SkyBus runs an express service between Melbourne Airport and Melbourne's city centre, 24 hours a day, 7 days a week. The service takes approximately 20 minutes to get from the airport to the city centre.

Arranging housing
Quite easy

Housing support by school
No

Cost of room in the city
Various

Cost of campus housing
n/a

Royal College of Art

Footwear is one of four possible specialisms.

Royal College of Art (RCA)
Kensington Gore
London SW7 2EU
United Kingdom

T +44 (0)20 7590 4444
info@rca.ac.uk
rca.ac.uk

The RCA's annual graduation show attracts a large audience.

Course
Fashion Menswear/Womenswear

School
Royal College of Art

Introduction

'We encourage students to develop their individual vision and design identity'

Wendy Dagworthy, head of the MA Fashion programmes

When was the school founded?
The School of Fashion was founded in 1948 by Madge Garland, a former editor of *Vogue*. Fashion Menswear was added in 1964.

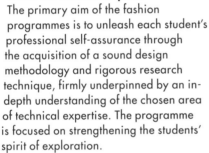

What can students expect?
The primary aim of the fashion programmes is to unleash each student's professional self-assurance through the acquisition of a sound design methodology and rigorous research technique, firmly underpinned by an in-depth understanding of the chosen area of technical expertise. The programme is focused on strengthening the students' spirit of exploration.

What kind of teaching method is applied?
The MA Fashion programmes encourage the development of students' individual design identity through the translation of their personal research into design. Within the discipline there are four areas of separate design specialisation: knitwear, footwear, accessory design and millinery. Students are given the opportunity to develop their individuality and creativity through concentrating on the following subjects: research and development of design ideas, colour, fabric and yarn sourcing, dedicated technical workshops relevant to the specialism selected, drawing and portfolio presentation.

Why should students choose this school?
Recognised for producing the most celebrated young designers in recent years, the fashion programmes encourage a fearless approach to creative expression, fanatical technique and an informed professionalism. The realisation of individuality within a global design context is enabled through our excellent links with practising designers, international fashion brands and a dedicated staff team.

What is the most important thing for students to learn during this course?
We encourage students to develop their individual vision and design identity. Technical courses relevant to the discipline and specialisms are integral elements to this process. Professional presentation and portfolio development focus on communication skills and the ability to present work coherently. Profile analysis and marketing clarify the students' aspirations through product, positioning and use of the media. Our aim for students is that they fulfil their potential and exert a creative influence on the future of fashion menswear and womenswear.

In what kind of jobs do your students mostly end up?
Many students have made names in their own right, such as Julien Macdonald, Erdem and Philip Treacy, while others are respected for their consistently innovative work for international companies such as Calvin Klein, DKNY, Louis Vuitton, Sportmax, Marc Jacobs, and many more. Research alumni have entered art and design faculties as lecturers, tutors and programme leaders across the world.

Programme

The MA Fashion Menswear/Womenswear programmes pursue regeneration and development by constantly adapting to the realities and needs of the designers of the future. We see this as a positive challenge and an inspiration to all the work we undertake. New ideas, materials, methods and design applications are continually originated and progressed by our students. Staff members endeavour to create an environment directed towards creative self-discovery, one that offers each student both the conceptual tutelage and technical guidance to achieve their 3D design objectives.

The primary aim of the programmes is to unleash each student's professional self-assurance through the acquisition of a sound design methodology and rigorous research technique, firmly underpinned by an in-depth understanding of the student's chosen area of technical expertise. The programmes are focused towards strengthening the students' spirit of exploration through unique technical expertise and sound industry awareness. We encourage a strong work ethic across a broad variety of personally driven and industry-oriented design projects.

Remarkable achievements continue to be made in all areas. The programmes and specialisms have advanced and developed successfully, achieving professional recognition for its graduates. We are assured of the success of the programmes through the high international employment profile secured by our graduates who, as they achieve seniority in their own careers, return to the college to recruit young designers. Many of our former students also establish their own businesses in all aspects of design.

The fashion studio is where students spend much of their time.

Student Union Terrace with Royal Albert Hall in the background.
Photo: Alys Tomlinson

Programme
Fashion Menswear / Fashion Womenswear

Leads to
Master of Arts

Structure
Both MA Fashion programmes encourage the development of students' individual design identity through the translation of their personal research into design. Within the disciplines, there are four areas of separate design specialisation, including knitwear, footwear, accessory design and millinery.

Head of programme
Wendy Dagworthy

Mentors and lecturers
Simon Foxton, Sarah Dallas, Heather Holford, Flora McLean, Ike Rust, Justin Smith, Noel Stewart, Iain R Webb and Tristan Webber.

Recent visiting lecturers
Wendy Baker, Manolo Blahnik, Sid Bryan, Katie Eary, Georgina Goodman, Sheilagh Hosker Brown, Betty Jackson, Peter Jensen, Brian Kirkby, Ulrich Lehmann, Matthew Miller, Erdem Moralioglu, Charlie Porter, Peter Sidell and Iain R Webb.

Notable alumni
Christopher Bailey, Boudicca, Peter Copping, Erdem, Holly Fulton, Julien Macdonald, Heikki Salonen, Sibling, Justin Smith Esq, Philip Treacy and Claire Waight-Keller.

School Facts

Duration of study
2 years

Full time
Yes

Part time
No

Female students
70%

Male students
30%

Local students
44%

Students from abroad
56%

Yearly enrolment
Fashion Menswear: 31
Fashion Womenswear: 52

Tuition fee
- GBP 9000 per year for UK and EU citizens (approx. EUR 10,562)
- GBP 13,450 per year for Channel Islands and Isle of Man citizens (approx. EUR 15,785)
- GBP 26,900 Post Experience Programme (approx. EUR 31,570)

Funding/scholarships
Yes, in addition to GBP 3 million of RCA bursaries offered annually, there is also the possibility of winning awards while at the College. GBP 500,000 worth of prizes, scholarships and awards are available to students on an annual basis.

Minimum requirements for entry
A high-quality undergraduate degree in fashion or a related discipline. Proficiency in written and spoken English.

Language
English

Application procedure
Apply by registering online and sending an application file containing:
- your personal and contact details
- a statement outlining why you have chosen this course and what you propose to gain from your studies,
- a copy of your degree and diploma (if you have graduated)
- the contact details of your academic referee
- a portfolio with examples of your recent work.
Shortlisted candidates will be invited to a formal interview.

Application details
applications.rca.ac.uk

Application date
End of January for priority applications

Graduation rate
96%

Job placement rate
90–95%

Memberships/affiliations
n/a

Collaborations with
Fashion Menswear: Bill Amberg, Manolo Blahnik, Brioni, IFF, LOCOG and Thierry Mugler.
Fashion Womenswear: Manolo Blahnik, Esprit, Sophie Hallette, IFF, Intel, Marks & Spencer, Monsoon, Swarovski and Umbro.

Facilities for students
A designated studio space, fabric and yarn stores, specialist sewing machinery, computer studio, high-tech printing, knitting and weaving equipment. In addition, technical support and extensive equipment is available from the School of Material and other programmes of the College.

Student Work

Graduation Collection (2012)
By Rachael Hall

Fashion Womenswear.
Photo RCA/Dominic Tschudin

Graduation Collection (2012)
By Hannah Morgan

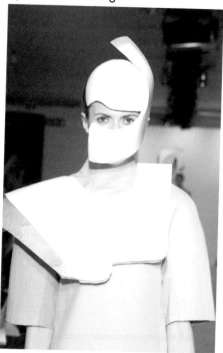

Fashion Womenswear – Millinery.
Photo RCA/Dominic Tschudin

Graduation Collection (2012)
By Yachne Serrano Rose

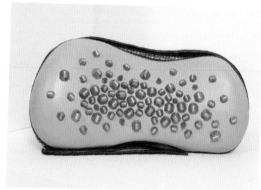

Fashion Womenswear – Accessories.
Photo RCA/Dominic Tschudin

Graduation Collection (2012)
By Benedicte Holmboe

Fashion Menswear.
Photo RCA/Dominic Tschudin

Course
Fashion Menswear/Womenswear

School
Royal College of Art

Graduation Collection (2012)
By Peter Bailey

Fashion Menswear.
Photo RCA/Dominic Tschudin

Graduation Collection (2012)
By Shubham Jain

Fashion Womenswear.
Photo RCA/Dominic Tschudin

Graduation Collection (2012)
By Aku-Petteri Bäckström

Fashion Menswear – Footwear.
Photo RCA/Dominic Tschudin

Graduation Collection (2012)
By Apu Jan

Fashion Womenswear.
Photo RCA/Dominic Tschudin

Graduation Collection (2012)
By Alex Mullins

Fashion Menswear.
Photo RCA/Dominic Tschudin

City
London

Country
United Kingdom

Alumnus

Name Nabil El Nayal
Residence London, United Kingdom
Year of birth 1985
Year of graduation 2008
Current job Designer at Nabil Nayal
Website nabilelnayal.co.uk

Why did you choose this school?
The Royal College of Art has a reputation for cultivating talent and nurturing students. I remember first visiting the RCA and feeling a sense of awe, which I still do to this day.

What was the most important thing you learned here?
To be open to the wonderfully different art and design disciplines in the world, which gave me the strength to express myself with honesty and confidence.

What was the most interesting project you did?
We were given the exciting brief of looking through the archives of the drawing and study rooms at the Victoria and Albert Museum. To my amazement, I discovered a taxidermy bat in one of the boxes.

Was there any class that you found particularly difficult?
Yes – in my final year at the RCA, I invested a lot of time in 3D printing. I had to learn how to use various software I had never even heard of! Thankfully I had the much-needed support of the technical team there. For my graduation collection, I was obsessed with achieving a very specific shade of 'smoke' grey. So I visited the textiles department where mixing chemicals and dyes seemed to come naturally.

What was your graduation project?
My graduation project was called 'She Smokes...'. It was centred around a rich aristocratic woman who one night is seen lying on her chaise longue in her opulent mansion house. A smoke-grey, cracked-leather glowing peach-and-crystal Swarovski collection was the result, with figure disfiguring molten skirt-trousers.

Any words of advice for future students?
Enjoy every single millisecond – time flies when you are amongst so many creative geniuses.

Do you have fond memories of the city?
Every day spent in London is a memory in the making. I met the Queen at the British Clothing Reception at Buckingham Palace while I was creating my graduation collection. I thought I was dreaming!

Where did you live/hang out?
I lived in Camden. Aside from the studio, I used to hang out in Greenwhich. I was obsessed with getting as close as possible to Elizabeth II.

Are you still in contact with the school or your fellow students?
I pop in as much as I can; I always seem to bump into my former tutor Julie Verhoeven. I recently met up with a few old classmates in Paris, which was lovely.

Was the transformation from graduation to working life a smooth one?
Yes and no. I have had the experience of both. I was lucky to be taken on as a designer straight away and, although I learnt so much, I have always wanted to 'do my own thing', so I am doing it! At the same time I lecture at various universities, which I love.

El Nayal credits the course with giving his work a confident, honest edge.

Course
Fashion Menswear/Womenswear

School
Royal College of Art

Current Students

'The professional feedback from practising designers is invaluable. The course is very focused on developing your ability to be critical about your work. The tutors give you the space to explore your own inspiration and guide you towards finding what makes you a unique voice in menswear.'
Alex Benekritis

'Looking for a flat can be really challenging, especially if you have never lived in London before. Luckily for me, I was house hunting with two close friends so we were able to share the responsibility. We share a flat in North London.'
Emma Hardstaff

'My advice for future students – be prepared to work really hard and give the course everything you've got. Enjoy it.'
Zoe Waters

'The time and space to develop your own work and the opportunity to figure out your own direction is very beneficial. We also have excellent technical help.'
Ellen Hedermann Pedersen

'London as a city is so exciting, busy, bustling and full of life. Also great are the hidden secrets that the city has to offer, whether a cafe in the East End's Broadway Market or a bar in Vauxhall. Personally for me, it's the museums that make London so great. The Victoria and Albert Museum, British Museum and the Tate Gallery have great collections that always inspire.'
James Kelly

City Life

With more than 7.5 million inhabitants, London is the biggest city of the United Kingdom. It's not just the geographical, but also the political, economical and cultural, capital of England. Together with New York, Paris and Tokyo, London is one of the four leading global cities.

London contains several UNESCO World Heritage Sites: the Tower of London; Kew Gardens; the site comprising the Palace of Westminster, Westminster Abbey, and St Margaret's Church. Other famous landmarks include Buckingham Palace, the London Eye, Piccadilly Circus, St Paul's Cathedral, the Tower Bridge, Trafalgar Square and Wembley Stadium. London is home to numerous museums, galleries, libraries, sporting events and other cultural institutions, including the British Museum, National Gallery, Tate Modern, British Library, Wimbledon and 40 theatres. The city offers a great variety of cuisine as a result of its ethnically diverse population. Gastronomic centres include the Bangladeshi restaurants of Brick Lane and the Chinese food restaurants of Chinatown. Besides RCA, London also features several other influential business, design, art, fashion, music and acting schools.

United Kingdom

The RCA campus is located in London on Kensington Gore, facing Hyde Park and next to the Royal Albert Hall.

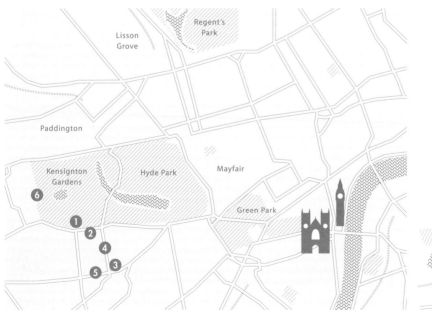

London

1 RCA
2 Royal Albert Hall
3 Victoria & Albert Museum
4 Science Museum
5 Natural History Museum
6 Kensington Palace

Park

Water

Railway

Main road

Course
Fashion Menswear/Womenswear

School
Royal College of Art

City Facts

See also more London City Facts on p.145

Royal Albert Hall ②
The hall, which was opened in 1871 to promote, understand and appreciate arts and sciences, hosts not only concerts of music but also exhibitions, public meetings, scientific conversations and award ceremonies.
royalalberthall.com

Victoria & Albert Museum ③
The museum features an extensive and extremely professional staff, which results in well-grounded research, careful preservation of the ever-changing collections and a well-developed educational service for students.
vam.ac.uk

Science Museum ④
The Science Museum in London is a free museum packed with interactive exhibits, awe-inspiring objects and an IMAX 3D Cinema.
sciencemuseum.org.uk

Natural History Museum ⑤
The mission of the Natural History Museum is to maintain and develop its collections, and to use them to promote the discovery, understanding, responsible use and enjoyment of the natural world.
nhm.ac.uk

Kensington Palace ⑥
Kensington Palace is a royal residence set in Kensington Gardens in the Royal Borough of Kensington and Chelsea in London. It has been a residence of the British Royal Family since the 17th century. It has undergone a huge refurbishment and has just reopened for the public.
hrp.org.uk/kensingtonpalace

Hyde Park
Being one of the largest parks in London, Hyde park is famous for its Speakers' Corner, and many other sides of interest, but mainly for the numerous events that take place. From several rock concerts to the London 2012 Summer Olympics.

Design Museum
The Design Museum shows how design is an integral part of every aspect of life: a way to understand the world around us, and to make it a better place to live. The museum is due to open a new building in Kensington in 2014 which will be a major resource for design students.
designmuseum.org

London Design Festival
Over 10 days in September, the London Design Festival features hundreds of events that take place across London, showcasing the city's pivotal role in global design.
londondesignfestival.com

Frieze Art Fair
Frieze Art Fair takes place every October in Regent's Park. It features over 170 contemporary art galleries. The fair also includes specially-commissioned artists' projects, a prestigious talks programme and an artist-led education schedule.
friezeartfair.com

New Designers
New Designers is the UK's most important graduate exhibition. Over 3500 of the most talented, newly-graduated designers from across the nation will come together in nine distinct design zones.
newdesigners.com

Clerkenwell Design Week
Clerkenwell is home to a series of talks, workshops, parties and special events in over 60 participating showrooms, a multitude of architectural and creative practices.
clerkenwelldesignweek.com

How to get around
With four airports (Heathrow, City, Stansted and Gatwick), London has the largest city airspace in the world. From London, you can fly directly to almost every destination in the world. Transportation around the city centre is either underground or overground by bus, tram or bike. Car travel is only common in the suburbs. The London Underground – dating from 1863 – is the oldest underground railway network in the world and has 270 stations.

London's bus network is also one of the largest in the world, running 24-hours a day, with 8000 buses, 700 bus routes, and over 6 million passenger journeys made every weekday. The distinctive red double-decker buses are internationally recognised, and are a trademark of London transport along with black cabs and the underground.

Cycling in London has enjoyed a renaissance since the turn of the millennium. Cyclists enjoy a cheaper, and often quicker, way around town than those using public transport or car, and the launch of the Barclays Cycle Hire scheme in July 2010 has been successful and generally well-received.

Arranging housing
Average

Housing support by school
Yes

Cost of room in the city
GBP 600 per month (approx. EUR 740)

Cost of campus housing
n/a

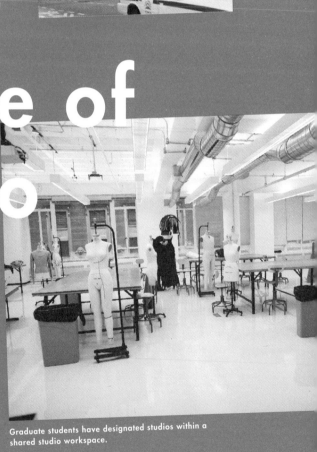

SAIC's fashion design programme is housed the building originally designed by Louis Sullivan in 1899.
Photo Noah Davies

School of the Art Institute of Chicago

School of the Art Institute of Chicago
Department of Fashion
Sullivan Center, 36 South Wabash Avenue
Chicago, IL 60603
United States

T +1 (0)312 629 6710
fashion@saic.edu
saic.edu

Graduate students have designated studios within a shared studio workspace.

Introduction

'Students explore a breadth of possibilities yet achieve an in-depth focus within their individual practice'

Conrad Hamather, graduate programme coordinator

When was the school founded and how has it changed?
Founded as the Chicago Academy of Design in 1866, the purpose of the School of the Art Institute of Chicago (SAIC) was to provide a challenging education in the studio arts and exhibition opportunities for its students. It is now one of the largest accredited independent schools of art and design in the United States, offering a broad, dynamic spectrum of study.

What is studying at this school all about?
To provide excellence in the delivery of a global education in visual, design, media and related arts, with attendant studies in the history and theory of those disciplines set within a broad-based, humanistic curriculum in the liberal arts and sciences. To provide instruction for this education in a range of formats: written, spoken, media and exhibition-based.

What is the learning environment like?
SAIC's fashion programme is housed in the redesigned, expansive space within the Sullivan Center, the building originally designed by Louis Sullivan in 1899. Graduate students have designated studios within a shared studio workspace.

What is expected from the students?
Students explore a breadth of possibilities yet achieve an in-depth focus within their individual practice. Studios progressively provide a space for a deeper individual investigation of fashion within the broader context of community, sustainability, technology and the industry. Four electives taken in the final year allow students to finely hone their interests and practice and may be utilised to support a more interdisciplinary practice. Issues in professional practice are built into the entire curriculum and supplemented by visiting designers from both the fashion industry and related fields.

What is the most important thing for students to learn during this course?
Today, ideas and concepts carry a product, an entity which must embody an experience and a lifestyle. Our programme provides a conceptual and intellectual context in which the nature of fashion is closely examined and re-imagined.

What is the focus of your programme?

Grounding individuals in their personal creative motivation and strengthening the context of their work through critical, theoretical, and practical studies, SAIC cultivates graduates who are highly sensitised, responsive fashion innovators.

City
Chicago

Country
United States

227

Programme

The MDes Fashion, Body and Garment programme is uniquely situated within a vibrant contemporary school of art and design associated with a world-famous museum of art and design. It builds on the connections and relationships between art and fashion that have been evolving in the past century and that reach an unprecedented level in contemporary practices today.

The course focuses on the designer's ability to work conceptually, allowing the body to be utilised as a vehicle for research and development working within a fashion-based studio setting. It manipulates a two-fold study doctrine, technical and conceptually into a hybrid thesis outcome, giving the genre of fashion a new breath.

Each student is encouraged to follow their own intuitive aesthetic response to the information that is derived from the programme, of either a Fashion, Body or Garment trajectory. It is this crucial point when the student makes his/her own developed decision, can they than be able to build into their final thesis project. Taking the three facets of Fashion, Body and Garment to a new aesthetic response is paramount to helping re-define the genre.

Fashion students have 24/7 access to great facilities.

Students have the pick of some select gallery spaces to show their work, with a video installation of Adam Van Eekhout shown here.
Photo Jim Prinz Photography

Fashion students have 24/7 access to great facilities at the school.

Programme
Fashion, Body and Garment

Leads to
Master of Design

Structure
The 2-year full-time course is divided into semesters. Fashion Design Studios, taken each semester, provide a place for an expansive investigation of fashion, body and garment projects. The course is made up of a combination of studios, topical seminars, self-directed research and technical labs. Students also take part in a summer studio to sharpen their technical skills on conceptual research and design, draping techniques as well as finishing details and flats. The second year is devoted to a final project, a distilled collection or body of work that is exhibited as appropriate to the form.

Head of programme
Conrad Hamather

Mentors
Nick Cave, Liat Smestad, Katrin Schnabl, Anke Loh, Mathew Ames, Shane Gabier, Carolin Lerch and Conrad Hamather. Visiting artists: Walter Van Beirendonck, Ralph Rucci, Dirk van Saene, Micha Kuball, Inge Grognard, Ronald Stoops, Paul Boudens, Isabel and Ruben Toledo, Liz Collins and Reiko Sudo.

Notable alumni
Cheryl Pope Justin LeBlanc, Kristina Januskaite, Adam von Eeckhout and Ana Ut Kei.

School Facts

Duration of study
2 years

Full time
Yes

Part time
No

Female students
80%

Male students
20%

Local students
20%

Students from abroad
80%

Yearly enrolment
20

Tuition fee
USD 39,810 per year (approx. EUR 29,830)

Funding/scholarships
Yes, partial and full scholarships available

Minimum requirements for entry
Bachelor's degree and proof of English language

Language
English

Application procedure
The following documents are required:
- application form
- copy of degree certificate/college transcripts
- digital design portfolio
- your curriculum vitae
- statement of purpose
- letters of recommendation
- a copy of your passport
- proof of language (if applicable), with a TOEFL score of 85 or IELTS of 6.5.
  Some candidates may be contacted for interview. International applicants are not required to have an in-person interview. Successful candidates will be informed by email.

Application details
saic.edu/admissions/grad

Application date
By 15 January

Graduation rate
100%

Job placement rate
High

Memberships/affiliations
Fashion Resource Center, Material Connexion, Stoll Knitwear Database, Video Data Bank and Roger Brown Study Center.

Collaborations with
Swarovski Ltd, Base Miami/Art Basel Miami Beach, SU_7 Pop-Up Shop and Sullivan Galleries.

Facilities for students
Graduate students have designated studios within a shared studio workspace. The Fashion Resource Center maintains a unique hands-on collection of late 20th and 21st century garments and accessories representative of extreme innovation. Students have use of 3D scanners, 3D rapid prototypers and laser cutters in the workshops, as well as large format printers and full access to all Media Center technology.

City
Chicago

Country
United States

Student Work

No Way Out (2013)
By Cher Jiang

This was a project realised with cast resin and found objects.
Photo Jim Prinz Photography

Read From Me (2013)
By Misha Lee

This project incorporated cast glass and video projection.
Photo Jim Prinz Photography

Digital Print Project (2013)
By Jieru Li

This was a research and development project that resulted in the realisation of a digital print garment.
Photo Jim Prinz Photography

Too Good to be True (2012)
By Kristina Sparks

This projected displayed reclaimed house paint cans covered with images of foreclosed homes as a response to the current US housing situation.
Photo Jim Prinz Photography

Course
Fashion, Body and Garment

School
School of the Art Institute of Chicago

Untitled (2013)
By Man Yuan

This is a process piece stemming from research and development informing a larger garment collection.
Photo Jim Prinz Photography

Bubble Life (2013)
By FuFu Tsao

This thesis project incorporated warp yarn, garments and found objects.
Photo Jim Prinz Photography

Stacks (2010)
By Cheryl Pope

Still from HD video for a project addressing specific questions that extend into social, political and global conversations.
Photo Jim Prinz Photography

Ga (2013)
By Joe Leamanczyk

This project was realised with the help of: peppermint candy, candy wrappers and a rocking chair.
Photo Jim Prinz Photography

Alumna

Name Kristina Januskaite
Residence Chicago, United States
Year of birth 1978
Year of graduation 2012
Current job Lecturer

Why did you choose this school?
It's a great interdisciplinary fine art school with an encyclopaedic art museum, and Nick Cave is the principal mentor of the MDes Fashion Body and Garment programme. He is a great role model.

What was the most important thing you learned here?
Experimenting with new media and overlapping disciplines.

What was the most interesting project you did, or the most fun?
The most fun was definitely a collaboration with the Swarovski.

Was there any class that you found particularly difficult?
No. However, critiques were very intense and at the same time super informative.

What was your graduation project?
It was a complete body of work is a response to the current US housing situation and its effect on those of various social class and their perceived status. Reclaimed house paint cans were covered with foreclosed/bank-owned home images collected from various internet sites. These 'dream homes' were interrupted with abstract floral and camouflage patterns referencing wallpaper that visualised the desire, reality and 'what's at stake' of owning this type of dream home. The work sought to reveal the hidden tragedies that lay underneath the false facade and illusion created by an image of a perfect home.

What was your favourite place to hang out?
My studio.

Are you still in contact with the school?
Yes. I am currently teaching in the undergraduate fashion design programme at SAIC.

Do you have any fond memories about the city?
For me, Chicago city is one of the most beautiful cities and SAIC is perfectly located in the heart of it all: Grant Park, a variety of great public art, as well as endless shoreline of Lake Michigan with impressive and sometimes unpredictable season changes.

Any words of advice for future students?
Continue to be a student for the rest of your life!

Januskaite's project work during her master's degree included fashion knitwear with a metallic sheen.

Course
Fashion, Body and Garment

School
School of the Art Institute of Chicago

Current Students

'Fashion can be a very narrow world, but at SAIC you are encouraged to incorporate all kinds of art forms into your studio work. I have never completely been an artist or fashion designer, I've been a little bit of both. This programme really helped someone like me find a voice.'
Lindsey M Whittle
Photo Aaron M Conway

'SAIC provides a broad range of possibilities and innovation. Bold art and design styles are encouraged and cherished here.'
Fei Nei

'On this course, I hope I can develop my process of thinking and my ability to analyse, not only clothing but also artworks.'
Hao Liu

'Future students can expect a highly intensive daily life, which results in a wonderful sense of achievement.'
Man Yuan

City Life

SAIC's buildings are interwoven into the fabric of Chicago's vibrant downtown, amidst the radically diverse neighbourhoods ready to be explored and find inspiration. The city is a patchwork of more than 70 neighbourhoods, some of which are identified by ethnic heritage (Ukrainian Village, Chinatown, Little Italy), some by location (Lakeview, Wicker Park, Near South Side, Lawndale), some by whim (Bucktown's residents used to keep goats, or 'bucks', in their yards). Together, the neighbuorhoods form the heart of Chicago's astonishing diversity.

Chicagoans are proud of their world-famous institutions, which include the DuSable Museum of African-American History, the Field Museum of Natural History, the National Museum of Mexican Art, the Museum of Contemporary Art, and the Adler Planetarium. All of these are within walking distance or a short bus ride from the SAIC. There are numerous smaller reasons to love the city: a delicate tile mural over the entrance of a Loop building, a cramped blues club on the South Side, a late-night performance at a storefront theatre, or a cutting-edge gallery in Pilsen.

It would be an exhaustive task to compile a list of restaurants, bars and cafes to cover every taste or type of food represented in Chicago. There are numerous delightful spots in each neighbourhood, and all tastes and different styles of cooking are catered for.

United States

In downtown Chicago is Millennium Park, a popular destination for SAIC students in the summer.

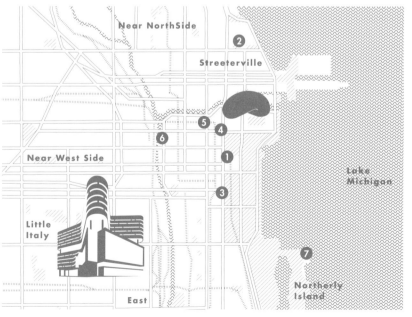

Chicago

1 SAIC
2 Museum of Contemporary Art
3 Museum of Contemporary Photography
4 Chicago Cultural Center
5 Gene Siskel Film Center
6 Lyric Opera
7 Adler Planetarium

///// Park

≈≈≈ Water

······· Railway

═══ Main road

Near NorthSide

Streeterville

Near West Side

Little Italy

East

Lake Michigan

Northerly Island

Course
Fashion, Body and Garment

School
School of the Art Institute of Chicago

City Facts

The Art Institute of Chicago
SAIC is located in the grounds of The Art Institute, which was founded in 1879. It has approx. 300,000 works of art in its permanent collection, with 30 special exhibitions and hundreds of gallery talks, lectures, performances and events taking place every year. It has one of the finest research libraries for art and architecture in the country.
artic.edu

Museum of Contemporary Art ②
This is one of the nation's largest facilities devoted to experiencing the work and ideas of living artists. The MCA documents contemporary visual culture through painting, sculpture, photography, video and film, and performance.
mcachicago.org

Museum of Contemporary Photography ③
The only mid-western museum dedicated solely to the medium of photography, it was founded in 1984 as a stimulating and innovative forum for the collection, creation and examination of contemporary image-making in its old-format camera tradition and in its expanded vocabulary of digital processes.
mocp.org

Chicago Cultural Center ④
A landmark building with two stained-glass domes, free music performances, dance and theatre events, films, lectures, art exhibitions and more.

Gene Siskel Film Center ⑤
For almost 40 years, the Film Center of the School of SAIC has presented world-class independent, international and classic films at this cinema. Renamed in honour of the late film critic, the complex has been operating in its unique, modern facilities since June 2001.
siskelfilmcenter.org

Lyric Opera ⑥
Lyric Opera of Chicago, founded in 1954, is renowned internationally for its artistic excellence and visually spectacular productions.
lyricopera.org

Adler Planetarium ⑦
Adler is America's first planetarium with a full programme of immersive sky shows and educational events regularly held in its three full-sized theatres.
adlerplanetarium.org

Fashion Resource Center
SAIC's Fashion Resources Center, a collection of late 20th and 21st century designer garments and accessories representative of extreme innovation plus videos of runway presentations and vintage magazines from the 1890's to present.

How to get around
As in many large cities, there are several options to get you around town. Having a car in Chicago can be useful at times, but it often takes special consideration because of limited parking downtown and in popular neighborhoods. Where parking garages and metered parking are available, the costs can add up quickly. Having a car is often unnecessary, and many Chicagoans don't own a car.

Public transportation via the elevated train/subway ('the L') or buses is often the most cost-effective and convenient option, especially if you are an SAIC student with a Chicago Transit Authority U-Pass.

Cycling is also an option – if you have a bike, you can take advantage of the wealth of cycle trails that runs along Lake Michigan from Hollywood Avenue on the North Side to 71st Street on the South Side.

Arranging housing
Average

Housing support by school
Yes

Cost of room in the city
Various

Cost of campus housing
Various

City
Chicago

Country
United States

Tama
Art
University

The textile building is a prominent feature of TAU's vast campus in Hachioji.

A gallery displaying student work greets visitors to the textile building.

Tama Art University (TAU)
Department of Product and
Textile Design
2-1723 Yarimizu
192-0394 Hachioji, Tokyo
Japan

T +81 (0)42 679 5625
tx@tamabi.ac.jp
tamabi.ac.jp/tx

Introduction

'We cultivate students' creativity and knowledge to think about the role of textile design for the society'

Kyoko Hashimoto, head of the textile design course

When was the school founded?
The history of our school dates back to 1935, when Tama Imperial Art School was founded in Tokyo. It changed its name to Tama Art University (TAU) in 1953. The Graduate School of TAU was inaugurated in 1964 as the first non-state funded art university in Japan to offer a master's degree course.

What is studying at this school all about?
Freedom and will is the ideology of TAU. Freedom is a matter of the greatest significance, not least because without it there can be no art. Will creates freedom, and freedom fosters will. This dialectic forms a strong current underlying the activities of TAU. The world today is in the midst of a seemingly never-ending cycle of intolerance, hatred and violence, but perhaps the human desire to create works of art can offer a solution. As its contribution to the pursuit of international peace and understanding, TAU is fully committed to fostering the creative spirit.

What kind of teaching method is applied?
We find it important to incorporate the teaching of traditional textile design techniques, as well as state-of-the-art textile technology – those of which are deeply rooted in the Japanese textile industry. Thus, we carry out two types of projects: one is with a textile association at a local level in society,

and another is a global project called Day-See Program that provides sustainable design toward developing countries, such as Laos.

Why should students choose this particular school?
We do not only teach printing, weaving and dress-making techniques but we also cultivate students' creativity and knowledge to think about the role of textile design for the society.

What opportunities do students have on your course?
Master's degree candidates have varied opportunities to carry out projects, have discussions and study specific topics with students from various fields, such as other design course and fine arts.

What is the most important skill to master for a textile designer?
Not to only gain textile-related skills but also to explore oneself and to solve a social issue by designing textiles.

What career paths do your graduates take?
Our former textile students mostly end up fashion, textile, graphic and industrial designers, artists or museum curators, as well as scholars at university faculties.

City
Tokyo

Country
Japan

237

Programme

The MFA Textile Design programme centres on the student's own research theme, which can be related to any field of textile design. The course is designed to equip students with a broad perspective and rich sensitivity in the fields of art and design that involve textiles. Fabric is part of our everyday lives. It continues to evolve today through the work of human hands and state-of-the-art technology. Teaching focuses not only on designing textile products but also creating works of art.

The programme offers students hands-on learning opportunities in the latest textile technologies as well as in traditional techniques. Guided by the key concepts of materials, expression and design, students produce textile works by 'thinking with their hands' and giving form to their original creative ideas.

While working on their themed projects, students are encouraged to join the 'Day-See Program', a collaboration with the Japanese International Cooperative Association and local corporations in order to develop textiles and other products in local communities.

By the time students finish the course, they will be independent in terms of establishing their own theories about textile design and art. They will also have gained skills in compiling information to verify their theories and to present their ideas and textile products or art to the public in a convincing way.

Facilities include a weaving lab which has about 90 looms, allowing students to explore various techniques including jacquard and computer weaving.

A printing lab boasts a digital garment-printing machine, full-length heated print tables, and heat presses.

Programme
Textile Design

Leads to
Master of Fine Arts

Structure
The 2-year, full-time course is split into modules (30 credits per year) and includes areas of study such as surface design, textiles and the environment, textile art production, traditional Japanese dyeing, textile materials and artistic expression in the textile arts. Students work on themed projects and plan research methods, while developing their theories and creative designs through experimentation, culminating in a final textile product or artwork. In the second year, students modify and further develop their theories. This results in a thesis and a final project that verifies the thesis.

Head of programme
Kyoko Hashimoto

Mentors and lecturers
Kyoko Hashimoto, Mayumi Higaki, Yasuko Iyanaga, Koh Kashiwagi, Yuka Kawai, Tadashi Takahashi and Yuko Fukatsu.

Notable alumni
Unknown

Course
Textile Design

School
Tama Art University

School Facts

Duration of study
2 years

Full time
Yes (30 hours a week)

Part time
No

Female students
87%

Male students
13%

Local students
96%

Students from abroad
4%

Yearly enrolment
5–10

Tuition fee
JPY 1,709,000 per year (approx. EUR 13,315)

Funding/scholarships
Yes

Minimum requirements for entry
Bachelor's degree

Language
Japanese and English (courses are in Japanese, tutorials can be in English)

Application procedure
Applications must be submitted by post with the following documents:
- a completed application form
- copy of your degree certificate
- three recent photographs
- official transcript of grades from the last school you attended
- proof of Japanese language knowledge (if applicable)
- a copy of a residence card
- a copy of your passport
- portfolio submission, including pencil drawing, colour composition and essay in Japanese
- a receipt for payment of entrance exam fee: JPY 35,000 (approx. EUR 275).
  Based on these documents, and the results of the entrance exam, candidates may be invited for an interview with the programme director. Successful applicants will be informed by email.

Application details
tamabi.ac.jp/english/admission/

Application date
Before 27 September

Graduation rate
100%

Job placement rate
100%

Memberships/affiliates
Design for Social Innovation Toward Sustainability, International Council of Societies of Industrial Design, Hachioji Textile Industrial Association and Japanese International Cooperative Association.

Collaborations with
Aalto University (Finland), Central Academy of Fine Arts (China), Berlin University (Germany), Kyoto University (Tokyo), Seoul National University and Hongik University (Korea), National Institute of Design (India), Malmo University (Sweden), Taipei National University of Arts (Taiwan), Silpakorn University (Thailand), Royal College of Art (United Kingdom) and Art Center College of Design (United States), as well as Dole Japan, Suzuki Motor Corporation, Tokyo Metropolitan Industrial Technology Research Institute and Unido.

Facilities for students
Weaving lab with 90 looms including Jacquard and computerised machines, plus spinning, yarn-twisting, recycling and fibre-opening machines; sewing and knitting machines; digital garment-printing machine, full-length heated print tables, and heat presses; dyeing, steaming and washing facilities; and paper making facilities.

City
Tokyo

Country
Japan

Student Work

Textiles for Interactive Tactile Experiences (2012)
By Saori Takashio

Banana Textile Project (2009)
By Hiroko Takano

This 'textile experience' does not limit itself to a single use. You can get into the tube, turn it into a cushion by stuffing it, or use as material to make other things. The rich tactile quality and versatility are intended to make you think about the relationship between yourself and your surroundings, hopefully inspiring your subconscious and creativity in life.
Photo Tama Art University

A use for the banana fibres left behind after harvesting the fruit, this fabric, called Sky, is used here for a simple wrap-around skirt. Not only are banana textiles sustainable, they also provide an opportunity for banana-producing countries to make clothing and other textile products locally.
Photo Tama Art University

Textiles for Interactive Tactile Experiences (201
By Yuri Himuro

This jacquard woven fabric contains a 'happy surprise' – cutting the green threads uncovers animals concealed beneath the yarn. This feature means that the fabric pattern is variable and customisable.
Photo Kazuya Shioi

Telling a Story Through Tapestry (2012)
By Miki Kihara

This tapestry depicts the act of crying – the greatest useless function of the human body and one with an unfathomable mystery to it. In this work, various things contained in the tears suggest the repressed ideas often behind the act of crying.
Photo Tama Art University

Clothes Soaked into a Piece of Cloth (2011)
By Tomoko Endo

This project explores the reasons why we dye to shape the form of our clothing. It is also an approach to human existence: people will continue to create, since creating expresses the wonder and mystery of being alive.
Photo Tomoko Endo

Japanese Visual Culture (2010)
By Christopher Zoellner Pinto

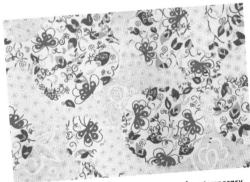

These textile patterns are visual evocations of contemporary Japan, as seen from an outsider's point of view, referencing traditional Japanese culture. A hybrid of peacock and demon, Taniuba, the entity which inspired the patterns along with Noh masks and other cultural manifestations, is the witch-goddess of consumption. The resulting fabrics are like visual poems for clothes and accessories.
Photo Ryan Bruss

City
Tokyo

Country
Japan

241

Alumna

Name Alisa Benfey
Residence Brooklyn, United States
Year of birth 1982
Year of graduation 2010
Current job Textile and surface designer at Designtex, owner of IROCOH
Websites irocoh.com, alisabenfey.com

Why did you choose this school?

I grew up in Tokyo, but I moved to the United States for high school and college. I was working at an environmental graphics design firm for a couple of years after graduating from my undergraduate degree, and I decided I wanted to focus on materials and pattern. I chose to study textile design in Japan because of the rich history of textile making there. I focused on TAU as my first choice because of the diverse interests and broad focus of the professors' theory and practice, and the amazing 10-m textile printing tables and the well-equipped weaving facility.

What was the most important thing you learned here?

I learned that working by hand is still the most important practice when you design. Even if it's something that ends up in digital format, it is important to practice working with your hands, especially for textile patterns. Sometimes digital vector drawings are too strong and give a mechanical appearance for the soft surface of textiles.

What are you doing now?

I am the main designer in a New York studio for all the digital printing projects, which include wall coverings wall coverings, upholstery and textiles. It is very exciting and educational to work at Designtex, because everyone here is very talented, resourceful and experienced. I also have my own start-up textile brand which I created during my study at TAU. I work in my spare time to create one-of-a-kind hand-printed textile products.

How did the school prepare you for what you are doing now?

I got to work on collaboration project with Nike. Fifteen students were invited to research and solve current problems of sports gear and propose new designs for Nike. It was like a true real-life working experience as a product designer.

What was your graduation project?

My thesis was 'Timeless Design in Printed Textiles', where I investigated the reasons some textile designs withstand the test of time. I designed patterns and created printed textiles in the spirit of timeless design, based on what I learned in my research.

How was the transition from graduation to working life?

I stayed in Tokyo for a few months after graduating but eventually I had a strong feeling about moving to New York to explore opportunities. Now I have a great network in the design world, and I am always excited and grateful for all the projects I'm asked to do.

Any words of advice for future students at TAU?

I recommend meeting with professors and fellow students as much as you can to discuss what you are working on. Use the library, printing and weaving facility to the max. You don't get that kind of space anywhere else!

For Benfey's graduation project, she designed colourful patterns and screen-printed printed textiles in the spirit of 'timeless design'.

Course
Textile Design

School
Tama Art University

Current Students

'I chose this school because I already knew that the university has one of the best school environments in Japan, in terms of facilities and professors.'
Aiko Inami

'I recommend Indonomegumi, a curry restaurant near to the school. The wide variety of dishes cooked by Indian chefs are really delicious.'
Rika Nojima

'I love the silk-screen printing workshop. We can print up to 10 meters of fabric at once!'
Keiko Nitta

'I found an apartment near school. There are many apartments for students around the nearby station, and it takes about 15 minutes by bicycle to the school.'
Mei Morioke

'The teachers are specialised in various textile fields giving us access to many different viewpoints.'
Akane Nishimaki

'Through the Banana Textile Project, I learnt about an interesting material, sustainable design and global thinking.'
Atsumi Yamada

'There are students from different majors in some of the classes, and exchanging ideas with them can be inspirational.'
Reina Nakazawa

City
Tokyo

Country
Japan

City Life

The 153,000-m² campus is located in Hachioji, a city with some 550,000 residents and some 9000 registered foreigners living in the city. Hachioji is the eighth largest city in the Greater Tokyo Area. Located about 45 km west, it is an hour's train ride from Tokyo. The city is a university town with 21 university campuses resulting in a young, vibrant environment. The city is also a residential area for people commuting to central Tokyo with all the amenities needed for daily life available, such as fresh groceries, hospitals, etc. Students are encouraged to go and see exhibitions, new shops, new venues, trends and general happenings in the central Tokyo area.

Hachioji is deeply rooted in Japanese textile culture. The area has long been involved in silk production, and a notable textile called *Tama-ori* originates from here.

Formerly, the city was famous for its production of kimono fabrics and for silk ties. Since the 1980s, various textile studios here have contributed to creating innovative fabrics for world-leading fashion designers, such as Issey Miyake.

The city is surrounded by nature with mountains on three sides. There is easy access to Takao mountain and Okutama gorge. Students can therefore enjoy both country life and city life.

Japan

Leading architect Ito Toyo's library for Tama Art University is an iconic new landmark for Hachioji.

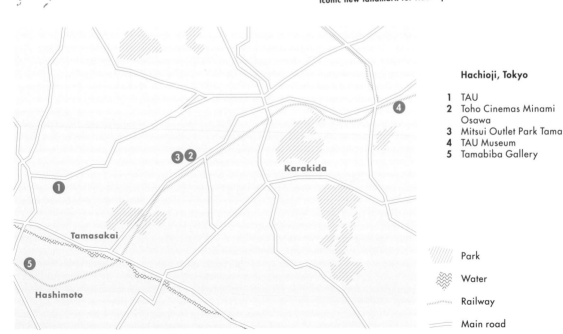

Hachioji, Tokyo

1 TAU
2 Toho Cinemas Minami Osawa
3 Mitsui Outlet Park Tama
4 TAU Museum
5 Tamabiba Gallery

Karakida

Tamasakai

Hashimoto

///// Park

≈≈≈ Water

········· Railway

— Main road

Course
Textile Design

School
Tama Art University

City Facts

See more Tokyo City Facts on p. 45

Toho Cinemas Minami Osawa ②
The cinema complex adjacent to Minami Osawa station on Keio line has nine screens, accommodating some 1900 seats with some screens up to 5.8 x 13.6 m in size.
tohotheater.jp

Mitsui Outlet Park Tama ③
Factory outlet of various brands, from Beams and United Arrows to international brands like J Ferry, with up to 80 per cent deducted from the retail price.
31op.com/english/index.html#tama

Tama Art University Museum ④
The Museum run by Tama Art University, aims to present to the public both historical works of art and contemporary art from various disciplines through exhibitions, workshops and seminars, as well as serving as a platform where the university researchers can present their findings.
tamabi.ac.jp/museum

Tamabiba Gallery ⑤
Literally meaning a place for Tamabi (Tama Art University), this cafe gallery sits in the neighbourhood supermarket. Run by university students and the supermarket, it is a place for Tama Art University students to show their research activity to the surrounding community by showing their work outside the university environment.

The Silk Roads Museum
A 10-minute walk from TAU, this museum showcases the fascinating history of the silk industry in Hachioji, exploring the area's rich traditional textile culture and trade routes (the silk roads).

Hachioji Textile Industry Association
In 1900, the HTIA was established to unite workers in weaving, spinning and dyeing studios in Hachioji. The association supports textile-related studios and also has its own brand, Mulberry City, as well as successfully promoting the traditional fabrics of Hachioji, such as Tama-ori.
hachioji-orimono.jp

Sanrio Puroland
In 1990, the Sanrio Company established an indoor theme park in Tama, Tokyo, with world-famous cartoon characters including the iconic Hello Kitty, My Melody, Cinnamoroll, Jewelpet and many others.
puroland.jp

Art Laboratory Hashimoto
The art laboratory is organised and curated with TAU and other universities in order to develop local neighbourhood communities through art and design.

Mount Takao
Mount Takao is one of the natural areas of central Tokyo and a national park with beautiful scenery, a temple and a hiking trail.

How to get around
Narita Airport (the new Tokyo International Airport), located 140 km east of Hachioji, is the easiest international gateway to the city. You can either use the Chuo Line – which takes just over 2 hours to the city – or you can take the limousine bus – which runs six times a day and takes 3 hours.
Public transportation within the city is well organised. There are plenty of bus services throughout the city and students living close to the station either take the bus or ride a bicycle to school.

Arranging housing
Average

Housing support by school
No

Cost of room in the city
JPY 50,000 per month (approx. EUR 515)

Cost of campus housing
n/a

City
Tokyo

Country
Japan

245

The
Hong Kong
Polytechnic
University

The school's main entrance on Cheong Wan Road.

Hong Kong Polytechnic University is located in Hung Hom, Kowloon.

The Hong Kong Polytechnic University, Institute of Textiles & Clothing
Room QT715, Q Core, 7/F
Hung Ham, Kowloon
Hong Kong

T +852 (0)2766 6500
tcgeneral@polyu.edu.hk
itc.polyu.edu.hk

Course
Fashion and Textile Design

School
The Hong Kong Polytechnic University

Introduction

'We want to develop graduates with design skills who can propose solutions to industry issues'

Joe Au, programme leader

When was the school founded and what is its mission?
The Hong Kong Polytechnic University first established the Institute of Textiles & Clothing in December 1977. Formerly, it was the Department of Textile Industries, founded in 1957. Its goal is to become a world-class academic department of fashion and textile education, research and knowledge transfer. Our key objectives include developing all-round graduates with vision and a global outlook, a sense of social responsibility, and critical and creative thinking ability.

What kind of teaching method is applied?
The institute has a strong team of staff with expertise in fashion and textiles design, technology and business. We teach in an integrated and multi-disciplinary manner, with an emphasis on both theory and practice. We have successfully developed all-round graduates who are highly regarded by local industries and have become a formidable force behind the economic success of the Hong Kong fashion and textile industries.

Why should students choose this school?
We offer a wide range of academic programmes covering disciplines including fashion and textile design, fashion technology, fashion retailing, fashion and textile marketing and merchandising, intimate apparel and knitwear design with technology.

These programmes are offered at levels ranging from higher certificates, bachelor's degree and master's degree programmes to doctoral degrees and in full-time and part-time learning modes.

What do students get out of your fashion/textile master's degree?
The MA Fashion and Textile Design programme began in September 2000. Ever since then, our goal has been to develop graduates with an appropriate set of professional design skills and the related knowledge required to propose solutions to contemporary industry issues.

What is the most important skill to master for a fashion designer?
They should be creative individuals, able to translate their design ideas into commercial fashion and textile products which can fulfil the market's wants and needs.

In what kind of jobs do your former students mostly end up?
As fashion designers (menswear and womenswear), knitwear designers, textile designers, bodywear designers or fashion educators.

City
Hong Kong

Country
Hong Kong

247

Programme

This programme aims to provide designers with an in-depth understanding of global fashion trends and requirements. It places the emphasis on design conceptualisation, independent research, creative application and artistic expression, and provides a design-focused environment for students to follow their chosen path to generate a range of design-oriented, decision-making skills that are required in the fashion industry.

Four major subject areas are available: fashion, knitwear and textile design, as well as bodywear. Students develop skills that underpin their existing design and industry knowledge, and learn to appreciate the demands placed on designers in this dynamic industry. In-depth personal projects allow students to explore issues of design practice, technology and theory. The programme fosters a broad range of critical thinking and creative awareness skills. When combined, these elements provide the basis for making our graduates highly sought-after design professionals.

Hard at work in the fashion design studio.

The campus has the advantage of being centrally located, so there's always a lively buzz around the school.

Programme
Fashion and Textile Design

Leads to
Master of Arts

Structure
The 1-year full-time programme is divided into core subject areas. Students complete four core subjects (evolution of design trends, design concepts, visual design communication, and fashion technology) in semester 1; three subjects (design collection preparation, innovative strategy for the fashion industry, and fashion business) in semester 2; and one subject (personal project) in the summer term. The personal project consists of a written report, design portfolio and design collection, developed in one of the four major subject areas (fashion design, knitwear design, textile design, or bodywear design), with advice from subject specialists. The programme culminates in a final assessment and presentation.

Head of programme
Joe Au

Mentors and lecturers
Chupo Ho

Notable alumni
Chen Dao

School Facts

Duration of study
1 year

Full time
Yes (40 hours a week)

Part time
No

Female students
80%

Male students
20%

Local students
40%

Students from abroad
60%

Yearly enrolment
26

Tuition fee
- HKD 99,000 per year for local students (approx. EUR 9500)
- HKD 110,100 per year for non-local students (approx. EUR 10,600)

Funding/scholarships
No

Minimum requirements for entry
Bachelor's degree or equivalent in fashion or textiles design

Language
English

Application procedure
Admission is by an online application with the following:
- a completed application form
- a curriculum vitae
- a statement of purpose
- a portfolio of projects
- a copy of your BA degree certificate
- a copy of your IELTS/TOEFL/CET language certificate or recognised equivalent certificate (if appropriate).

Shortlisted candidates are invited to an interview conducted in English, for which candidates are expected to bring a selection of their design work for discussion. Candidates must convince the committee of their creative, intellectual and reasoning skills required to complete the programme.

Application details
polyu.edu.hk/study

Application date
By end of October

Graduation rate
100%

Job placement rate
Unknown

Memberships/affiliations
The Textile Institute

Collaborations with
Fashion Institute of Technology (United States) and Institut Francais de la Mode (France).

Facilities for students
Fashion & Textiles Resource Centre, 4D Fashion Digital Communication Theatre, Fashion Design Studio, multimedia centre and photographic studio, along with various teaching and research laboratories.

City
Hong Kong

Country
Hong Kong

Student Work

Show Your Bones (2012)
By Eno Fang

Graduate project which included a tailored fashion collection.

Humanoid (2012)
By Justin Tam

This project included printed textiles in a contemporary fashion collection.

ooops (2012)
By Kenax Leung

This project was inspired by the artworks of the installation artist Felix Schramm and his works which exhibited destroyed structures. The collection is a fall/winter contemporary fashion collection which incorporates the experimentation of shape and form using different kinds of materials, to develop a flat construction by the silhouette and both constructive and decorative fasteners and trimmings.

Son of the Unknown (2013)
By Erin Jin

The concept was based around 'thinking like a baby' – from a brand new perspective – in order to open creativity, enhance sensibility and spark new ideas. The project aimed to break the conventional mode of thinking, which resulted in a collection inspired by the curiosity of the unknown universe. Specifically, inspired by some natural phenomena, such as black holes and galaxies.

Course
Fashion and Textile Design

School
The Hong Kong Polytechnic University

Indian in the Jungle (2013)
By Joyce Liu

This collection is inspired by mysterious and uncanny ancient Indian art and land-based spiritual belief. The collection incorporates colours and prints that are based on jungle elements which have an intrinsic connection with the Native American.

Ben Yuan (2012)
By Joya Shen

A fashion collection which included bright, colour blocks in different materialities.

Four-Dimensional Fashion (2012)
By Connie Wu

This graduate project resulted in a womenswear fashion collection which incorporated contemporary forms.

Backstreet Girls (2012)
By Heidi Wu

A modern and street-wise womenswear collection included splashes of colour in the printed textiles incorporated into the designs.

Alumnus

Name Chen Dao
Residence Hong Kong
Year of birth 1977
Year of graduation 2008
Current job Fashion designer, stylist, writer, lecturer, clown, actor
Website chendao.com

'40 under 40' by *Perspective* and in 2013 I was amongst Hong Kong's top ten designers.

How did the school prepare you for what you do now?
It prepared me for making the most of chances and opportunities.

Any words of advice for future students?
Life is short, live your dream. And go travel, getting lost will help you find yourself!

Why did you choose this school?
It is a very stylish school and the location is in the midst of all the high-fashion brands. Everyone speaks fashion, walks in fashion and dresses stylishly there. The school is fashion.

Are you still in contact with the school?
Yes, I have tea with the professors, I go to shows there and I give talks.

What was the most important thing you learned at this school?
That it's vital to share your passion.

What are you doing now?
I'm preparing my 10th anniversary project, Croxx. It's an exciting crossover fashion collaboration project, with two key focuses – I will work with 10 up-and-coming artists from different fields to create 10 exaggerated fashion art-pieces. Also, I will design cross-dressing styling concepts for a photo exhibition.

What was your graduation project?
It was called Ultramania, it was inspired by Ultraman, the Japanese comic-book hero.

Was the transition from graduation to working life a smooth one?
Yes, I was lucky. In 2003, I opened my own studio and retail store, and the following year I was named one of the New Future Talents by *i-D* magazine. In 2008, I was named one of the

Since graduating, Chen Dao has been named one of Hong Kong's top designers.

Course
Fashion and Textile Design

School
The Hong Kong Polytechnic University

Current Students

'I think the most valuable aspect is that the design process – from the initial concept to making the actual garments – is all decided by myself. Teachers just give us some guidance and suggestions.'
Tinna Cai

'I remember our programme leader Dr Joe Au said 'Welcome to the hell' the first time he met us in the design studio, and later we began to understand what it really meant! During the year, there are so many projects with tight deadlines. Only 12 students from the course can get the chance to showcase their final collection during Hong Kong Fashion Week, so the competition is fierce.'
Joyce Liu

I chose this school because it is the most professional fashion school in Asia. It has so many fantastic resources, like great professors, good quality of teaching, excellent commercial activities, etc. I aim to improve my design skills and develop a strong sense of fashion trends.
Amy Jiang

'In my spare time, I like to hang out on the small islands that are far away from the central city. There, I can eat delicious sea food and drinking natural juices, whilst admiring the beautiful scenery.'
Yelena Wang

City Life

Hong Kong is a special administrative region of the People's Republic of China. It is situated on China's south coast, enclosed by the Pearl River Delta and South China Sea. Hong Kong is frequently described as a place where East meets West reflecting the country's mix of Chinese roots and influences from its time as a British colony.

There are a number of art and cultural museums in Hong Kong. The government supports cultural institutions such as the Hong Kong Heritage Museum, the Hong Kong Museum of Art, the Hong Kong Academy for Performing Arts, and the Hong Kong Philharmonic Orchestra. The government's Leisure and Cultural Services Department subsidises and sponsors international performers to visit in Hong Kong.

All these activities stimulate creative thinking and impact design studies.

The Hong Kong Polytechnic University (PolyU) is strategically located in Hung Hom, Kowloon, on a 9.34-hectare site adjacent to the Cross Harbour Tunnel. As it is located at the centre of the city, PolyU is easily accessible by various means of public transport. With the motto, 'To learn and to apply, for the benefit of mankind', PolyU's vision is be a leading university that excels in professional education, applied research and partnership for the betterment of Hong Kong, the nation and the world.

Hong Kong is justly famous for its spectacular and vertiginous view

Hong Kong

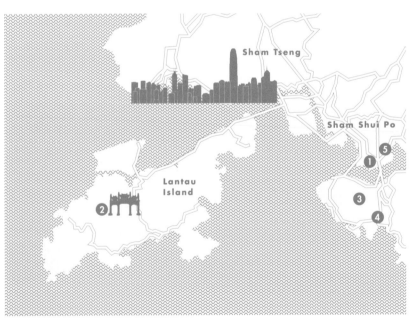

Hong Kong

1 Hong Kong Polytechnic University
2 Ngong Ping 360
3 The Peak
4 Ocean Park Hong Kong
5 Tsim Sha Tsui Promenade

Sham Tseng

Sham Shui Po

Lantau Island

Park

Water

Main road

Course
Fashion and Textile Design

School
The Hong Kong Polytechnic University

City Facts

Ngong Ping 360 ②
The highest point of Hong Kong Island. The view from the top view makes it one of the most popular attractions in Hong Kong.
thepeak.com.hk

The Peak ③
The highest point of Hong Kong Island. The view from the top view makes it one of the most popular attractions in Hong Kong.
thepeak.com.hk

Ocean Park Hong Kong ④
A popular marine-life theme park featuring animal exhibits, thrill rides and shows.
oceanpark.com.hk

International Arts Carnival
The International Arts Carnival is held during the summer months to provide children, young people and their families with cultural diversions during the summer holiday. The performances include dance, musical theatre, acrobatics and puppet shows.

Tsim Sha Tsui Promenade ⑤
Starting at the colonial-era Clock Tower and stretching all the way to Hung Hom, a stroll along the Tsim Sha Tsui Promenade takes you past the Hong Kong Cultural Centre, the Hong Kong Space Museum, the Hong Kong Museum of Art and Avenue of Stars. But like most of the love birds and shutterbugs on the promenade, your gaze will be drawn south to the dramatic topographical and architectural spectacle that is the Hong Kong Island skyline towering over the busy waters of Victoria Harbour.

Hong Kong Arts Festival
The Hong Kong International Film Festival is one of Asia's most reputable platforms for film makers, film professionals and film goers to launch new works and view fresh features.
hk.artsfestival.org

International Arts Carnival
The International Arts Carnival is held during the summer months to provide children, young people and their families with cultural diversions during the summer holiday. The performances include dance, musical theatre, acrobatics and puppet shows.

How to get around
Students generally use, trains and buses to get around. To reach the campus by metro (MTR), head for Hung Hom Station on the East Rail Line, then take the footbridge at Exit A1 to reach the main campus (mtr.com.hk).
To reach the campus by bus, head for the Cross Harbour Tunnel and get off at the stop at the entrance/exit of the tunnel on the Kowloon side (kmb.hk, wstbus.com.hk, nwstbus.com.hk). Alternatively, take a taxi to the entrance on Cheong Wan Road.

Arranging housing
Difficult

Housing support by school
No

Cost of room in the city
HKD 6000 per month (approx. EUR 600)

Cost of campus housing
HKD 3600 per month (approx. EUR 360)

The Swedish School of Textiles University of Borås

The school has just moved into the new, dedicated Textile Fashion Center in Borås.

Textilhögskolans,
Högskolan i Borås
Skaraborgsvägen 3
501 90 Borås
Sweden

T +46 (0)33 435 4170
ths@hb.se
hb.se/ths

Facilities, like those in the knitting lab, are second to none.

Introduction

'What sets us apart from other textile schools is our access to extraordinary technology'

Lars Hedegård, director of studies

When was the school founded?
The Swedish School of Textiles was established in 1866 as a weaving school. In 1936, the Textile Institute was founded, which in 1986 turned into one of the departments of the University of Borås.

How has it changed over the years?
In 2008, we received funding from the Swedish research institute Vinnova for work in smart textiles. In 2010, we started a general research degree plus an artistic research degree in textiles and fashion.

What is studying at this school all about?
What sets us apart from other textile schools is our access to extraordinary technology with our specially equipped labs, workshops, studios, sewing rooms and computer facilities. We are unique in the fact that all of our programmes are within the field of textiles and fashion and are housed under one roof.

Why should students choose this school?
We are a strong centre for textile education and research, with programmes of fashion and textile management and engineering in the same building, with good connections to the Swedish – and international – fashion and textile industry.

What can students expext from your master's programme?
It combines individually planned studies in four major design projects with common courses in design methodology and artistic development, as well as joint design seminars that run parallel to other courses throughout the entire course of study. The individually planned study plan is based on the student's application project which also directs in which textile techniques the student should deepen their skills. Since the programme has a strong focus on experimental work, students should demonstrate and further develop their three-dimensional artistic skills.

What is the most important thing for students to learn during this course?
To not only have their own artistic expression and motives, but to be also able to develop the field through exploratory work.

What jobs do your students go on to?
They work within the fashion and textile industries in Sweden, Europe and worldwide.

Programme

The programme has a strong focus on experimental design and students are given the chance to explore and develop throughout their studies. Through design work, the students' individual projects are continuously and progressively defined, developed and discussed in all the project courses of the programme, and finalised in their degree work. Examples of students'

Students hard at work in the sewing lab.

design projects include demonstrating new ways of constructing form and expression, identifying an ideological direction, exploring design methods or introducing new expressive possibilities in materials and techniques. Students reflect critically on their way of working, articulating their motives and discussing their results from a professional and experimental perspective, in their design work and in words.

There is the option to either specialise in fashion design or in textile design. Both tracks deepen the students' knowledge of textile techniques and materials. Courses are offered based on the students' prior textile background or specialisation. The school offers ateliers and has a significant knitting and weaving machine park with skilled technicians on hand to help. In addition, hand knitting, hand weaving and dyeing, printing and finishing facilities offer strong possibilities for both qualitative production and experimental design work. Since the school awards artistic degrees at all levels up to PhD in fashion and textile design, this programme is part of a dynamic design environment in an artistic research context.

Students can experiment with a wide range of equipment.

Programme
Fashion and Textile Design

Leads to
Master of Arts

Structure
The 2-year full-time course equates to an educational programme of 120 credits, split equally over the two years. The master programme combines individually-planned studies throughout four major design projects with common courses in design methodology and artistic development, as well as joint design seminars that run parallel to other courses throughout the entire course of study. The teaching methodology is strongly focused on tutoring, seminars and workshops, with all students assigned a main tutor.

Head of programme
Hanna Landin

Mentors and lecturers
Delia Dumitrescu, Lars Hallnäs, Anna Persson, Clemens Thornquist, Linda Worbin and Margareta Zetterblom.

Notable alumni
Unknown

Course
Fashion and Textile Design

School
The Swedish School of Textiles University of Borås

School Facts

Duration of study
2 years

Full time
Yes (40 hours a week)

Part time
No

Female students
85%

Male students
15%

Local students
40–60%

Students from abroad
40–60%

Yearly enrolment
15

Tuition fee
- Free for EU citizens
- SEK 270,000 per year
  for non-EU citizens (approx.
  EUR 31,280)

Funding/scholarships
Yes

Minimum requirements for entry
Bachelor's degree in design or equivalent

Language
English

Application procedure
Your application should include the following:
- your personal and contact details
- your curriculum vitae
- portfolio
- application project (textile or fashion design) with a description of the issues you wish to focus on in the frame of the design project courses of the programme.
A number of applicants will be called to interview, where the application is discussed with regard to artistic qualities in the portfolio and the direction of the application project.

Application details
www.hb.se/ths/masterdesign/apply

Application date
Before 15 January

Graduation rate
90%

Job placement rate
High

Memberships/affiliations
n/a

Collaborations with
n/a

Facilities for students
Various ateliers for students, a knitting and weaving machine park with skilled technicians, plus state-of-the-art hand weaving and dyeing, printing and finishing facilities.

City
Borås

Country
Sweden

Student Work

Living With Him (2012)
By Rapeeparn Kitnichee

This work aims to transform Andy Warhol's life into a design process for making textiles. A set of tablecloths and table runners shows the process of repetition. These textiles possess a certain functionality that invites people to get to know them, and Warhol.
Photo Jan Berg

Your Balance (2012)
By Barbro Scholz

What could be the role of textile user-interfaces in the digital age? This interactive, textile jewellery, inspired by insects, is a critical design project that questions the expectation of efficient time-use and our passive acceptance of that in our daily life. Are we like worker bees, labouring for the hive?
Photo Jan Berg

Fraction (2013)
By Karin Schneider

An investigation of the principles of functional design and its expressive potential deals with the interaction between the body, the worn garment and the space around it.
Photo Karin Schneider and Daniel Walenius

Triptych (2011)
By Sarah Torkelsson

An experimental fashion collection exploring how rhythm and transformation of silhouettes could create movement in between garments.
Photo Karin Schneider and Daniel Walenius

Course
Fashion and Textile Design

School
The Swedish School of Textiles University of Borås

A Soundscape Parade (2013)
By Abril Vergara Lozano

A textile study on the sounds of clothes explores fashion as a performative art. New ways are found to express the sounds of clothing through the study of surface design using non-traditional materials and knits to exploit their sonic possibilities.
Photo Abril Vergara Lozano

Unfolded (2013)
By Emelie Johansson

The aim of the project, a small collection of six looks, was to explore materiality as the origin of form, through the technique of pleating, in order to find new ways of constructing form and expressions.
Photo Emelie Johansson

Ambiguous and Unexpected (2013)
By Maiko Tanaka

The creation of aesthetic expressions through hand weaving is explored with the aim of evoking certain feelings by focusing on the tactility of the textile.
Photo Jan Berg

X (2013)
By Johan Nordberg

An examination of fundamental structures and construction principles in dress. The work aims to explore the functional and expressive potential of a cross-disciplinary approach to material from a fashion perspective.
Photo Johan Nordberg

Alumna

Name Anna Lidström
Residence Borås, Sweden
Year of birth 1983
Year of graduation 2011
Current job CEO of Another Studio
Website anotherstudio.se

Why did you choose this school?
Because of its creative environment, high level of artistic expression, the technical facilities, international contacts and its reputation.

What did you learn there?
A lot! It gave me contacts in fashion and helped me develop as a designer and artist. I also learned a lot in terms of different perspectives, analysis, critical thinking and the ability to turn and twist, whilst also giving me the skills to discuss form, composition and concepts.

What did you go on to do?
I founded my company Another Studio. I work as a consultant, designer and stylist with clients in advertising, fashion and home furnishings industry, organising art exhibitions, giving lectures, teaching, etc.I also published a book with my sister on how to rethink and rework your wardrobe, and I'm working on a Re:design project making upholstery fabrics from textile industrial waste.

How did the school prepare you for what you are doing now?
In many ways... The high pace prepares you for the deadline-driven fashion industry. The design methodology is advanced and you are given a wide range of tools and methods for designing, communicating and 'framing' your work. It is also a great preparation on how to work in both a commercial and artistic context. The projects I worked on were related to how I work as a freelance designer today.

Was the transition from graduation to working life a smooth one?
Yes, because of the great contacts I made at the school, I have been able to get interesting assignments. There is also an organisation here in Borås which supports small fashion companies and freelance designers.

Are you still in contact with the school?
Yes. I supervise BA fashion students there more or less every semester.

Any words of advice for future students at the college?
Work hard and experiment as much as you want. At the same time, think of who you are and what you like to do and don't be afraid to specialise. Then do as much research as you can. Use your fellow students as an audience and discuss your work with them. Do internships at different companies during your education. That helps you to understand how and where you want to work and in which context you want to be. That gives you more ideas on how to best use your time in school.

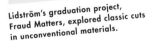

Lidström's graduation project, Fraud Matters, explored classic cuts in unconventional materials.

Course
Fashion and Textile Design

School
The Swedish School of Textiles University of Borås

Current Students

'I chose this school mostly for its incredible facilities: it has a huge variety of machines for making textiles, manually and industrially.'
Jo-Anne Kowalski

'The opportunities in the labs – combined with the technical support – are amazing, plus there's a strong focus on the design process.'
Karin Schneider

'Borås is quite a small city, so you can go anywhere by bike, and it's easy to take the bus to Gothenburg, which is Sweden's second biggest city.'
Nilla Berko

'The course is built on your own definition of your individual design programme, so you must be truly motivated and willing to challenge yourself.'
Emelie Johansson

'One thing I really like about Borås is that it is surrounded by beautiful forests. There is always a perfect spot for relaxtion.'
Daniel Bendzovski

'My advice for future students is to be open to new input and perspectives, while daring to follow your own idea and instincts.'
Ida Klamborn

'The single most valuable class for me is Design Methods, which gives useful tools for formulating your own working methods and design programme.'
Riikka Saarela

City
Borås

Country
Sweden

City Life

While Borås, in south-west Sweden, is small (population: 100,000), it's only 60 km to Gothenburg, Sweden's lively second city. Western Sweden's main international airport is within easy reach, and train and bus services link Borås with destinations all over Sweden and Europe.

Borås is sometimes referred to as the textile capital of Sweden. The city became the centre of Sweden's textile industry several centuries ago, and although manufacturing has now moved abroad, it remains the centre for textile design. Many leading fashion and textile companies are based in and around the city, and The Swedish School of Textiles leads the way in research and education. The city centre is lively, with plenty of shops, cafes and restaurants, all within walking distance. Borås is a multicultural city with a large immigrant community, which influences the food on offer.

Nature is also nearby – a short bus or cycle ride from the city centre takes you to forests, lakes and farmland.

Sandwalls Plats, next to the river Viskan, is located in the middle of the town with restaurants, gardens and palm trees.

Sweden

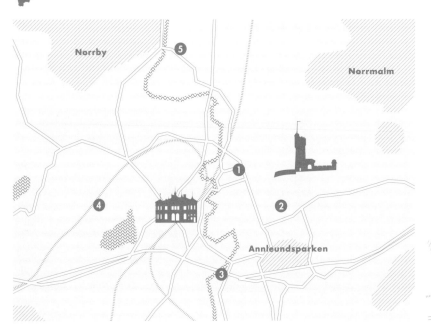

Norrby

Norrmalm

Annleundsparken

Borås

1 University of Borås
2 Borås Konstmuseum
3 Textile Museum Borås
4 Borås Museum
5 Abecita Art Museum

////// Park

〜〜 Water

········· Railway

═══ Main road

Course
Fashion and Textile Design

School
The Swedish School of Textiles University of Borås

City Facts

Borås Konstmuseum ②
The art museum in Borås is a cultural centre with a focus on recent Swedish art, as well as a theatre and library.
boras.se/textilmuseet

Textile Museum Borås ③
A fascinating collection illustrates the history of the textiles industry in Sweden and explores Swedish textile design.
boras.se/textilmuseet

Borås Museum ④
At this open air museum, visitors can explore Swedish history and past lifestyles through a collection of traditional buildings in the beautiful park setting of Ramnaparken.
boras.se/borasmuseum

Abecita Konst Museum ⑤
This art museum, to the north of the city, has good collection of 20th-century graphics and photography with a varied exhibition programme, cafe and bookshop.
abecitakonst.se

Ramnasjön lake
In the heart of tranquil Ramnaparken is Ramnasjön lake – a piece of nature, complete with resident bird colony, in the heart of the city.

Borås Zoo
Covering 40 hectares, this is reputedly Sweden's best zoo, with a large Savannah area and spacious enclosures for the animals.
boraszoo.se/en

Sommartorsdagar
This is a weekly event, which translates as Summer Thursday. On every Thursday during the summer, there is a free concert in the middle of the city.

Way Out West
This is a popular music festival which is organised annually in the neighbouring city of Gothenburg.
wayoutwest.se

Liseberg
This is the largest amusement park in Scandinavia which you can find located in Gothenburg. It is open from April to October.
liseberg.se

How to get around
It's easy to walk everywhere in Borås or take the bus – Sweden has excellent public transport. Borås has a citybus network, and good train and bus connections to other cities. A major airport (Göteborg Landvetter) is reachable in 40 minutes by bus, while frequent buses to Gothenburg transport you to Sweden's lively second city in just 50 minutes.

Arranging housing
Average

Housing support by school
No

Cost of room in the city
SEK 3000 per month (approx. EUR 350)

Cost of campus housing
n/a

City
Borås

Country
Sweden

University of Leeds School of Design

The Worshipful Company of Clothworkers has supported the school since its foundation and constructed one of the earliest buildings on the campus, the entrance to which is shown here.

University of Leeds School of Design
Leeds LS2 9JT
United Kingdom

T +44 (0)113 34 33700
texpg@leeds.ac.uk
design.leeds.ac.uk

The University of Leeds is recognised worldwide for its teaching and research activities, and has excellent library and studio resources.

Introduction

'Our work in design spans aesthetic and functional dimensions underpinned by high-quality research in the textile and fashion sectors'

Chris Carr, head of the School of Design

What is the history of the school and how has it changed?
Our school at the University of Leeds dates back to 1874, with a historical connection to the tremendous number of textile mills and related industries in the region. Recent developments have seen the school expand its well-established textile activities to also include fashion design, contemporary art practice, and design and technology management.

What approach to education is applied?
For us, teaching and research go hand-in-hand. The school works with business, public and third-sector partners to create social and economic benefit that influences developments in industry, society and culture. These activities are extremely diverse, ranging from the creation of new businesses to the formation of not-for-profit associations that address international megatrends such as sustainability.

Why should students choose this school?
The experience we have gained in technology transfer, entrepreneurship, high-profile network participation, consultancy and research collaboration continues to influence our approach to teaching and the provision of tomorrow's creative specialists, business leaders and technologists.

What is the focus of your fashion/textiles graduate programme?
Our work in design spans aesthetic and functional dimensions underpinned by high-quality research in textile and fashion sectors, including fashion enterprise in society, textile design and materials technology.

What is the most important thing for students to learn?
The unique study programme provides a rich diversity of multidisciplinary experience and reflects the vision and intellect of our school's participating designers and researchers.

In what industries do your graduates mostly end up?
The sectors are many and varied, anything from designers in large, international fashion firms to textile designers in new start-up collectives. Some continue to undertake further postgraduate research and end up as lecturers or mentors in the field.

Programme

The MA Design programme with specialism in fashion and textiles meets global design needs in relation to marketing, management and manufacture. The unique study programme provides a rich diversity of multidisciplinary experience for our students, and reflects the vision and intellect of its participating designers and researchers. An MSc Design course is also available which fosters both creativity and technological or scientific endeavour and is structured to enable students to focus on their chosen design specialism.

The programme has the flexibility and depth to respond to individual student interests, whilst fully reflecting external contextual trends – so broadening the employment prospects of master's degree-qualified professionals. The School of Design is recognised worldwide for its teaching and research activities, and has excellent library and studio resources.

This course is structured to enable students to focus on their own chosen design specialism. It comprises three related elements: a choice of taught modules that will enable you to develop a range of conceptual and practical design tools; a specialist design project chosen by you and negotiated with staff, in which the tools and skills are applied; and a reflective report through which you will critically reflect on the design project and the application of the design tools. There are a wide range of specialist areas to choose from through the negotiated project. These include: fashion design; textile design; fashion marketing; and printed textile design.

The linkage of creativity and innovation leading to the active exploitation of new ideas and understanding is at the heart of the school's mission.

At Leeds, design students develop skills to pursue a careers in a full range of fashion and textile sectors.

Programme
Design

Leads to
Master of Arts, Master of Science

Structure
The 1-year full-time course operates over two semesters (180 credits). Alongside a choice of taught modules to develop conceptual and practical design skills, students are prepared to negotiate a chosen project. Research Methodology, the core module, introduces students to methodologies and tools employed in design research and the issues surrounding them. This module will also determine the aims and objectives of their negotiated project – the core module undertaken in the second semester.

The second semester is dedicated to the core project, presented at the end of the programme. Assessment is carried out by coursework, a negotiated project and a reflective report/dissertation.

Head of programme
Vanessa Walker

Mentors and lecturers
David Bromilow, Tracy Cassidy, Thomas Cassidy, Vien Cheung, Philip Henry, Dian Li, Edel Moore, Tang Tang and Vanessa Walker.

Notable alumni
Unknown

School Facts

Duration of study
1 year

Full time
Yes

Part time
Possible

Female students
65%

Male students
35%

Local students
40%

Students from abroad
60%

Yearly enrolment
26

Tuition fee
- GBP 5100 per year for EU citizens (approx. EUR 6000)
- GBP 13,100 per year for non-EU citizens (approx. EUR 15,500)

Funding/scholarships
Yes

Minimum requirements for entry
Bachelor's degree in a relevant discipline and/or professional experience

Language
English

Application procedure
Your application should include the following:
- your personal and contact details
- your curriculum vitae
- application form
- portfolio
- mission statement
- proof of language (if applicable)
Successful applicants will be informed by email.

Application details
texpg@leeds.ac.uk

Application date
By 1 September

Graduation rate
High

Job placement rate
High

Memberships/affiliations
Society of Dyers and Colourists

Collaborations with
Marks and Spencer, Lancaster University and The Hong Kong Polytechnic University.

Facilities for students
Modern, spacious studios offering extensive workshops and specialist equipment, including: traditional and CAD fashion/textile design facilities industry standard manufacturing technology PC, Mac and CAD suites, laser-cutting technology; and traditional and digital textile facilities.

City
Leeds

Country
United Kingdom

Student Work

Girls from Wonderland (2011)
By Zi Young Kang

Three aims were set for this project: to investigate Lolita fashion and subculture; to understand the qualities of British Lolitas; and to produce Lolita fashion garments for UK consumers. To achieve these goals, a literature review, interviews and a survey were conducted and the data was used to create designs and to analyse British Lolitas.

Modern Corset for Vietnamese Market (2012)
By Thi Thu Hanh Pham

This project aimed to examine the origins of corsetry, to find its benefits and problems then to produce a modern corset for the Vietnamese market. Research included a literature review, focus group, interviews and surveys. Based on the findings, a modern collection was designed and the outcomes were assessed by fashion experts and Vietnamese customers.

Achieving the Perfect Fit (2011)
By Hye Won Lim

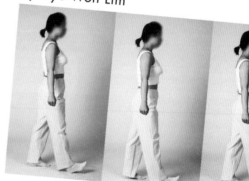

Sizing is one of the major concerns for pattern making in the clothing industry. Various pattern making methods have been introduced to define the sizing of clothing by body measurements. This study evaluated four pattern making methods which are known as ESMOD, Bunka, Aldrich and Armstrong methods. Fit evaluation for experimental garments made by suggested patterns were also conducted.

Style Details in Womenswear: Dresses (2012)
By Susan Welsh

Fireland (2012)
By Aylel Azizova

The aim of this project was to analyse 'mandala' and its common elements within traditional Azerbaijan ornaments. The outcome was applied to the idea of creating the range of scarves design that included common features relating to such ornamentation.

This project investigated the predominant style details in dresses within the late 1940 to early 1970 periods, utilising the Marks and Spencer Archive Collection. The emphasis is on developing style detail shapes, then re-positioning in a different part of a dress. The resulting dresses show contrasting silhouettes and developed details, entirely based on customer preferences.

Colour Effects of Marl Yarns (2012)
By Yiting Duan

Marl yarn is commonly made by twisting together two or more ends of different coloured yarns, and is often used in knitwear. Whilst there is obviously appreciation of the colour effects that marl yarn contributes to knitted fabrics, there is relatively little understanding on the formation of such colour effects. This study investigates different knitting parameters with marl yarn so as to allow effective ways to produce knitted fabrics with satisfactory colour effects.

Alumna

Name Hye-Won Lim
Residence Leeds, United Kingdom
Year of birth 1979
Year of graduation 2011
Current job PhD candidate

Why did you choose to study at this school?
I focused on searching for good places to study fashion and related subjects. I preferred an English-language course with a study duration of 1 year. The University of Leeds is a Russell Group university and has a high reputation in my home country.

What was the most important thing you learned here?
The teaching style here compared to my home country (or in Asia generally) is very different. I was impressed the teaching very much encourages individual creative talents. This helped me further develop independent thinking which is an asset for my current research study.

How was the programme divided?
In the MA study, we had to gain in-depth fundamental knowledge and to learn a variety of generic skills in the first term. We could also choose other modules and I went for the option of digital practice for fashion and textiles.

What was your graduation project?
My project evaluated four major pattern-making methods for the pattern-making of trousers. There has been a concern in the fashion and textile industry that different

pattern-making methods lead to significant different degrees of fit and comfort. The four methods I compared where ESMOD, Bunka, Aldrich and Armstrong, using both subjective and objective assessments in order to suggest a 'right' pattern.

Do you have any fond memories about the city?
Leeds is a nice city and easy to explore. Its city centre is rather compact and that makes it a centralised and vibrant place. The mixture of historical and modern buildings in the city and University is interesting.

What was your favourite place to hang out?
I enjoyed trying different cuisines that Leeds' large number of restaurants offered. Local pubs in city centre are good to visit too – the atmosphere, the beer and the popular pub food, such as fish and chips presented distinctive British culture.

Was the transformation from graduation to working life a smooth one?
I decided to carry on studying for a PhD degree after my master's studies Leeds, for which I received a scholarship from the School of Design. Many of my MA class mates have found work in design companies and I have heard that the MA degree has provided them with an advantage when job hunting.

Any words of advice for future students?
Generally, I think having some work experience before going on to undertake graduate study will be more advantageous. This is because the work experience will allow a better understanding on needs in the industry.

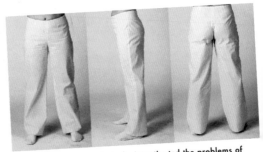

In Lim's graduation project, she investigated the problems of sizing and pattern-making for trousers in the clothing industry.

Current Students

'I have been interested in studying design in-depth, so I looked for a school in the United Kingdom. As the school here has an expertise in 'colour in design', this was very attractive to me. I feel colour is the most important element in terms of design. Therefore, I didn't hesitate to apply for this school. Compared to other design schools, this course focuses on academic aspects in terms of design research.'

Yoojin Kyong

'The sense of achievement from doing this intensive 1-year course is immense. It is challenging, and you develop your own self as a designer. I have met some great friends from all around the world and from all design backgrounds. This course provides a well-based design knowledge, with great support from the team of supervisors and professors.'

Douha Youssef Attiah

City Life

Leeds is a lively and exciting city, with an enterprising atmosphere. It is the location of some of the most exciting start-up companies and is at the heart of research and development in many sectors.

It is a city rich in heritage, being home to numerous musumes and galleries, along with one of the UK's largest regional repertory theatres, the West Yorkshire Playhouse. Other theatres include the splendid Victorian Leeds Grand Theatre and the City Varieties, which is a Grade II listed building. The city is well-known for its sophisticated shopping experience from new centres to historic arcades, there is a vast choice within a short walking distance across the city centre.

With a student population of over 200,000, Leeds is vibrant and cosmopolitan. Its clubs and drinking places cater for every taste, from student haunts and trendy wine and cocktail bars to friendly traditional pubs. The university Student Union has its own nightclub, Stylus, and the city centre has more than 10 clubs with everything from soul funk nights to dance, indie and hip-hop.

All tastes in dining are also catered for, whether you're after Japanese or Italian cuisine, a noodle bar or a sophisticated eatery, like the Harvey Nichols cafe, Leeds has something for every taste and budget. For something different, the Granary Wharf has a selection of restaurants with waterside views or the Corn Exchange also houses a stunning restaurant location.

Leeds City Gallery and City Hall dominates the skyline in the heart of the city.

United Kingdom

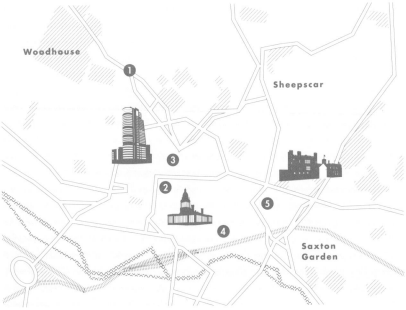

Woodhouse

Sheepscar

Saxton Garden

Leeds

1 School of Design
2 City Gallery
3 City Museum
4 The Corn Exchange
5 West Yorkshire Playhouse

Park

Water

Railway

Main road

Course
Design

School
University of Leeds School of Design

City Facts

Leeds City Gallery ②

This art gallery is in the heart of the city, adjacent to Leeds City Hall, and houses a world-class collection of 20th century British art. The gallery includes work by Francis Bacon, Stanley Spencer, Henry Moore and Barbara Hepworth, as well as contemporary art and design. It has a beautifully restored Victorian tiled hall cafe which is well worth a visit, as is the Craft Centre and Shop downstairs.
leedsartgallery.co.uk

Leeds City Museum ③

This museum takes visitors through the city's 800-year history with hands-on and audio-visual displays, exhibitions and interactive games.
leedsmuseum.co.uk

The Corn Exchange ④

This is an example of Britain's finest Victorian buildings, designed by Cuthbert Brodrick and completed in 1864. Nowadays, it is a proud champion of the very best in creative, innovative and independent retail enterprises including Village, an independent art bookstore and publishing house. The nearby Victorian Quarter and Grand Arcade

is also well worth a visit to marvel at the architecture, as well as the Leeds City Market.
leedscornexchange.co.uk

West Yorkshire Playhouse ⑤

This venue has an international reputation for producing exciting new work and has strong connections with major writers such as John Godber and Alan Bennett. Its award-winning productions attract leading performers such as Dr Who actor Christopher Eccleston, Patrick Stewart and Lenny Henry.
wyp.org.uk

Roundhay Park

This is one of the biggest parks in Europe and covers 700 acres of parkland, lakes and woodland. It is adjacent to Tropical World which is home to the largest collection of tropical plants outside Kew Gardens, as well as some resident fish, monkeys and reptiles.

Leeds Industrial Museum

Housed in what was once the world's biggest woollen mill in Armley, this museum relates the history of manufacturing in Leeds, including textiles, clothing, printing and

engineering. Exhibits include industrial machinery, locomotives and an old working cinema.

Yorkshire Sculpture Park

The Yorkshire Sculpture Park in parkland close to the neighbouring city of Wakefield is an open-air gallery showing work by UK and international artists, including Henry Moore and Barbara Hepworth.
ysp.co.uk

Kirkstall Abbey

This historic location not far from the city centre is one of the best preserved Cistercian monasteries in the country. Its dramatic architecture, which dates back to 1152, is set in beautiful parkland along the banks of the River Aire. Regular events such as theatre productions, craft fairs and farmers' markets take place in the grounds.
kirkstall.org.uk/abbey

How to get around

Leeds has a compact city centre and excellent public transport making it easy to get around. There is also a free city bus which operates every few minutes Monday to Saturday. It does a loop of the city, linking the train and bus stations with the southern end of the campus and other key locations. Many buses run to the north of the city, where the university campus is located, including a night bus which collects students from the entrance of the union building and takes them to their doorstep for just 50 pence (less than EUR 1.00). A good local train network links Leeds with nearby cities

and outlying towns and villages. The campus is 5 minutes' drive by taxi from the railway station, or a pleasant 40 minute walk. There is also a fast and efficient rail service to London Kings Cross. The nearest airport is Leeds-Bradford International Airport, accessble by regular bus service. It is easy to get from campus into the city by bus, although cycling is an ever-increasing popular option. There are cycle lanes throughout the city centre with many secure bike racks avalaible on campus.

Arranging housing
Quite easy

Housing support by school
Yes

Cost of room in the city
GBP 400 per month (approx. EUR 470)

Cost of campus housing
GBP 300 per month (approx. EUR 350)

University of Manchester School of Materials

The School of Materials is located in the heart of the central Manchester campus, very close to the city centre.

The clothing lab is open for textile students to use 24/7.

University of Manchester
School of Materials
Oxford Road
Manchester M13 9PL
United Kingdom

T +44 (0)161 306 4826
pg-materials@manchester.ac.uk
materials.manchester.ac.uk

Course
Textile Technology

School
University of Manchester School of Materials

Introduction

'We embrace emerging technologies, with a textiles science and technology focus'

Paul O'Brien, head of school

When was the school founded and how has it changed?
The University of Manchester was founded as early as 1824, with textiles a core discipline from the outset. It has evolved over the years to embrace emerging technologies and knowledge with a textiles science and technology focus. These days, we embrace both the performance textiles end (e.g. technical textiles) and the traditional aspects (e.g. fashion and design).

What is studying at this school all about?
The main focus of our textiles activity is to provide education and training in the science and technological aspects of this field. Our mission is to tool our graduates with understanding and know-how. Through fully appreciating the working principles of textile manufacture, testing, etc., we enable our graduates to excel in both aspects of management and innovation.

What kind of teaching method is applied?
We utilise numerous teaching methods: lectures, tutorials, seminars, etc. We also have a particular focus on laboratory sessions where our students learn through hands-on experience in our comprehensive facilities.

Why should students choose this particular school?
Our strength resides in the scientific and technological aspect of textiles. We have a unique offering as we provide the fundamental understanding of all textile processes, and apply these at the design/technology interface.

What is expected from the students?
Our master's programme provides an intensive schooling. We expect our students to engage with the material and actively participate in all aspects of the course. We believe a key aspect for the students to master is the ability to innovate with new technology.

When did you start offering the master's degree course in fashion/textiles?
The MSc Textile Technology has been offered since the 1940s, with the programme constantly evolving to reflect the latest knowledge and practices. We now also offer the MSc International Fashion Retailing degree, which marries some of the technical aspects of textiles with the business and retailing aspects.

What is the most important skill for a textile designer?
A thorough understanding of the material that is being used, naturally leads to appreciating its potential and limitations. This in turn enables a fashion or textile designer to innovate and work at the frontier of what can be achieved with current technologies.

Programme

The MSc Textile Technology programme aims to develop a high level of understanding of modern textile technology. Graduates of the programme are expected to understand the whole process of converting fibre materials to end products including those for specialised technical applications, and to have the expertise and skills to conduct quality evaluation of textile products. During the course, students develop the ability to exploit new technology, such as 3D weaving and knitting, smart textiles and nanotechnology in order to meet new consumer, fashion and legislation demands.

The programme is made up of individual taught units, followed by an individual research project. The taught units cover the latest developments of technical textiles, performance enhancement and testing of surface and mechanical properties, and applied manufacturing processes (fabric technologies) and techniques (3D weaving and flatbed knitting, CAD systems, converting 2D fabrics to 3D products, etc.), plus yarn and coloration technology. The course also provides information on effective supply chains and an understanding of diverse product sectors, such as textile composites, protective wear, filtration, sportswear, medical textiles and the integration of electronics into textile structures.
Graduates of this programme typically become managers or researchers in industry or university academics. Many graduates have become owner–managers of their own textile companies.

Interesting clothing types are studied in the classes on advanced materials, including the fabrication of police helmets.

Manchester has a wide range of textile machinery available for students to make the most of during their time at the school.

Programme
Textile Technology

Leads to
Master of Science

Structure
The 1-year full-time course is divided into semesters. The course is split between six taught units (90 credits) and a final project on a technical textiles topic (90 credits), to be undetraken over 5 months and incorporating a research dissertation. Assessment is by a combination of exams and coursework. The final project topic is selected by each student, in consultation with their personal tutor, and will include investigatory and problem-solving work, through studies of state-of-the-art technology and current practice, to experimental and analytical research. Students with advanced textile education can choose to carry out an extended research project and graduate with the degree of MSc by Research.

Head of programme
Hugh Gong

Mentors and lecturers
Xiaogang Chen, Anura Fernando, Richard Kennon, Huw Owens, Prasad Potluri, Muriel Rigout and Franz Wortmann.

Notable alumni
Unknown

School Facts

Duration of study
1 year

Full time
Yes (35 hours)

Part time
Yes

Female students
60%

Male students
40%

Local students
20%

Students from abroad
80%

Yearly enrolment
15

Tuition fee
- GBP 7200 per year for EU citizens (approx. EUR 8350)
- GBP 18,100 per year for non-EU citizens (approx. EUR 21,000)

Funding/scholarships
Yes

Minimum requirements for entry
Bachelor's degree or approved combination of educational qualifications/industrial experience

Language
English

Application procedure
The following documents are required:
- application form
- copy of degree certificate/college transcripts
- your curriculum vitae
- statement of purpose
- letters of recommendation
- a copy of your passport
- proof of language (if applicable). Some candidates may be contacted for interview. International applicants are not required to have an in-person interview. Successful candidates will be informed by email.

Application details
pg-materials@manchester.ac.uk

Application date
Throughout the year

Graduation rate
100%

Job placement rate
100%

Memberships/affiliations
n/a

Collaborations with
n/a

Facilities for students
Full range of textile laboratory facilities, 24-hour computer cluster, CAD facilities and extensive textile library, plus access to numerous central facilities (learning commons, student support offices, etc.).

Student Work

Visual Effects on Denim (2013)
By Celina Jones

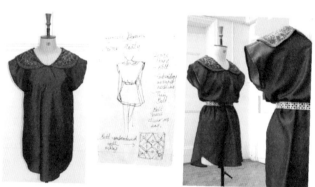

Celina employed a newly developed technology to achieve eco-friendly and innovative visual effects on denim, including distressing effects and other visual effects.

3D Design Using a Virtual Mannequin (2013)
By Abu Sadat Muhammad Sayem

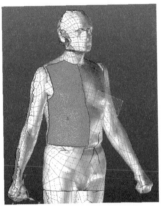

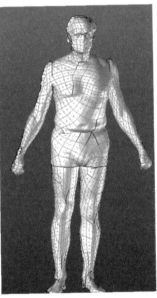

This project developed a digital reverse engineering technique as an effective approach for the creation of a system to support the design of garments in 3D. A body scanner was used to generate point-cloud data from a human model and this was used to develop a virtual mannequin. Designers can then draw clothing directly onto this virtual mannequin, placing the seam lines wherever they wish. The individual clothing panels are then peeled from the mannequin by the computer and flattened into 2D pattern pieces that may be used to create actual garments.

Course
Textile Technology

School
University of Manchester School of Materials

Design Implications for Apparel Applications (2013)
Kate Lloyd

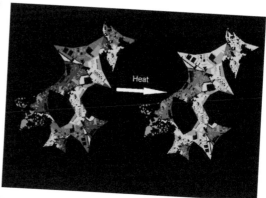

Kate studied the technical profiles of microencapsulated thermochromic colorants (hand, thermal response, etc) in view of informing the design constraints of these colorants on apparel; another aspect of her project was to investigate ways to remedy the technical limitations of these colorants which detrimentally impacted on design potential.

Fully-Shaped Nonwoven Articles (2013)
By Tingting Zhang

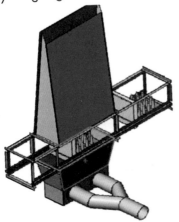

This project employed a newly developed non-woven technology to create complex fully-shaped and seam-free 3-dimensional articles in a single step.

Braided Cord (2013)
By Sabahat Nawaz

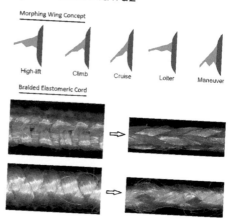

This project was aimed at working towards reinforcing flexible composites. It included the development of high-performance hyper-elastic triaxial and biaxial braided cords. These cords are used to make shape-changing skins for morphing wing structures for aerial vehicles.

Alumnus

Name Barry Tai
Residence Hong Kong, Hong Kong
Year of birth 1984
Year of graduation 2007
Current job Business development manager

Why did you choose this school?
The University of Manchester is one of the world renowned universities in the area of fashion and textiles. I know this school because it has exchange programme with my undergraduate university.

Are you still in contact with the school?
Yes. I keep in touch with both my classmates and supervisor, and I also still have contact with the head of school through my current job. I work as the business development manager at the Hong Kong Research Institute of Textiles and Apparel.

What was the most important thing you learned here?
The learning experience at Manchester was great, with its dedicated teachers and excellent facilities and educational resources. I learnt how to work proactively and to solve problems by myself. These skills have certainly helped me in my career and life after graduation.

What was the most interesting project you did?
Advanced Materials was my favourite workshop, because I could learn all about the latest development of materials in the world. The applications of these technical materials is also exciting, from firemen's uniforms to bullet proof vests, and even space suits.

What subject do you wish you paid more attention to?
Apart from fashion related subjects, the course also providing me with knowledge of technical textiles, which were all new to me. The courses equipped me with fundamental knowledge in these areas and these are useful for my career.

Was there any class you found particularly easy during the course?
Fashion-related subjects, such as spinning, weaving, knitting, etc., because I already knew fundamentally about them through my undergraduate studies.

Do you have any fond memories about the city?
I developed many good friendships during my time there, and I also travelled a lot. Manchester is fairly centrally located in the country and so it easy to have a one-day trip to north like Edinburgh or south to Brighton. I travelled to almost 30 cities across the country during my time in Manchester.

Was the transformation from graduation to working life a smooth one?
Yes. I entered into a textiles job quite easily, where I apply the knowledge I learnt from Manchester. I have been working here for almost 6 years now.

Any words of advice for future students?
Enjoy the city and – because it's Manchester – take the opportunity to watch at least one football match there!

Tai discusses with a delegation from Sri Lanka in his business development role in Hong Kong.

Course
Textile Technology

School
University of Manchester School of Materials

Current Students

'After following this course, I hope to have an in-depth understanding of technical textiles. I wish to continue studying this area as I develop my academic career.'
Yuhua Wang

'I chose this school because I needed to learn more about the technical aspects of textiles. The course is well rounded and exceeded my expectations as it laid for me a solid foundation in technical textiles, which complements my fashion design undergraduate degree.'
Hend Almoghunni

'My advice for future students? Plan your time effectively and it will ensure that you enjoy and experience everything the University of Manchester has to offer!'
Celina Jones

'I am interested in recent research trends regarding textiles, as well as material science. The research module here has enabled me to develop a new approach towards learning in these fields. Critical reasoning and analytical views are great skills to gain for my future in research.'
Ashiqul Islam

'I found the lab work in both the weaving and knitting workshops really interesting. It is possible to learn more through observing the machines at first-hand and seeing exactly how they work.'
I-Chen Chen

City Life

Manchester's undeniable buzz, cosmopolitan character and varied ethnic mix make it a popular student city.

From culture and music to sport, there's always something to do. World-class museums, international cinemas, theatres, opera, ballet and comedy clubs all feature regional, national and international talent. There are many music venues, from the small and intimate to a vast 21,000-seater arena, alongside hundreds of pubs, bars and nightclubs.

Manchester is a truly multicultural city, with established Asian, Caribbean, Chinese, Jewish and Polish communities. Cafes and restaurants are plentiful and suit all budgets and tastes. The city offers an array of restaurants with menus from around the world, including the famous Chinatown in the city centre, and the Curry Mile, home to over 150 Asian eating establishments and businesses.

Manchester's sporting reputation is famous, with its two football clubs, rugby clubs, the Lancashire Cricket Club, National Squash Centre, Sportcity, National Cycling Centre and a Hockey Centre. Sports fans will find a wide range of international and national sports events across the North West of England.

United Kingdom

Built in the 1930s, Manchester Central Library is one of the most instantly recognisable structures in the city.
Photo Michael Beckwith

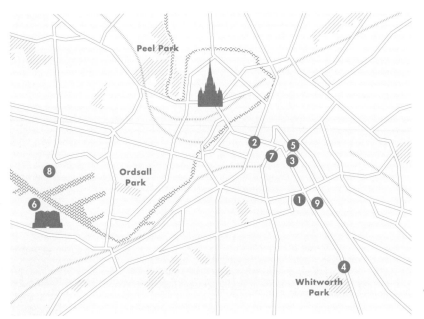

Manchester

1 University of Manchester
2 Great Northern Contemporary Craft Fair
3 Cornerhouse
4 Whitworth Art Gallery
5 Cube
6 Imperial War Museum
7 Bridgewater Hall
8 MediaCityUK
9 Manchester Aquatics Centre

Park
Water
Railway
Main road

Course
Textile Technology

School
University of Manchester School of Materials

City Facts

Great Northern Contemporary Craft Fair ②
The GNCCF showcases cutting edge contemporary craft to buy from over 150 selected designer-makers in ceramics, glass, jewellery, interior and fashion textiles, wood, paper, silver, metal, product design, print-making and more.
greatnorthernevents.co.uk

Cornerhouse ③
With film director Danny Boyle, artist Damien Hirst and actor Helen Mirren as its high-profile patrons, Cornerhouse is a major force in British contemporary arts comprising a cinema, gallery, bookshop and cafe bar.
cornerhouse.org

Whitworth Art Gallery ④
A visit to the Whitworth guarantees variety. Modern and historic fine art prints are displayed alongside prints, textiles and a rare collection of wallpapers.
whitworth.manchester.ac.uk

Cube ⑤
With three gallery spaces, there is always something interesting and unusual on display. From innovative graphic design to showcases of the best new architectural work, Cube is dedicated to the fusion of art and architecture.
cube.org.uk

Imperial War Museum ⑥
The museum is unique in its coverage of conflicts, especially those involving Britain and the Commonwealth, from the First World War to the present day.
iwm.org.uk/visits/iwm-north

Bridgewater Hall ⑦
This state-of-the-art 2400 seat auditorium, with magnificent Marcussen pipe organ, opened in September 1996. Concerts range from classical and jazz through to world and popular music.
bridgewater-hall.co.uk

MediaCityUK ⑧
The vision of MediaCityUK is to become a leading international hub for the creative and digital sectors, and a vibrant destination to work, live and play.
mediacityuk.co.uk

Buy Art Fair
Buy Art Fair brings together galleries and artists from across the United Kingdom in a purpose-built marquee. With over 50 galleries exhibiting pieces from over 500 artists.
buyartfair.co.uk

Manchester Aquatics Centre ⑨
The centre has been host to a number of international swimming events and galas. It is also the training facility for the British Paralympics Swimming Squad.
manchestersportandleisure.org

How to get around
Manchester Airport is the largest airport outside London. Over 100 airlines offer direct flights to over 190 destinations worldwide. The airport is approx. 14 km to the south of the city with excellent transport links including a direct train service into the city.

Manchester boasts the busiest bus route in Europe, a tram network, and four key train stations (Deansgate, Piccadilly, Oxford Road and Victoria). There are also free shuttle buses that link to all the main rail stations, shopping districts and businesses in the city centre.

Manchester is a bike-friendly city with many marked cycle lanes and dedicated routes throughout the city centre and beyond, but it is also easily explored on foot, with plenty of pedestrian-only zones. It is possible to traverse the main central locations within around 20 minutes, end-to-end.

To get to the University of Manchester, there are numerous buses heading towards the campus.

Arranging housing
Average

Housing support by school
Yes, for international students only

Cost of room in the city
Between GBP 275 and GBP 560 per month (approx. EUR 350 to EUR 700)

Cost of campus housing
GBP 430 per month (approx. EUR 550)

<u>Map</u>

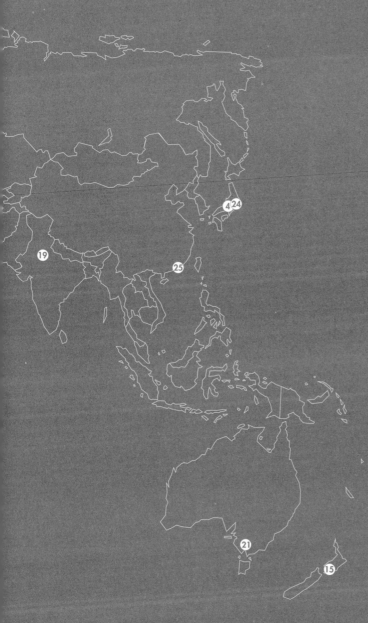

School Summary

School	Location	Leads to	Duration of study*
Aalto University School of Arts, Design and Architecture	Helsinki, Finland	MA Fashion and Clothing Design	2 years
Academy of Arts, Architecture and Design in Prague	Prague, Czech Republic	MA Applied Arts	2 years
ArtEZ Institute of the Arts	Arnhem, the Netherlands	Master Fashion Design	2 years
Bunka Fashion Graduate University	Tokyo, Japan	MA Fashion Design	2 years
De Montfort University	Leicester, United Kingdom	MA Fashion and Bodywear	1 year
Domus Academy	Milan, Italy	Master in Fashion Design	1 year
École nationale supérieure des Arts Décoratifs	Paris, France	MA Fashion Design	2 years
ELISAVA Barcelona School of Design and Engingeering	Barcelona, Spain	MA Fashion Design	1 year
Edinburgh College of Art	Edinburgh, United Kingdom	MA Fashion Design	1 year
ESMOD Berlin	Berlin, Germany	MA Sustainability in Fashion	1 year
HDK School of Design and Crafts at Steneby	Dals Långed, Sweden	MFA Applied Arts	2 years
Heriot-Watt University School of Textiles & Design	Galashiels, United Kingdom	MA Fashion and Textiles Design	1 year
Institut Français de la Mode	Paris, France	MA (equiv.) Fashion Design	1.5 years
London College of Fashion, UAL	London, United Kingdom	MA Fashion Design Technology: Menswear MA Fashion Design Technology: Womenswear	1.25 years
Massey University	Wellington, New Zealand	MDes Fashion Design	1 year
NABA/Nuova Accademia di Belle Arti Milano	Milan, Italy	MA Fashion and Textile Design	2 years
NC State University College of Textiles	Raleigh, United States	MSc Textiles	2 years
Oslo National Academy of the Arts	Oslo, Norway	MDes Fashion and Costume Design	2 years
Pearl Academy	New Delhi, India	MA Design (Fashion and Textile)	1.5 years
Rhode Island School of Design	Providence, United States	MFA Textiles	2 years
RMIT University	Melbourne, Australia	Master of Fashion and Textiles	2 years
Royal College of Art	London, United Kingdom	MA Fashion Menswear/Womenswear	2 years
School of the Art Institute of Chicago	Chicago, United States	MDes Fashion, Body and Garment	2 years
Tama Art University	Tokyo, Japan	MFA Textile Design	2 years
The Hong Kong Polytechnic University	Hong Kong, Hong Kong	MA Fashion and Textile Design	1 year
The Swedish School of Textiles University of Borås	Borås, Sweden	MA Fashion and Textile Design	2 years
University of Leeds School of Design	Leeds, United Kingdom	MA Design	1 year
University of Manchester School of Materials	Manchester, United Kingdom	MSc Textile Technology	1 year

*Full time

Full time	Part time	Language	Tuition fee	Funding/ scholarships	Yearly enrolment	Female students	Male students	Local students	Students from abroad	Arranging housing	Housing support by school
Yes	No	English	No	No	10	88.5%	11.5%	80%	20%	Never a problem	No
Yes	Possible	English, Czech	No**	Yes	12	52%	48%	70%	30%	Quite easy	Yes
Yes	No	English	Yes	Yes	10	81%	19%	53%	47%	Average	No
Yes	No	Japanese	Yes	Yes	53	76%	24%	36%	64%	Average	Yes
Yes	Yes	English	Yes	Yes	15–20	80%	20%	37.5%	62.5%	Average	Yes
Yes	No	English	Yes	Yes	25	88%	12%	0%	100%	Quite easy	Yes
Yes	No	French	Yes	Yes	8	87.5%	12.5%	87.5%	12.5%	Difficult	No
Yes	No	English, Spanish	Yes	Yes	15	90%	10%	30%	70%	Never a problem	Yes
Yes	No	English	Yes	Yes	4	100%	0%	25%	75%	Quite easy	Yes
Yes	No	English	Yes	Yes	18	90%	10%	15%	85%	Average/ quite easy	No
Yes	No	English, Swedish	No (EU), Yes (non-EU)	No	13	60%	40%	85%	15%	Never a problem	Yes
Yes	No	English	Yes	Yes	10	70%	30%	50%	50%	Average	Yes
Yes	No	English	Yes	Yes	20–30	60%	40%	20%	80%	Average	No
Yes	Yes	English	Yes	Yes	44	87%	13%	45%	55%	Average	Yes
Yes	Possible	English	Yes	Yes	22	100%	0%	90%	10%	Average	Yes
Yes	No	English	Yes	Yes	34	76%	24%	41%	59%	Quite easy	Yes
Yes	No	English	Yes	Yes	50	67%	33%	80%	20%	Never a problem	No
Yes	No	English, Norwegian	No	Yes	6	73%	27%	89%	11%	Average	No
Yes	No	English	Yes	Yes	20	80%	20%	100%	0%	Average	Yes
Yes	No	English	Yes	Yes	12	90%	10%	76%	24%	Never a problem	Yes
Yes	Yes	English	Yes	Yes	100+	80%	20%	40%	60%	Quite easy	No
Yes	No	English	Yes	Yes	31/52	70%	30%	44%	56%	Average	Yes
Yes	No	English	Yes	Yes	20	80%	20%	20%	80%	Average	Yes
Yes	No	Japanese, English	Yes	Yes	5–10	87%	13%	96%	4%	Average	No
Yes	No	English	Yes	No	26	80%	20%	40%	60%	Difficult	No
Yes	No	English	No (EU), Yes (non-EU)	Yes	15	85%	15%	40–60%	40–60%	Average	No
Yes	Possible	English	Yes	Yes	26	65%	35%	40%	60%	Quite easy	Yes
Yes	Yes	English	Yes	Yes	15	60%	40%	20%	80%	Average	Possible

**Free for students with basic level of Czech language

Credits

Masterclass: Fashion & Textiles
Guide to the World's Leading Graduate Schools

Publisher
Frame Publishers

Production
Carmel McNamara, Sarah de Boer-Schultz and Marlous van Rossum-Willems

Author
Jane Szita

Editor
Carmel McNamara

Graphic Design Concept
Cathelijn Kruunenberg

Graphic Design
Smel design & strategy
Federica Ricci (intern)

Prepress
Beeldproductie

Printing
Tiger Printing

Trade distribution USA and Canada
Consortium Book Sales & Distribution, LLC.
34 Thirteenth Avenue NE, Suite 101
Minneapolis, MN 55413-1007
T +1 612 746 2600
T +1 800 283 3572 (orders)
F +1 612 746 2606

Distribution rest of world
Frame Publishers
Laan der Hesperiden 68
1076 DX Amsterdam
the Netherlands
frameweb.com
distribution@frameweb.com

ISBN: 978-90-77174-99-9

© 2014 Frame Publishers, Amsterdam, 2014

Whilst every effort has been made to ensure
accuracy, Frame Publishers does not under any
circumstances accept responsibility for errors or
omissions. Any mistakes or inaccuracies will be
corrected in case of subsequent editions upon
notification to the publisher.

The Koninklijke Bibliotheek lists this publication
in the Nederlandse Bibliografie: detailed
bibliographic information is available on the
internet at http://picarta.pica.nl

Printed on acid-free paper produced from
chlorine-free pulp. TCF ∞
Printed in China

987654321

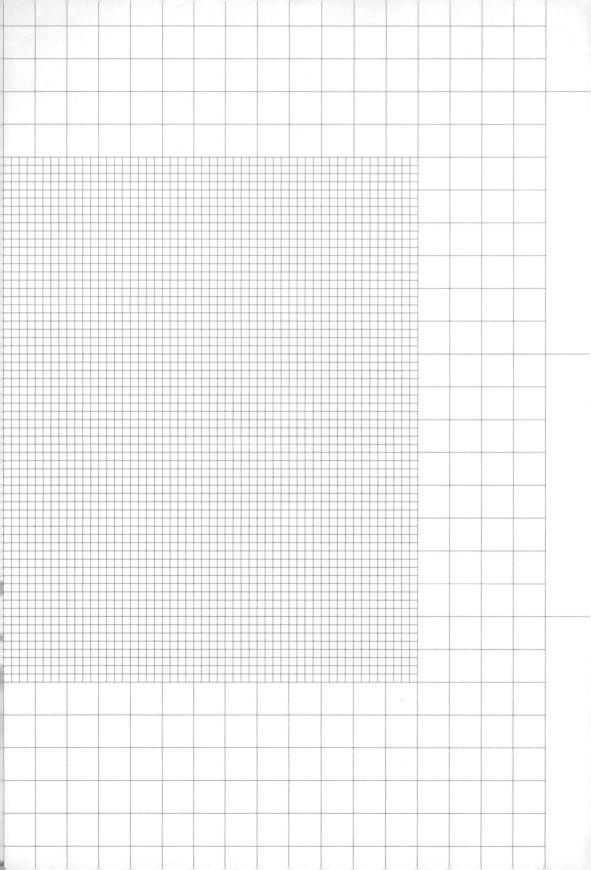

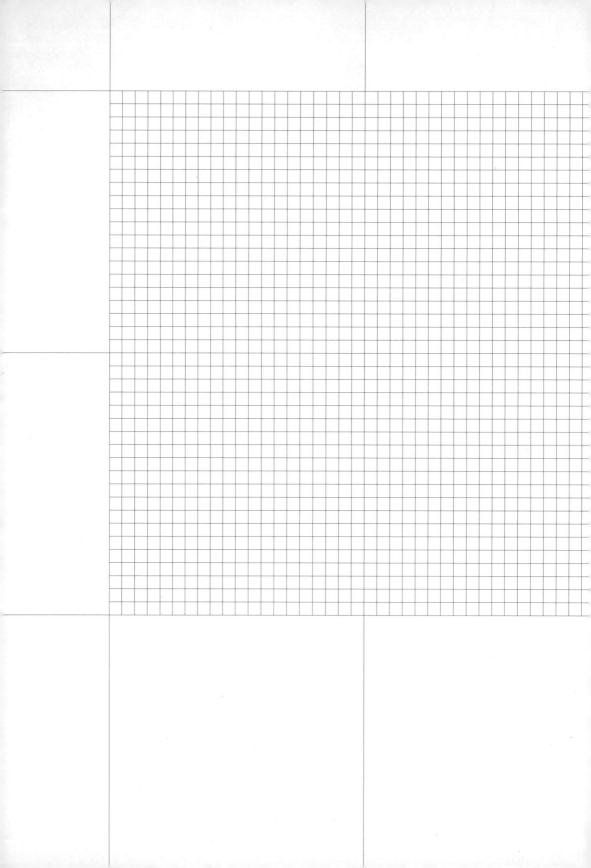

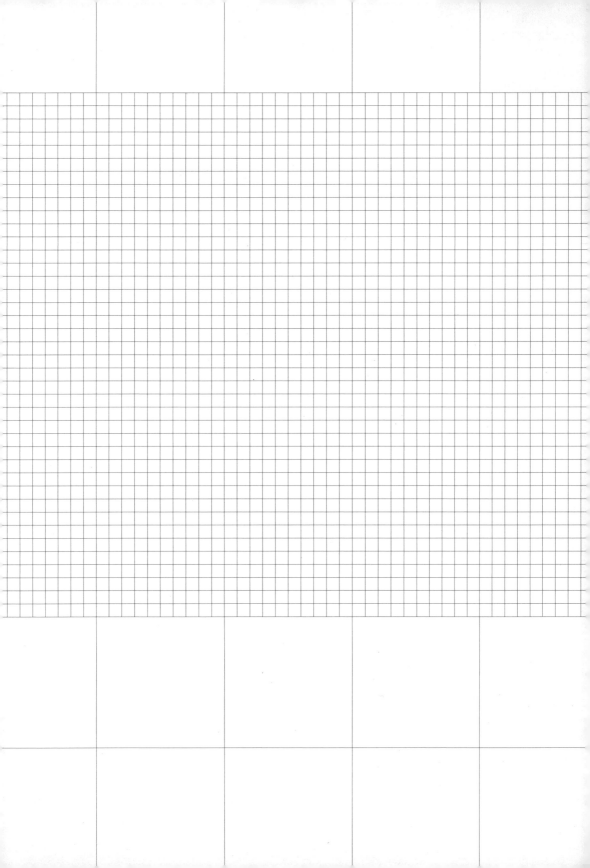

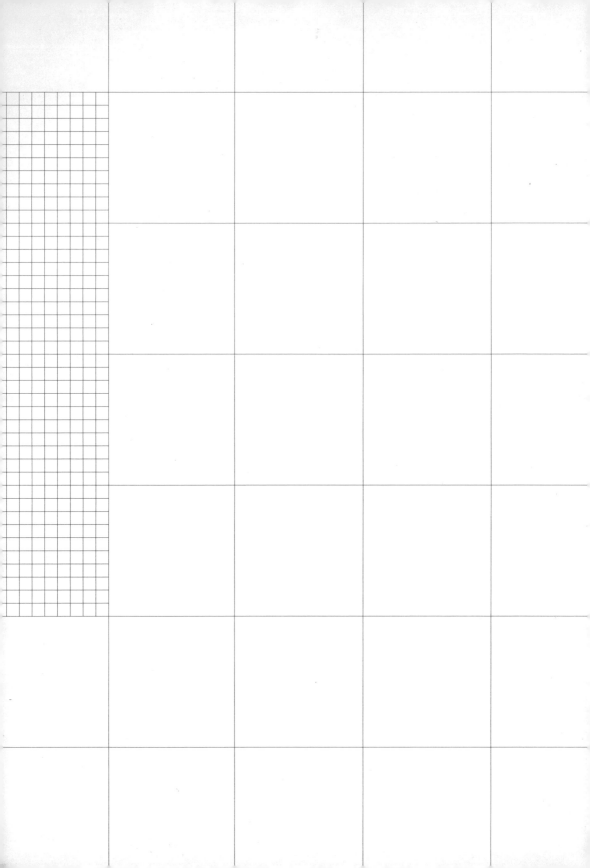